28 June
Sarajevo 1914–Versailles 1919
The War and Peace that Made the Modern World

28 June
Sarajevo 1914 – Versailles 1919
The War and Peace that Made
the Modern World
Edited by Alan Sharp

First published in Great Britain in 2014 by
Haus Publishing
70 Cadogan Place
London SW1X 9AH
www.hauspublishing.com

ISBN 978 1 908323 75 0
eISBN 978 1 908323 76 7

Typeset in Sabon by MacGuru Ltd
info@macguru.org.uk
Series design by Susan Buchanan
Interior maps by Martin Lubikowski, ML Design, London

A CIP catalogue record for this book is available from the British Library

Printed and bound by CPI Group Ltd, Croydon CR0 4YY

Cover and endpaper map from: *The Great War: The Standard History of the World-Wide Conflict*. The Amalgamated Press, London, 1919.

For Jamie and Chloe

Contents

Acknowledgements

I am very grateful to the contributors to this volume for making the editor's task so straightforward. Since many of them are friends and colleagues from our earlier *Makers of the Modern World* series it has been a particular pleasure to resume our collaboration. Chapters have arrived on time and any requests for adjustments have been met with unfailing courtesy and cooperation. Jaqueline Mitchell, who manages to combine quiet efficiency with sensitivity for her authors, is the most sympathetic of commissioning editors. Colleagues at Haus have advanced this venture with their usual friendly and effective manner, with particular thanks due to Ellie Shillito and Aran Byrne. Professors Tom Fraser, Tony Lentin and Sally Marks, together with Baroness Ruth Henig, have been, as ever, enormously supportive and generous with their encouragement, comments and suggestions.

When our publisher, Dr Barbara Schwepcke, asked me to edit the *Makers* series I envisaged it as an appropriate final project before I retired. This was clearly not her intention and I have been kept busy ever since, for which I am – on most days – suitably appreciative. Her vision and support remain inspirational and her friendship has brought a unique flavour to our various endeavours. As always my principal debt is to my wife Jen who creates the calm, space and stability which remains the foundation of everything. This book offers her some proof, I hope, that not all my time on my computer is spent playing bridge.

Alan Sharp
University of Ulster

1

Introduction

Alan Sharp

On Sunday 28 June 1914 Gavrilo Princip, a young Bosnian Serb, assassinated Archduke Franz Ferdinand, the heir to the Austro-Hungarian Empire, and his wife, Sophie, in Sarajevo in Bosnia. Thirty-seven days later Europe was at war. Although as recently as May 1914 Sir Arthur Nicolson, the Permanent Under-Secretary of the British Foreign Office, had written 'Since I have been at the Foreign Office, I have not seen such calm waters', a tsunami was about to overwhelm Europe.[1]

On Saturday 28 June 1919, in the Hall of Mirrors at Versailles in France, representatives of Germany and 30 Allied and Associated Powers signed the treaty re-establishing peace between them.[2] Although neither literally the beginning nor the end of the First World War, 28 June symbolically marks the parameters of the world's most costly conflict to that date. Its economic, political and international effects were seismic, making it the single most important event of the 20th century. How had it come about?

In 1898 the British Prime Minister, Lord Salisbury, in words redolent of the social Darwinism then in vogue, had suggested that the international balance of power was changing: 'You may roughly divide the nations of all the world as the living and the dying ... the weak states are becoming weaker and the strong states are becoming stronger ... the living nations will gradually encroach on the territory of the dying and the seeds of conflict among civilised nations will appear.'[3] Demographic and economic developments offered some clues as to which states might prosper or decline, with population and coal and steel production figures as crude indices of power. States' abilities to maintain their inner cohesion in the face of the problems created by industrialisation, urbanisation and the growth of new ideological challenges from liberalism, socialism and democratisation also provided important indications of their capabilities. Nationalism, and the aspirations of subject national minorities, posed a particular problem for the multi-national autocracies of Russia and, especially, Austria-Hungary. The key question was whether the international system could cope with these challenges without, as Salisbury feared, resort to war.

In addition to changes in the relative strengths of the European states, the emergence of new powers such as the United States and Japan complicated the international scene. Rapid – and expensive – technological innovation, coupled with a growing number of naval powers, challenged the supremacy of Britain's Royal Navy, the main arm of its defence. European conscript armies were increasing in size, with greater killing power. Nonetheless, the division of Africa and the subsequent competition for concessions in China were resolved without conflict in the 1880s and 1890s. Both offered, however, examples of a perceived need to secure gains in the present in the face of pessimism about an uncertain future – a trait which had a major role to play in the thinking of several states in 1914. Germany, by 1914 an urbanised industrial giant, rich in steel, coal, chemical and electrical industries, and with a well-educated population of 66 million, seemed secure. Yet Theobald von Bethmann Hollweg, the Chancellor, refused to plant trees on his Prussian estate, predicting that the Russians would occupy it within 30 years.

Europe experienced a number of crises in the new century, each of which was resolved peacefully, perhaps contributing to complacency amongst decision-makers that this would always be the case. France and Germany clashed twice over Morocco in 1905 and 1911, each time leaving Germany feeling humiliated despite its apparent success in obtaining recognition of its right to be consulted and compensated. Austria-Hungary's annexation of Bosnia-Herzegovina in 1908 ended the period of Austro-Russian détente in the Balkans, leaving Russia embarrassed and with a grievance. Russia was embarrassed because its abandonment of Serbia's ambitions in the two provinces, for the promise of Austrian support for Russian control of the Straits, had exposed the hollowness of its claim to be the protector of Slav interests. Its grievance arose because Austria reneged on its promise, subsequently relying on Germany to face down an indignant Russia. Such legacies of perceived failure limited actors' options in future confrontations, causing them to lose confidence in compromise solutions.

The growth of long-term peacetime alliances rendered the European international system less flexible than in the classic balance of power era earlier in the 19th century. Although the 1882 Triple Alliance of Germany, Austria-Hungary and Italy and the rival 1894 Franco-Russian Dual Alliance were never rigid or exclusive combinations they did constrain their

Europe 1914

Petrograd (St Petersburg)

Riga

Moscow

Sea

Vilna

Königsberg

anzig

RUSSIAN EMPIRE

Warsaw

Brest-Litovsk

Kiev

Budapest

Odessa

NGARY

ROMANIA

Belgrade

Bucharest

Black Sea

SERBIA

BULGARIA

NEGRO

Sofia

ana

ALBANIA

Constantinople

GREECE

OTTOMAN EMPIRE

Athens

members' freedom to act. Both were defensive in nature, in theory providing a strong motive for any member to avoid provoking a war because its partners would then be under no obligation to support it. Paradoxically such agreements, which were meant to offer security to their members, were often a source of anxiety as each suspiciously watched any contact by its partners with rival powers, fearing desertion. The need to keep partners faithful provided another motive for action in 1914.

The existence of these alliances influenced the military and defence planning of their members. The principle of 'getting there firstest with the mostest' underlay the elaborate mobilisation schemes of the continental Great Powers, posited upon an expanding network of strategic railways. This was particularly true of Germany, faced, after 1894, with the nightmare of fighting on two fronts. The solution was to seek defensively to contain one of its enemies until it had defeated the other, but the order in which France or Russia should be tackled altered several times. By 1914 the ideas of Count von Schlieffen as modified and adapted by his successor as Chief of the Great General Staff, Helmuth von Moltke the Younger, proposed the rapid defeat of France within six weeks by an attack through neutral Belgium, thus bypassing the main French defences. Russia would then be defeated in six months. For Germany, mobilisation meant war, there was no pause between the assembly of its armies and their despatch to fight. The requirements of war plans constituted another major restraint on the freedom of decision-makers in July 1914.[4]

Britain, the major non-committed power, had, since 1901 and the collapse of its second attempt to conclude an alliance with Germany become increasingly associated with the Dual

Alliance, concluding an Entente with France in 1904 and a Convention with Russia in 1907. Both agreements regulated a number of long-standing imperial differences, but neither constituted an alliance – a commitment to go to war in specified circumstances. However, as Britain and other states discovered in 1914, the fear of being perceived as an unreliable friend and hence the danger of future isolation, meant that commitments often extended beyond the formal obligations of treaties.

By 1914 some of the antagonisms that had divided Europe had lost their edge. Germany had given up its naval race with Britain, and French leaders, even the redoubtable Lorrainer, President Raymond Poincaré, accepted that Alsace-Lorraine, lost to Germany in 1871, would not be recovered. Other crises came and went, but the Eastern question of who would inherit the spoils of the supposedly dying Ottoman Empire (though it was taking an unconscionable time to do so) created one of the 19th century's enduring problems and had a major role in the growing tensions leading to the outbreak of war in 1914. In the 15th and 16th centuries the Ottoman Turks had swept into the Balkans and eastern Europe, conquering Hungary and posing a constant menace to the Habsburg Empire. As Ottoman power waned and its grip on the Balkans weakened, first Greece, in 1821, then Serbia, Romania, Montenegro and Bulgaria in 1878, achieved independence or autonomy, often proving adept at manipulating one or other of the Great Powers in their struggles to achieve recognition and territory.

Prominent among these were Austria-Hungary and Russia, for whom the Balkans assumed increasing importance as their other options for expansion or spheres of influence were blocked. After 1815 Austria was the pre-eminent power in both the Italian peninsula and the German territories but its ambitions in both regions were thwarted in the 1850s and 1860s by defeats by first France and then Prussia. Russia's pretensions in Asia were undermined by its surprise defeat by Japan in 1904–5 and the ensuing revolution at home, and further curtailed, at least temporarily, by the agreement reached with Great Britain in 1907 which established a *modus vivendi* in the disputed territories of Persia (Iran), Tibet and Afghanistan. Both empires hoped to benefit from the decline of Ottoman power, with control of the Straits and Constantinople being of particular importance to Russia for both strategic and ideological reasons.

Italy's attack on the Ottoman province of Libya in 1911 exposed both the military and diplomatic weakness of that empire. Bulgaria, Serbia, Romania and Greece were quick to react, forming the Balkan League in 1912, and between October and December in the first Balkan war came close to driving the Turks out of Europe. Then the victors fell out and a second war from June to August 1913 saw Bulgaria losing almost all its recent gains and the Ottomans able to retrieve some of their lost territory. The major winner was Serbia, which doubled its 1912 size and increased its population by 64 per cent. Its attempt to gain still further territory from newly independent Albania was only thwarted by an ultimatum from Austria in October 1913, the success of which encouraged those in Vienna, such as General Conrad von Hötzendorf, the Imperial Chief of Staff, who saw force as the answer to the empire's problems.[5]

After some prevarication as to whether to adopt Bulgaria or Serbia as its main client in the Balkans, Russia opted for the latter, which had, in turn, become the particular object of Austrian hostility because of its perceived ambitions in the region and its encouragement of Slav dissent within the empire. The fate of this small state became crucial for both powers, with Austria increasingly intent on its destruction and the prestige of Russia resting on its ability to prevent this happening. It was, as Bismarck had gloomily predicted, 'some damned fool thing in the Balkans' that set Europe ablaze. The Austrians knew that their determination to settle accounts with Serbia after the assassinations in June 1914 would almost inevitably precipitate Russian action. The fateful transformation of their defensive alliance with Germany into one in which Germany agreed to support Austria even if it provoked war was sealed by the so-called 'blank cheque' issued by the Kaiser on 5 July. Thereafter a series of ultimatums, mobilisations and declarations of war, partly triggered by the formal or perceived obligations of alliances and partnerships, transformed what might have been the third Balkan war into the First World War.

The following chapters explain the reactions of the major powers and alliances to the 28 June assassinations and how each of the states entered a war that few had anticipated and whose magnitude and duration none had predicted. The book concludes with a description of the signature of the Treaty of Versailles and an overview of the broader settlement in its post-war context.

28 June 1914: Assassination of Franz Ferdinand in Sarajevo
Serbia, Sarajevo and the Start of Conflict
Dejan Djokić

Nikola Pašić awoke on Saturday 28 June 1919 at his Paris hotel ready to sign the German peace treaty at Versailles. The erstwhile Serbian Prime Minister knew this had enormous significance for the Kingdom of Serbs, Croats and Slovenes (the official name for Yugoslavia 1918–29) whose peace delegation he led in Paris, with his deputy Ante Trumbić, a Dalmatian Croat who was Yugoslavia's first Foreign Minister and one of the leaders of the 'Yugoslav movement' in former Austria-Hungary. The Treaty of Versailles named the Serb-Croat-Slovene state, thus effectively constituting the country's international recognition – something for which Pašić and the Yugoslavs, hitherto regarded as representatives of the old Kingdom of Serbia (which in fact had ceased to exist with the unification of Yugoslavia on 1 December 1918), had continuously campaigned during the previous six months.[1]

Exactly five years previously on a warm and sunny Sunday, 28 June 1914, Serbia and Montenegro celebrated the 525th anniversary of the Battle of Kosovo, an event central to Serbian *and* Yugoslav national ideology.[2] That year's St Vitus's Day celebrations differed from previous commemorations, since Kosovo had been recently re-incorporated into Serbia, following the Balkan Wars of 1912–13, when much of 'old Serbia' was added to the modern Serbian state. Montenegro, the other independent South Slav state, which shared medieval history and a sense of common identity with Serbia, also received parts of 'old Serbia'. 'The day of defeat and sorrow for the lost freedom had now become a day of pride due to glorious victories and a day of joy because the Serbian people have been liberated from the Turkish rule', wrote an eyewitness.[3] Delegations of South Slavs from Austria-Hungary and from Montenegro turned Belgrade into a symbolic Yugoslav capital. When choirs and members of singers' societies sang the Croatian national anthem outside a restaurant in central Belgrade, there was spontaneous applause.[4]

'For the first time since [the] Kosovo [Battle of 1389], Serbia celebrated the *Vidovdan* [St Vitus's Day] as a day of the resurrection of the Serbdom ... many Serbs and Croats, especially from Dalmatia, went to Kosovo, and across Serbia people swam in a [sea of] patriotic fervour', recalled another contemporary.[5] South Slav students went on a pilgrimage to Kosovo, visiting the site of the medieval battle and nearby monasteries.[6] En route for the Kosovo celebrations Pašić, who was in the midst of a parliamentary election campaign, learned of Franz Ferdinand's assassination in Sarajevo.[7] The Austro-Hungarian authorities had, rather tactlessly, that day organized military manoeuvres in Bosnia, attended by Archduke Franz Ferdinand, his wife Duchess Sophie, and senior political and military officials, including General Oskar Potiorek, Bosnia's Habsburg Governor. By midday Franz

Ferdinand and Sophie were dead.[8] Following an unsuccessful attempt by Nedeljko Čabrinović, whose grenade missed the intended target, another assassin, Čabrinović's friend Gavrilo Princip, was unexpectedly presented with an opportunity to fire revolver shots at Franz Ferdinand's car, killing the archduke and, accidentally, the duchess. Both assassins were immediately arrested and it soon emerged that six – or, according to some sources, seven – would-be assassins intended to kill the heir to the Habsburg throne. All were detained, except Muhamed Mehmedbašić, who escaped across the Montenegrin border. The official investigation discovered a wider revolutionary network, with a central cell in Sarajevo, and established that three of the assassins, including Čabrinović and Princip, had recently been in Serbia where they had decided to assassinate the archduke.[9]

All members of the revolutionary network came from Bosnia-Herzegovina and thus were citizens of Austria-Hungary; most were ethnically Serb, but there were also Croats, Muslims and even the odd Slovene. They belonged to Young Bosnia, one of several South Slav nationalist youth organizations; it sought inspiration from contemporary European nationalist movements, such as Giuseppe Mazzini's Young Italy. Vladimir Gaćinović, one of the leading Young Bosnians, began calling himself a *garibaldinac* from the age of 15, and was something of an expert on Giuseppe Garibaldi and the *Risorgimento* (Leon Trotsky commissioned him to write an article on Italian nationalism). Princip cited Mazzini during his trial in 1914, while the police in Sarajevo discovered a note written shortly after the assassination by one of his associates, quoting Mazzini: 'There is no more sacred thing in the world than the duty of a conspirator, who becomes an avenger of humanity and the apostle of permanent natural laws.'[10]

The Young Bosnians sought the liberation of Bosnia-Herzegovina from the Habsburg rule and its unification with Serbia, Montenegro and other Habsburg South Slav territories in an independent state. They were Yugoslav nationalists, inspired by a romanticized interpretation of the past; they lamented the loss of the South Slavs' medieval independence from foreign invaders, in particular the Austrians, Hungarians and Ottoman Turks. It was especially the history of medieval Serbia and its struggle against the Ottomans, symbolised by its perceived defeat at the Field of Kosovo on 28 June 1389, the rich South Slav epic tradition and 19th-century romantic literature (including works by the Montenegrin prince-bishop Petar Petrović Njegoš) that inspired them. The cult of Miloš Obilić, the alleged assassin of Sultan Murad I at Kosovo, resonated powerfully among the Young Bosnians. They read widely: from Bakunin, Chernyshevsky, Kropotkin, Stepnyak and other Russian socialists and anarchists, through Marx, Lenin and Trotsky, to Herzen, Dostoyevsky, William Morris, Schiller, Ibsen and Jean-Marie Guyau.[11] Aspiring poets, writers[12] and philosophers, they believed their goals were noble and their revolutionary means justified, and hoped Serbia would play the role of a South Slav Piedmont.

§

Anti-Serb riots and demonstrations erupted in Bosnia, Croatia and elsewhere in the empire as the news of the assassination spread. Propaganda against Serbia and the Serbs reached new proportions. Prominent Serbs (as well as pro-Serb and pro-Yugoslav Croats, Slovenes and Muslims) were arrested and their property, schools and churches were damaged or destroyed, while the Serb Cyrillic script was banned in

Bosnia-Herzegovina. By the end of July, up to 5,500 Serbs had been interned, of whom between 700 and 2,200 were to die during the First World War of maltreatment, while another 460 Serbs were executed, some by the *Schutzcorps*, a militia composed of local Muslims and Croats. Many Serbs from eastern Bosnia (near the border with Serbia) were forcefully resettled into north-western parts of the province and as many as 5,200 Serb families may have been expelled to Serbia. The anti-Serb violence continued after the war broke out.[13] To avoid reprisals, Trumbić and several other South Slav leaders from Austria-Hungary fled to Italy, where they organized the Yugoslav Committee, which from 1915 advocated the creation of a Yugoslav state from London.[14]

Throughout the empire, the popular assumption was that Serbia was to blame for the assassination, though the Habsburg investigation failed to implicate the Serbian government. Friedrich von Wiesner, a high official of the Austro-Hungarian Foreign Ministry, concluded on 13 July that while there was evidence that the Bosnian nationalists drew support from Serbian organizations tolerated by the Belgrade government, the government itself was 'without any doubt not involved in the assassination, its planning or in providing weapons [to the assassins]'. Wiesner stated there were 'many reasons' to believe that any involvement by the Serbian government was 'out of the question'.[15]

Yet the Habsburg leadership was determined to act. On 5 July Alexander von Hoyos, another high official of the Austro-Hungarian Foreign Ministry, arrived in Berlin and secured Germany's support for radical measures against Serbia, though this was likely to antagonize France and Russia, and possibly Britain. The assassination, Serbia's possible involvement in it or indeed the unfortunate archduke and duchess were hardly mentioned during the talks.[16] The Imperial Foreign Minister Count Berchtold neutralised the more cautious Hungarian Prime Minister, Count Tisza, who opposed further action without German support. After the assassination Kaiser Wilhelm declared, 'It was high time that a clean sweep was made of the Serbs!', so the outcome of the 'Hoyos mission' was unsurprising.[17]

§

Austria-Hungary was determined to take action against Serbia despite no evidence of Belgrade's complicity being found (or even seriously sought, as historian Andrej Mitrović implied). Habsburg imperialism, combined with Austro-German and Hungarian nationalisms, clashed with Serbian and Yugoslav nationalisms. Vienna and Budapest feared South Slav irredentism, but for economic and strategic reasons still wished to expand further into the Balkans, even if that meant incorporating yet more Slavs into the empire.[18] The occupation of Bosnia-Herzegovina (formerly an Ottoman province) in 1878 had offered some compensation for humiliating defeats by France in 1859 and Prussia in 1866, leading to the unification of Italy and Germany, respectively, and to the transformation of Austria into Austria-Hungary. It seemed logical that the Dual Monarchy would seek further expansion into south-east Europe where another one of its rivals, the Ottoman Empire, was in decline. The British writer Edith Durham, travelling in the region before the First World War, observed that '"Nach Salonik" ["To Salonika", in Greek] was the favourite topic of conversation'.[19]

Bosnia-Herzegovina, which the Habsburgs occupied in 1878 under the terms of the Congress of Berlin, and then unilaterally annexed in 1908, was a major source of tension between Austria-Hungary and Serbia. Its annexation nearly led to war with Serbia, further radicalizing nationalist and anti-Habsburg sentiment among Slavs. Its population was overwhelmingly South Slav and Serbo-Croat-speaking, religiously mixed and predominantly rural. According to the Habsburg population census of 1910, there were 825,418 (43.5 per cent) Orthodox Serbs, 612,137 (32.2 per cent) Muslims and 434,061 (22.9 per cent) Catholic Croats.[20] The Serbs, many of whom lived in the countryside, in particular resented Austro-Hungarian rule, partly for economic reasons, while the Muslims, many of whom were urban dwellers, initially resisted the Habsburg occupation militarily, before eventually reluctantly accepting the new authorities.[21] Tens of thousands of Muslims emigrated to Ottoman Turkey between 1879 and 1910, leading Aleksa Šantić, an ethnic Serb poet from Mostar in Herzegovina to write in 1896 'Ostajte ovdje' (Stay here), one of the best-known Yugoslav poems. He pleaded with his Muslim neighbours to remain in Bosnia because 'The sun that shines in a foreign place, / Will never warm you like the sun in your own'.[22]

South Slav nationalists claimed Bosnia-Herzegovina on the 'nationality principle' and saw Austria-Hungary as a foreign occupier despite the socio-economic improvements which it introduced; but rivalry over Bosnia-Herzegovina was not the only reason for the difficult relationship between Belgrade and Vienna-Budapest. During the 1880s Serbia became a de facto Austro-Hungarian satellite, and the dependency on Vienna was in part responsible for the violent overthrow of the Obrenović dynasty in 1903, when a group of Serbian army officers massacred King Aleksandar and Queen Draga, and brought back the exiled Karadjordjević dynasty. Post-Obrenović Serbia drew closer to Russia – the Habsburgs' imperial rival – creating further tension between Vienna and Belgrade. Disagreements over railway credits and army purchases combined with an economic and political rapprochement between Serbia and Bulgaria, led to Austria-Hungary imposing a trade embargo on Belgrade in 1906. Serbia successfully developed new industries and found new markets (including Germany) for its wheat, corn and meat during the Tariff War (or the 'Pig War', named after Serbia's main livestock export). By 1911 Austria-Hungary was forced to concede a defeat and conclude a favourable trade agreement with Serbia.[23]

The annexation crisis showed that, despite domestic nationalist opinion, Serbia was not prepared to fight a war against its powerful neighbour, especially without Russia's support. It also showed that nationalism and increased military interference with politics threatened Serbia's fledgling democratic institutions.[24] The key figure in the 'military party' was Lieutenant-Colonel Dragutin Dimitrijević Apis, Chief of Army Intelligence. Dimitrijević was also one of the leaders of the 'Unification or Death' secret society (known by its enemies as the 'Black Hand'), a militant nationalist group formed in 1911 by politicians and officers who conspired against King Aleksandar before 1903. 'Unification or Death' had close links with another nationalist organization, the 'National Defence'. The two groups advocated an enlarged Serb or a South Slav state at the expense of the Austro-Hungarian and Ottoman empires. Believing the government incapable of fulfilling 'national goals', they began to challenge its authority. In early 1914, a civil-military conflict between Pašić's government and the Black Hand (who were supported by the opposition) led to the fall of the government. It probably also led to King Petar stepping aside, citing old age and poor health; his son, Crown Prince Aleksandar, reigned in his name as prince-regent (until 1921, when he became the King of Serbs, Croats and Slovenes, following Petar's death). The tensions between the military, specifically the officers involved in the 1903 conspiracy, and the political leadership were important factors in Serbia's behaviour in June–July 1914.

Increased political cooperation between Croat and Serb parties in the Habsburg Monarchy also contributed to growing tensions between Belgrade and Vienna. In 1906 a Croat-Serb Coalition won elections for the Croatian Diet and it was to dominate Croatian politics until 1914; one of its leaders was Trumbić. Belgrade became a South Slav cultural centre, with some leading Habsburg Yugoslav intellectuals and artists visiting or moving to the Serbian capital. They included the celebrated Croatian sculptor Ivan Meštrović, arguably the best-known advocate of Yugoslavism at the time, who drew inspiration from the Kosovo battle as the symbol of South Slav struggle against foreign domination and oppression.[25]

Serbia doubled its territory and significantly enhanced its prestige among Slavs living under the Habsburg Monarchy as a result of the Balkan Wars. Only the threat of Austro-Hungarian military intervention prevented Serbia and Montenegro taking over more territory in what is now northern Albania, the Habsburgs backing the creation of an Albanian state. Some Habsburg Slovenes and Croats viewed Serbia's successes with unease – especially those who had hoped to see a Habsburg mini-Yugoslavia emerge within a 'trialist monarchy', a solution that was favoured by, ironically, Franz Ferdinand. However, leaders of the Croat-Serb Coalition publicly celebrated Serbia's military successes against the Ottomans, as did many Bosnia's Serbs, which in turn made the local Muslim population uncomfortable.

The Ottoman defeats against Italy and the Balkan states in 1911–13, which led to the loss of territory in Libya and the Balkans, and an internal crisis caused by the Young Turks' revolution, did not go unnoticed in Austria-Hungary. Approaching 1914, the Habsburg leadership perceived an increasing threat from the South Slav nationalisms. The Serbian government indirectly supported the South Slav leaders in Austria-Hungary, but had to be careful not to provoke the empire and give it excuse to accuse Belgrade of working against its territorial integrity.[26] The Habsburgs attempted to discredit the leaders of the Croat-Serb Coalition, especially the Serbs, in two staged trials for high treason, but in the process only humiliated themselves and strengthened the resolve of the growing Serb-Croat front.[27]

This was the context in which the Austro-Hungarian military manoeuvres took place in Bosnia in June 1914. The potential risk to Franz Ferdinand was clear to many, including Baron Rumerskirch, a senior member of the archduke's entourage, who believed the visit should be postponed. Similarly, a member of the Bosnian assembly advised Potiorek that the archduke's visit on 28 June risked provoking Serbs.[28] Belgrade's minister to Vienna also allegedly advised against the visit (as discussed below), but it went ahead.

§

Whether Pašić gave a defiant speech upon learning of the assassination in Sarajevo is not clear, though it seems that he responded with a characteristic mixture of composure and caution. In Belgrade, Prince-regent Aleksandar reacted to the news with shock and disbelief, only saying, 'Poor woman, they could have at least spared her', before promptly retiring to his study.[29] The Serbian authorities halted the festivities throughout the country that same evening, an official state of mourning was proclaimed and the government sent its condolences immediately to Vienna, promising an investigation of any Serbian citizen involved in the murder.[30] In Montenegro the *Vidovdan* celebrations were immediately abandoned, condolences were sent, including from King Nikola to Emperor Franz Josef, while an official publication described the assassination as a 'mindless terrorist act [carried out] by isolated daydreamers'. A Montenegrin minister later recalled how the country's leaders received the news from Sarajevo with a mixture of 'joy and anxiety', while the people were 'just joyful', a description that, according to Mitrović, also applied to Serbia.[31]

The initial reaction of Serbia's leadership to the news from Sarajevo was paradigmatic of Belgrade's position over the next few weeks: it condemned the murder, distanced itself from the assassins, and was careful not to antagonize Austria-Hungary. It could do little about the general sense of jubilation – mixed with a sense of anxiety – among the Serbian public, though it did appeal for public restraint and tried to curb anti-Habsburg propaganda in the nationalist press. It proclaimed that it would try any person found in Serbia who was involved in the assassination, but in reality did little to carry out a full-scale investigation. Austria-Hungary also made no specific requests before its ultimatum to Serbia on 23 July. The Serbian government hoped to avoid war, and its hopes increased as time passed. Indeed, in late July politicians were campaigning for parliamentary elections called for 14 August (which were aborted by the war), while normal business and trade links between the two countries continued. Serbia's military leadership was hardly prepared for war, relying on outdated defence plans, while Field Marshal Putnik, the Chief of Staff, was on holiday in Gleichenberg, a spa in Austria.[32] Indeed, many of Europe's leaders and diplomats went on holiday in July – it was to be the last peaceful summer in five years.

Serbia's view, that the assassination was an internal Austro-Hungarian affair, since the assassin and his associates were all citizens of Austria-Hungary, may have been based on a literal reading of the facts, but it was naive wishful thinking to expect the Habsburgs to adopt the same position. Belgrade treated the assassination as a murder, while Vienna saw it as a product of pan-Serb nationalism, emphasizing the political background to the murder. As much as Belgrade attempted to argue otherwise, and as hard as the conspirators tried to protect Serbia during their trial by denying or minimising their Serbian contacts, in Vienna and Budapest there was no doubt who was responsible for the assassination. Serbia was to be punished not just for the murder of Franz Ferdinand, but also for its aggressive, anti-Habsburg nationalism.

The ultimatum presented on 23 July was designed to be rejected. The ten-point document blamed Serbia for not accepting the annexation of Bosnia, it (rightly) claimed that the assassination of Franz Ferdinand was planned in Serbia, where the assassins received financial support, training and weapons, and that Serbia's border officials secured a safe passage for the assassins. It demanded that Serbia ban all publications which spread anti-Habsburg propaganda, dissolve the National Defence and remove all military personnel who were involved in anti-Habsburg activities. Points 5 and 6 demanded that Serbia agree to the participation of Austro-Hungarian officials in the suppression of anti-Habsburg activities inside Serbia and a full *joint* investigation of all persons involved in the conspiracy found on Serbia's territory.[33] These two points were deemed – not just by Serbs – as directly challenging Serbia's independence. Upon receiving the ultimatum on Pašić's behalf, Finance Minister Lazar Paču cabled Serbia's diplomatic representatives abroad: '[t]he Serbian government has not made a decision [on how to respond] yet because not all cabinet ministers are presently in Belgrade, but I can say now that the demands are such that no Serbian government can accept them in full.'[34] Only with reluctance did Pašić abandon the election campaign and return to Belgrade early the following morning. The Cabinet convened rapidly as time was short – a reply was needed by 6 pm the following day.

Aleksandar asked the Tsar for Russia's help, fearing an immediate Austrian attack after the ultimatum expired. The government sought other allies, informing the British minister in Belgrade that Austro-Hungarian demands 'were such that no government of an independent state could ever comply fully', and seeking British influence for their modification.[35] The Serbian Cabinet worked on the text of the reply almost non-stop and finished drafting it shortly before the deadline. Jovan Jovanović wrote later: 'The hope in Russia [coming to protect Serbia] was significant, and it was justified, but it did not have any influence on Serbia's reply'.[36] The Tsar's reply to Belgrade's plea arrived two days after Serbia had responded to the ultimatum. Despite popular perception, Serbia's decision-making was more independent from St Petersburg than is often assumed.

Pašić went to the Austro-Hungarian legation carrying the reply, 'a long envelope, with Serbia's destiny sealed inside'. He returned calm and composed. After a short meeting with the Cabinet, the Prince-regent appeared, 'pale-faced and distraught', after learning that Baron Giesl, the

Austro-Hungarian minister to Serbia, stopped reading the reply as soon as he realised that not all demands were met. Giesl left Belgrade almost immediately, his luggage already packed. Expecting an imminent attack on Belgrade, the government moved to Niš, some 150 miles south of the capital, while the army headquarters decamped to Kragujevac, in central Serbia, albeit without the Chief of Staff, who was still in Austria-Hungary.[37]

Just before replying to the ultimatum, Belgrade informed its allies that it would accept all demands that it could, that the reply would be conciliatory and should satisfy Austria-Hungary, 'unless it wishes war at all costs'.[38] Each word of the reply was measured carefully, its tone in stark contrast to the aggressive language of the ultimatum. The Serbian government accepted all demands, but claimed that it did not understand Point 5 fully, while as regards Point 6, it was prepared to accept it so long as it did not contravene international law of domestic judiciary – in effect rejecting these two demands. The reply ended with a note stating that 'The Royal Government considers it to be in the interest of both parties not to hurry in deciding this matter', adding that it was prepared 'in the event that the Imperial and Royal Government is not satisfied with this reply', either to bring the dispute 'before the International Court in the Hague' or to ask for mediation by 'the Great Powers' which had assisted in solving the post-annexation crisis.[39] The Serbian reply was so well put together that one of the authors of the Austro-Hungarian ultimatum described it as 'The most brilliant specimen of diplomatic skill' he had ever seen.[40]

The reply indeed impressed the Great Powers, while Kaiser Wilhelm stated that there was no longer any reason for war, so Austria-Hungary should call off its military mobilisation. Serbia followed Russia's advice and withdrew its forces from the border with the Dual Monarchy, although still carrying out a full mobilisation. The government explained that the mobilisation was ordered in the aftermath of Austria-Hungary's decision to break off diplomatic relations with Serbia. 'If we are attacked, the army will perform its duty', the statement read. Montenegro offered its support, King Nikola declaring, 'Our Serb People will emerge from the tribulation that has been imposed on us, and secure a bright future. My Montenegrins are already at the border, ready to die for the defense of our independence.' Prince-regent Aleksandar replied, claiming that Serbia had 'tried everything to avoid new losses and new burdens [being imposed] on the Serb people, but we have failed because Austria-Hungary demanded that we sacrifice our dear independence.'[41]

⁂

These statements portray Serbia (and Montenegro) as acting merely in self-defence, unsurprisingly neglecting to mention the South Slav nationalist aspirations vis-à-vis Austria-Hungary. But was 'official' Serbia involved in the assassination? There is no evidence to suggest that Serbia's leadership wished to involve the country in a dangerous confrontation by organising or even encouraging the assassination of the heir to the Habsburg throne. Did Belgrade know about it? If so, could it have prevented the crime and warned Austro-Hungarian authorities? On the occasion of the tenth anniversary of the outbreak of the war, Ljubomir-Ljuba Jovanović, Minister of Education in 1914, published his recollections of the events of June–July 1914 in an obscure volume produced by Russian émigrés in Yugoslavia. Jovanović claimed that 'at the end of May or the beginning of June [1914]', Pašić revealed 'that there were people who were preparing to go to Sarajevo to kill Francis Ferdinand, who was to go there to be solemnly received on *Vidov Dan* [St Vitus's Day].' The plot was allegedly 'hatched by a group of secretly organised persons and in patriotic Bosno-Herzegovinian [sic] student circles in Belgrade.' Pašić and Interior Minister Stojan Protić tried to prevent the illegal border crossings, but it was too late as frontier officials working for Apis had already facilitated a safe passage for the Bosnian students.[42]

Despite Jovanović's claim receiving attention from con-temporaries,[43] specialists such as R W Seton-Watson were not persuaded of its credibility.[44] Jovanović subsequently clarified that the conversation did not take place during a Cabinet meeting, but that Pašić revealed his knowledge of the plot to a few ministers only, which would explain why no minutes of the meeting exist. Protić had died before the publication of the article and Pašić never commented publicly, let alone denied, the claim. In the mid-1920s the relationship between Jovanović and Pašić was not amicable. The former had emerged as a rival leader within the Radical Party, forming his own faction, and, in King Aleksandar's eyes at least, as an alternative candidate to replace Pašić as prime minister. Pašić managed to have Jovanović expelled from the party in early 1926, at the time when he was forced by Aleksandar to resign as prime minister.[45] It seems plausible that Jovanović either misremembered or made up the part of the story that alleges that Pašić knew of the plot to assassinate Franz Ferdinand, but he did not invent the entire story.

Serbian government papers first revealed by historian Vladimir Dedijer in the late 1970s show that Pašić had some knowledge of armed Bosnian students crossing the border. In a letter to Pašić dated 15 June, Protić warned that although arms smuggling had been proceeding without the Cabinet's approval, it was the government that would bear all responsibility if these clandestine activities became public knowledge. Pašić agreed, adding that such 'crossings ought to be prevented ... for they are very dangerous for us.' They were aware that Apis's agitation in Bosnia 'could provoke a war between Serbia and Austria-Hungary, which in the present circumstances would be very dangerous'.[46] It seems unlikely the Serbian ministers knew details of the plot, though they probably suspected Franz Ferdinand's life could be in danger. Illegal border crossings by armed men were a common occurrence at the time, but Pašić ordered an internal investigation into the Black Hand-Young Bosnia activities in Serbia. An anonymous note found by Austro-Hungarians in Pašić's papers speculated that Austrians might arrange to have 'that foolish Ferdinand' assassinated during the military manoeuvres in Bosnia as an excuse to attack Serbia.[47]

The Serbian government did not officially inform the Austro-Hungarian authorities of the border crossings or of its internal investigation. Pašić did not wish to put his country at risk by revealing anything to an unfriendly neighbour he believed was looking for excuses to attack Serbia. Moreover, if it became public that Pašić warned Vienna, accusations that he sided with Austria-Hungary against the South Slavs in the Monarchy would have seriously weakened his position at home at the time of the election campaign and the conflict with Apis and the nationalist organisations. Pašić knew that Jovan Jovanović had links with the Black Hand and the officers would likely find out from his minister in Vienna if he had warned Austria-Hungary.[48] Did Pašić fear losing more than his political support? It is hard to say, but he was aware of the methods employed by the Black Hand.

Yet an unofficial warning appears to have been delivered by the Serbian minister in Vienna. On or around 21 June, Jovan Jovanović went to see Finance Minister Leon Biliński, responsible for Bosnia-Herzegovina, to express his concern that something might happen during the archduke's visit to Sarajevo, given the date chosen for the event. Biliński did not take this to be a clear warning and so apparently did not report the conversation to his superiors, and after the war he refused to talk about the whole episode. In correspondence with Seton-Watson after the war, Jovanović maintained that he went to warn Biliński on his own initiative. The Austro-Hungarian minister, in his view, should have interpreted this as a formal visit and treated his warning as official.[49] In an interview with a Hungarian paper given in early July 1914, Pašić strongly denied that he could have issued any warnings.[50]

Members of the Black Hand and the National Defence believed that murdering a tyrannical ruler was justified, and they perceived the Habsburgs as tyrants. It is probable that, independently from the Young Bosnians, they had planned to assassinate Franz Ferdinand and other leading Habsburg officials. Dedijer demonstrates convincingly that Princip and his friends approached the Black Hand and the National Defence for help, not the other way around, and that eventually Apis and his associates agreed to assist them.[51] It is unlikely Apis would have chosen untrained amateurs to carry out a political assassination of such magnitude. He was, however, willing to provide them with training and weapons, and to facilitate their safe passage into Bosnia. Apis's involvement was probably not in his capacity as Chief of Army Intelligence, but as a member of the Black Hand.[52] Yet, during the July crisis, such nuances would count for little. The very fact that prominent individuals and organisations in Serbia had direct contact with the assassins – even if Apis appears to have never met Princip – meant that the Serbian government had little chance of countering accusations, only too readily fired from Vienna, that Serbia was responsible for the arch- duke's murder and must be punished.

§

Serbia, with its secret societies and a nationalist government and public opinion, was not an innocent victim, as some have maintained, while Austria-Hungary was not a peaceful empire provoked into war by sinister Balkan nationalism, as others have argued. The Belgrade government did not organise the assassination and most probably did not know of the plot, but it was unable, or unwilling, to remove figures such as Apis from positions of power and influence or to close down the nation- alist associations, despite clashing with them. This conflict would be resolved in 1917, when Aleksandar and Pašić, them- selves involved in a political struggle, joined forces to bring Apis to a show trial, when the colonel was sentenced to death for an alleged attempt on the Prince-regent's life. Aleksandar and Pašić would later resume their rivalry, which would reach a climax in early 1926, when Pašić was forced to resign as prime minister. Pašić died before the end of the year, while Aleksandar was assassinated in 1934, when on a state visit to France, by a Macedonian revolutionary working with the Croatian Ustaša. Apis was rehabilitated by Tito's Communist government after the Second World War, while Princip and the Young Bosnians were celebrated in socialist Yugoslavia as fighters against foreign, imperial oppression, even proto-communists. Princip died in prison just months before the end of the war, his young age and Habsburg laws sparing his life in 1914.[53]

Serbia was not ready for a war in 1914, but a future confrontation with Austria-Hungary, the 'prison of (South Slav) nations', was widely expected in Belgrade. In the end, Serbia was attacked by Austria-Hungary, the Sarajevo assassination providing the Habsburgs with an opportunity to eliminate the threat they believed the South Slav nationalisms posed. It is likely the two countries would have clashed sooner or later even without the assassination because of their incompatible goals in the Balkans. When and if such a war would have broken out and whether it would have spread globally, as it did in summer 1914, will remain speculation.

Not satisfied with Serbia's reply to the ultimatum, it was only a matter of time before Austria-Hungary would attack its south-eastern neighbour. The Foreign Minister Berchtold used a false report of a Serbian attack on Habsburg troops to persuade the reluctant Franz Josef to support a declaration of war on Serbia. Written in French, it was sent on 28 July by ordinary telegraph service via Bucharest and reached Niš around midday. According to eyewitnesses, it was delivered to 'Evropa', a restaurant where Pašić was having lunch. Not sounding the least surprised, he allegedly said: 'Austria has declared war on us. Our cause is just. God will help us.'[54] Hours later Austro-Hungarian troops shelled Belgrade, while cries of *Serbien muss sterbien* ('Serbia must die') echoed throughout the empire. Neither Serbia nor Austria-Hungary survived the First World War which began that day, with both sides suffering heavy casualties, Serbia's losses being particularly high.[55] At the end of the war Austria-Hungary disintegrated, its South Slav territories joining Serbia and Montenegro in a new Yugoslav state, as Princip and the Young Bosnians had once dreamed.

3

28 July 1914: Austria-Hungary declares war on Serbia
The Dual Monarchy Stumbles into War
Bryan Cartledge

In the last week of June 1914, the Prime Minister of Hungary, Count István Tisza, was enjoying his first holiday since assuming office, for the second time, a year earlier. In the late afternoon of Sunday 28 June, while relaxing on his family estate near the village of Geszt in eastern Hungary, he received a telegram telling him that Archduke Franz Ferdinand, heir to the imperial throne since the suicide of Crown Prince Rudolf 25 years earlier, and his wife Sophie, had been assassinated in Sarajevo. Tisza was immediately driven to the nearest railway station, caught the first train to Budapest and then travelled overnight to Vienna. On the following morning, he called on Emperor Franz Josef at the Schönbrunn Palace to express his condolences; the Emperor had returned to the capital from his country retreat at Bad Ischl. Tisza was then driven to the Ballplatz and sought out the Monarchy's Foreign Minister, Count Leopold von Berchtold, who had also rushed back to Vienna from his country estate.[1] Their conversation inaugurated four weeks of the most intense diplomatic activity and political crisis that Europe had known.

§

István Tisza, whose father Kálmán had dominated Hungarian politics during the last quarter of the 19th century, was a man of great strength of character with three unshakeable convictions. The first was that Hungary's survival depended on its continued partnership with Austria in the Dual Monarchy and on the Monarchy's alliance with Germany, where he had studied during the era of his hero, Bismarck. The second was his belief in the mission of the Magyar nobility to lead their nation and to preserve its Magyar character; he therefore resolutely opposed any move towards greater democracy in Hungary, and any significant concessions to the national minorities – Slovaks, Romanians, Serbs, Croats and Saxons – who by 1910 made up nearly half the country's population. Tisza's third conviction, related to the second, was that the Dual Monarchy should eschew any policy which might, by annexation or incorporation, increase the Slav or Romanian elements in the population of Hungary, thereby endangering the nation's slim Magyar majority which had been created by the government's controversial policies of 'Magyarisation'.[2]

Tisza was nevertheless all too aware of the potential threat posed to the Monarchy by the ambitions of Serbia, its southern neighbour, which had significantly enlarged its territory in the second Balkan war at the expense of Bulgaria and had been dislodged from its partial occupation of newly independent Albania only by the Monarchy's threat of war in its ultimatum of 18 October 1913; the Monarchy was determined to deny Serbia access to the Adriatic. Ethnic Serbs made up a significant proportion of the population of southern Hungary and presented a constant temptation to Serbian irredentism. In March 1914, Tisza had presented a memorandum to Franz Josef warning against the threat of the formation of a Balkan League, led by Serbia and backed by Russia. Tisza urged that Germany should be encouraged to take this threat more seriously and to consider wooing Bulgaria into the Triple Alliance (Germany, Austria-Hungary and Italy) as a counterweight to Serbia, given that Romania's secret commitment to the alliance could not be relied upon. Franz Josef approved the memorandum which, with minor amendments made by Berchtold's officials, had by 24 June become a formal statement of the Monarchy's Balkan policy for transmission to its German ally.[3]

Tisza's journey from Geszt to Vienna had given him time to reflect on the implications of the Sarajevo assassinations. Despite his strong religious faith – he was a devout Calvinist – he must have reacted to the news with considerable relief. Franz Ferdinand's fierce hostility towards Hungary, and towards Tisza personally, was no secret. He had expected before very long to succeed his uncle, who was now 83 and had been seriously ill in the spring, and he had openly discussed with his intimates plans for restructuring the Dual Monarchy immediately after his accession. Although these plans were unformed and frequently changed, their common theme was the demotion of Hungary from equal partner to subordinate; Hungary would become just one among other members of an Austrian-led imperial federation. The Compromise (Ausgleich) of 1867 would be dismantled. The Archduke remarked that he would not allow Tisza to remain Prime Minister for more than a day, since within two he would be leading an uprising of the Hungarian gentry against their new Emperor and his reforms. Hungary, he declared, 'will have to be conquered once again at the point of the sword'.[4]

Tisza knew, however, that he had made a good impression on the German Kaiser, Wilhelm II, when they had met for the first time in March. The Kaiser had described him afterwards as 'this real statesman'.[5] Tisza did not know (but would not have been surprised to learn) that when Franz Ferdinand had met the Kaiser in mid-June, just two weeks before the arch-duke's murder, he had done his best to undermine Wilhelm's favourable opinion of Tisza, describing him as a dictator who persecuted the Romanian minority and planned to form an independent Hungarian army.[6] From the Hungarian per-spective, therefore, the Sarajevo assassinations had removed a potent threat to the nation's future. Initially Tisza, who lacked experience in foreign affairs, does not appear to have given much thought to the wider implications of the Sarajevo tragedy. His conversation with Berchtold in the Ballplatz on 29 June opened his eyes.

Count Leopold von Berchtold was rich, cultivated, elegant and charming. Despite having served as the Monarchy's ambassador in St Petersburg, he knew very little about foreign affairs, which ranked third in his interests behind horse racing and aristocratic society. He was indecisive and inclined to share the opinion of the last person to whom he had spoken. As a minister, he was over-dependent on his officials in the Ballplatz. He was well aware that the Monar-chy's feeble showing during the Balkan wars had called into question its status as a Great Power and that he personally bore much of the responsibility for this. Serbia had called the Monarchy's bluff and won. In 1914, therefore, Berchtold was determined that history would not repeat itself; he would be tough and decisive. Having repeatedly deflected the insistence of the Monarchy's Chief of General Staff, General Conrad von Hötzendorf, for a settling of accounts with Serbia by force, Berchtold was now, after Sarajevo, more than ready to contemplate the punitive war that was being urged upon him by his officials.[7]

This was the new Berchtold whom Tisza encountered in the Ballplatz. There is no record of their conversation; but Tisza was sufficiently alarmed by Berchtold's uncharacteristic bellicosity to compose another memorandum to the Emperor, which Franz Josef received on Wednesday 1 July. In it, Tisza claimed to have told Berchtold that to use the Sarajevo assassinations as a pretext for war against Serbia would be 'a fatal mistake'. He argued that there was so far insufficient evidence of official Serbian complicity in the crime to justify military action, and that the Monarchy would 'appear before the whole world as a disturber of the peace, kindling the fires of a major war in the most unfavourable conditions'. Before launching an attack, the Monarchy should use diplomacy to create a more favourable constellation of forces in the Balkans: Germany must be persuaded to make a public declaration of its allegiance to the Triple Alliance or, failing that, to join the Monarchy in wooing Bulgaria. Only then would war become a viable option.[8]

For tactical reasons, Tisza did not include in his memorandum his three most powerful reasons for opposing an immediate war with Serbia. He perceived, correctly, that Romania was sliding away from the Triple Alliance into Russia's orbit; and that if, as was likely, Russia intervened in the Balkans to defend her fellow Slavs and Orthodox believers in Serbia, Romania might take advantage of hostilities on the Monarchy's eastern front to pounce on Transylvania and reunite its large Romanian population with their ethnic motherland, an ambition as old as the Romanian state itself. Secondly, Tisza was all too aware of the Monarchy's military weakness; for it was his own Hungarian Parliament which had for the past decade denied funding for the common defence of the Dual Monarchy – Tisza owed his appointment as premier to his success in breaking this political deadlock. And, finally, Tisza feared that a victorious war against Serbia would result in annexations that would increase the Slav element in Hungary's population. He also had a deep moral aversion to war. In a letter to his niece in August 1914, he wrote, 'War, even if victorious, is terrible. For my soul, every war means misery, suffering, destruction, the shedding of innocent blood, the suffering of innocent women and children.'[9]

Tisza's arguments seem to have impressed Berchtold because when, on the evening of 29 June, Conrad proposed the mobilisation of the Monarchy's armies on 1 July, he found that Berchtold's martial ardour had significantly cooled. Berchtold expressed concern that, in the absence of firm evidence of Serbian guilt, public opinion was insufficiently prepared for war. A strongly worded diplomatic note, demanding among other things the dismissal of the Serbian minister responsible for the police, would be a necessary prelude to mobilisation. Conrad contemptuously dismissed this suggestion and demanded war. Both men agreed, however, that the final decision was the Emperor's; and that, in view of the risk of Russian intervention, a declaration of war required the assurance of full German support.[10]

There was now a pressing need to ascertain Berlin's, and in particular the volatile Kaiser's, reactions to Sarajevo. Wilhelm II's expected attendance at the funeral of Franz Ferdinand and Sophie on 3 July would offer an ideal occasion both to sound him out and also to present him with the final version of Tisza's memorandum on Balkan policy. But at the last minute the Kaiser, fearing a terrorist attack, decided not to attend – the Germans understandably had a low opinion of Austrian competence in security matters. Berchtold therefore was persuaded to send to Berlin his *chef de cabinet*, Count Alexander Hoyos, a young, ambitious diplomat who was a vocal member of the 'war party' in the Ballplatz. Hoyos carried two important documents: the revised version of Tisza's memorandum, to which Berchtold now added a post-Sarajevo addendum stressing 'the need for the Monarchy with a firm hand to sever the threads which its enemies seek to draw close into a net over its head'; and a personal letter from Franz Josef to the Kaiser which concluded by urging the elimination of Serbia 'as a political power factor in the Balkans'.[11] With these two documents, of which Tisza was kept in ignorance until after their dispatch to Berlin, the Monarchy nailed its colours to the mast. Any retreat from its stated commitment to punitive action against Serbia would involve a humiliating loss of face which could be fatal to the German alliance.

In Berlin on 5 July, working in tandem with the Monarchy's veteran ambassador to Germany, Count Ladislaus Szögyény, Hoyos found that he was pushing against an open door. After a pause for reflection and with the proviso that he would have to consult his Chancellor, Theobald von Bethmann Hollweg, Kaiser Wilhelm assured Szögyény over lunch that the Monarchy 'could reckon on full support from Germany', despite the acknowledged risk of Russian intervention. Moreover, the Kaiser urged that action against Serbia should be undertaken without delay; he would deplore the Monarchy's 'not taking advantage of the present moment which is so favourable to us' – by which Wilhelm meant that Russia was not yet ready for war.[12] Hoyos, meanwhile, was engaged in parallel discussions with Alfred Zimmerman, Under-Secretary at the German Foreign Ministry. Hoyos took it upon himself to inform Zimmerman that the Monarchy intended to launch a surprise attack on Serbia, without any preliminaries, and that Serbian territory would then be portioned between Austria-Hungary, Bulgaria and Albania. Zimmerman expressed full sympathy with the Monarchy's refusal to tolerate further provocation, advising that if the Monarchy intended to act it should do so immediately: diplomatic preliminaries would give the Entente (France, Russia and Great Britain) time to mobilise its own diplomacy. Later the Kaiser consulted both Bethmann Hollweg and leaders of the German military establishment, neither raising any objections to the provisional promise of support given to Szögyény. On 6 July, therefore, while the Kaiser departed for his annual northern cruise, Bethmann Hollweg could confirm to Szögyény and Hoyos Germany's backing in whatever action the Monarchy might take against Serbia; and that the present was more favourable for such action than later. With this affirmation, Germany signed the notorious 'blank cheque', which Hoyos bore triumphantly back to Vienna.[13] Had the Germans known that the Hungarian Prime Minister, with his constitutional right of veto over policies of common interest, was adamantly opposed to war, they might have hesitated.

Tisza, having been apprised of the contents of Franz Josef's letter to Wilhelm and of Berchtold's bellicose postscript to the memorandum on Balkan policy only when it was too late to amend them, immediately requested a meeting of the Common Ministerial Council. This body, the highest political institution of the Dual Monarchy, comprised all the ministers responsible for policy areas of common interest – foreign affairs, finance and defence – together with the premiers of Austria and Hungary and, on occasion, the commanding officers of the imperial and royal army and navy. Berchtold scheduled the Council meeting for Tuesday 7 July. Meanwhile Conrad, in a private audience on Sunday, had secured Franz Josef's agreement that if German support was forthcoming, war could be declared on Serbia. Bolstered by this knowledge and by Szögyény's reports from Berlin, Berchtold asked Tisza and his Austrian counterpart, Count Stürgkh, to meet him for a pre-Council briefing. The German Ambassador, Heinrich von Tschirschky, was also invited. Berchtold and Hoyos, who had just returned from Berlin, gave the two Prime Ministers a full account of the Berlin conversations, including that of Hoyos with Zimmerman. Tisza was livid. He demanded that the Germans must be told that Hoyos had been expressing his personal views about attacking and partitioning Serbia, not those of the Monarchy. Berchtold had no option but to agree.[14] Tschirschky took careful note.

When the Common Ministerial Council assembled in the Ballplatz on the afternoon of 7 July, therefore, Berchtold had to build the case for early military action against Serbia from scratch: Tisza had neutralised the advantage which, if unchallenged, the Hoyos report would have given him. Berchtold confirmed Berlin's assurance of unconditional support for whatever action the Monarchy might decide. He conceded that Russia would probably intervene on Serbia's behalf, but argued that this strengthened the case for prompt action: delay would give an impression of weakness and give Russia time to form a league of Balkan states hostile to the Monarchy. Tisza's response was initially conciliatory: the facts revealed by the inquiry into the Sarajevo assassinations together with the defiant tone of the Serbian press had, he said, persuaded him that the possibility of 'military measures' against Serbia was less remote than he had first thought. But he would 'never agree to a surprise attack on Serbia without preliminary diplomatic preparation'; such a course would discredit the Monarchy in the eyes of Europe and incur the hostility of the whole of the Balkans apart from Bulgaria. Demands should certainly be made of Serbia and an ultimatum should follow if these demands – which must be stiff but not impossible of fulfilment – were not met. If they were rejected he favoured military action, provided this was not aimed at Serbia's destruction. As Hungarian premier, he could never agree to the Monarchy annexing any part of Serbia. Timing, Tisza added, was not for Germany to determine. He saw no compelling reason to go to war yet.[15]

Count Karl Stürgkh, the Austrian Prime Minister, then inserted a skilful probe into what later transpired to be Tisza's Achilles heel. Stürgkh argued that Tisza should reflect that 'by a policy of hesitancy and weakness we run the risk at a later time of being no longer so sure of this unreserved support from the German Empire'. Tisza stood firm and the Council agreed that 'mobilisation should only take place after concrete demands have been placed before and rejected by Serbia and an ultimatum has been presented.' But only Tisza believed a purely diplomatic success would suffice. His colleagues were united in considering such a success to be worthless, even if Serbia suffered 'a resounding humiliation'; they therefore envisaged demands of Serbia so severe that they were bound to be rejected. Tisza nonetheless insisted that the text of the note to Serbia should be submitted to him before dispatch so that he could check that its demands were not framed so as to ensure its rejection.[16] After the meeting Tisza, his voice trembling with anger, told the Monarchy's ambassador to Serbia, von Giesl, that if the action taken resulted in war and the destruction of Serbia's sovereignty, he would resign.[17]

Since a decision to go to war had to be made jointly by both halves of the Dual Monarchy, Tisza had effectively stymied the possibility of the surprise attack favoured by all his colleagues – and, apparently, by Germany. He consequently thought it prudent to argue his case in yet another memorandum to the Emperor, which was submitted on Wednesday 8 July. Tisza stated that an attack on Serbia would result in 'the intervention of Russia and with it a world war', in which the Monarchy would find itself fighting not only Russia but Romania as well, a profoundly unfavourable situation. Serbia, Tisza argued, should therefore 'be given the opportunity to avoid war by means of a severe diplomatic defeat'; if war nevertheless resulted, the Monarchy would at least be in a stronger position before world opinion. To the same end, Tisza continued, the Monarchy should declare publicly that it had 'no intention of annihilating, let alone of annexing, Serbia'. Serbia should be obliged only to disgorge territory it had seized from Bulgaria, Albania and Greece; the Monarchy should content itself with 'strategic frontier rectifications'. He could not, he concluded, associate himself with responsibility for going to war as the only solution to the crisis – another veiled threat of resignation.[18]

Berchtold – who, for all his indecisiveness, was an astute politician – now embarked on a subtle campaign to wear down Tisza's opposition. On 8 July, he informed Tisza that, according to the German ambassador, the Kaiser expected the Monarchy to act against Serbia and would not understand failure by the Monarchy to seize this opportunity. At the same time – whether at Berchtold's instigation or not is unclear – pressure was applied to Tisza from another quarter. Baron István Burián was a former professional Hungarian diplomat who had held the post of Common Minister of Finance for nine years until 1912; in 1913 Tisza, on taking the Hungarian premiership for the second time, had appointed him 'Minister at the King's Side (*a latere*)', the archaically named post which combined responsibility for representing Hungary's interests at the imperial court with that for handling Hungary's foreign affairs, to the extent that these could be separated from the Monarchy's. Tisza, whose experience of foreign affairs was limited, at first used Burián as his personal adviser in this field. Burián enjoyed the confidence of Franz Josef who later, in 1915, appointed him to succeed Berchtold as the Monarchy's Common Foreign Minister. On 10 July, Burián discussed the crisis with Tisza in Budapest; and on 12 July Burián turned up at Bad Ischl, where he is likely to have had a conversation with the Emperor and to have informed Tisza of its content. Significantly, Tisza had received no response from the Emperor to his memorandum of 8 July – an indication that it had not met with whole-hearted imperial approval.[19]

On 10 July, Berchtold gave Conrad an account of his previous evening's meeting with the Emperor, telling him: 'Tisza … is urging prudence and opposes war; but Baron Burián is in Budapest for discussions with Tisza.' The 'but' is significant: it points to the probability that Berchtold had sent Burián to Budapest to change Tisza's mind. Berchtold also arranged to meet Tisza himself, in Vienna on 14 July, when he would have an initial report from Dr Wiesner, Legal Adviser to the Ballplatz, who had been dispatched to Sarajevo to investigate Serbian links with the assassination plot.[20]

When they met, Berchtold held strong cards. First, although

Wiesner had found no evidence to indicate complicity of the Serbian Government in the assassinations, he reported that it was beyond doubt that the murderers had been equipped and smuggled across the frontier by Serbian railway and customs officials. Secondly, Berchtold was able to quote from two telegrams from the Monarchy's ambassador to Berlin, Szögyény, confirming German support, from the Kaiser downwards, for 'vigorous measures against Serbia' which should be taken without delay.[21] Russian intervention, in the German view, was not inevitable; and British involvement in a Balkan war even less likely. Germany would ensure Romania's good behaviour – the Kaiser had sent a stiff letter to King Carol. Tisza does not seem to have put up much of a fight. Burián's softening-up exercise had evidently been effective; the evidence of Serbian guilt was becoming stronger; and the reports from Berlin seemed to discount the threat of Russian intervention to which Tisza, with the security of Transylvania in mind, had been so sensitive. Above all Tisza, with his profound attachment to the German alliance, was vulnerable to the argument that if the Monarchy failed to take decisive action it would be seen in Berlin as 'unfit for alliance (*bündnisunfähig*)'. Personal vanity was also a powerful factor: Tisza greatly valued the Kaiser's good opinion of him and had no wish to jeopardise it. For all these reasons, Tisza dropped his opposition to war and accepted a two- rather than three-stage diplomatic scenario: a 48-hour ultimatum would now be incorporated in the note making specific demands of Serbia, rather than following it. On one point, however, Tisza remained immovable: the Common Ministerial Council must approve a declaration, to be made public before the outbreak of hostilities, forswearing any annexation of Serbian territory apart from necessary frontier adjustments. Berchtold was obliged to accept this.[22]

Tisza rushed to the German embassy to inform Tschirschky of the meeting's outcome, clearly hoping that the Kaiser would quickly be informed of his conversion to the 'war party'; he would have been gratified to know that the Kaiser did scribble on Tschirschky's subsequent report: 'Well, a real man at last!'[23] On 15 July Tisza explained his change of heart to the Hungarian Parliament in Budapest: 'War is a very sad *ultima ratio*, which should not be used until all other means are exhausted but, naturally, every nation and state, if it wishes to remain what it is, has to be prepared to be able and willing to fight a war if necessary.'[24]

Berchtold could now determine the content of the note to the Serbian government and consider, in consultation with Conrad, the timing of its delivery. Drafting was entrusted to a senior official in the Ballplatz. A number of factors complicated the question of timing. First, nearly half of the imperial and royal army was scattered throughout the Austro-Hungarian countryside on 'harvest leave', which had recently been introduced as a sop to the Monarchy's landowners. The army would not return to full strength until 25 July.[25] Secondly there was French President, Raymond Poincaré's imminent state visit to Russia, where he would be Tsar Nicholas II's guest from 20 to 23 July; Poincaré would make the five-day voyage to St Petersburg and back in a French battleship. The delivery of the Monarchy's ultimatum to Serbia during Poincaré's visit would not only be seen as a direct affront to the Tsar but would also stimulate a spirit of solidarity between the two leading members of the Triple Entente and facilitate a coordinated response to the Monarchy's aggressive act. Berchtold, Tisza, Burián and Stürgkh thus agreed to deliver a 48-hour ultimatum only on 23 July, the day of Poincaré's departure, so that it would expire on 25 July when he and his Prime Minister would be virtually incommunicado on the high seas.[26]

It was essential that the Monarchy's plans remain secret until Poincaré's state visit ended. To create an impression of normality, Conrad left Vienna for the country; Alexander Krobatin, the Common Minister of War, was already on leave and remained undisturbed. Half the army continued to help with the harvest on the Monarchy's great estates. No officers were recalled. When the Common Ministerial Council assembled on 19 July, at Tisza's insistence, to approve the final text of the ultimatum to Serbia, it met at Berchtold's private residence, with the ministers arriving individually in private cars.[27]

In drafting the note-cum-ultimatum, Ballplatz officials and Berchtold himself had to tread a fine line between ensuring its rejection by Serbia and making its terms so obviously unacceptable that Tisza would refuse to endorse it. Berchtold's wife told her family that 'poor Leopold could not sleep on the day when he wrote [finalised] his ultimatum to the Serbs, as he was so worried that they would accept it. Several times in the night he had got up and altered or added some clause, to reduce this risk.'[28] The text which the Common Ministerial Council approved on 19 July contained a number of demands relating to the disavowal and suppression by the Serbian Government of activities and organisations hostile to the Monarchy. The two clauses, numbers 5 and 6, which Berchtold and his officials hoped would make rejection of the ultimatum a virtual certainty, read as follows:

[The Royal Serbian Government further undertakes]:
5. To accept the collaboration in Serbia of organs of the Imperial and Royal Government in the suppression of

the subversive movement directed against the territorial integrity of the Monarchy;

6. To take judicial proceedings against the accessories to the plot of 28 June who are on Serbian territory; organs delegated by the Imperial and Royal [Austro-Hungarian] Government will take part in the investigations relating thereto.

These clauses represented, and were intended to be seen as, clear violations of Serbian sovereignty.[29]

Tisza accepted the text but continued to insist, as a condition of his approval of the ultimatum, that 'no plans of conquest by the Monarchy are linked with the action against Serbia and that except for frontier rectifications for military reasons not an inch of Serbian territory will be annexed by us.' After a vigorous debate in which all Tisza's ministerial colleagues opposed his demand on the grounds that it was an unnecessary hostage to fortune, the Council had no choice but to accede to it. It was accordingly resolved that 'immediately on the outbreak of war the foreign Powers shall receive a statement that the Monarchy is not waging a war of conquest and does not purpose to annex the Kingdom [of Serbia]. Strategically necessary frontier rectifications and such temporary occupation of Serbian territory as may eventually become necessary are not ruled out by this resolution.' At the end of the meeting, Conrad quietly commented to General Krobatin, the Common Minister for War: 'Well, we shall see. Before the Balkan war the Powers talked about the *status quo* – after the war, nobody bothered about it any more.'[30] Other members of the Council, apart from Tisza, doubtless shared the view that when Serbia had been defeated the Monarchy's self-denying declaration would be quietly forgotten.

As the members of the ministerial Council left Berchtold's house on the afternoon of Sunday 19 July, it would have seemed to them that, with the text of the ultimatum finally approved, nothing could be expected to happen until its delivery to the Serbian Government at 6 pm on 23 July. Harvesting could continue, summer vacations were briefly resumed. The Ballplatz, of course, was busy. On Monday 20 July, the ultimatum was despatched under seal to the Monarchy's minister in Belgrade, Baron Giesl, in good time for its formal presentation three days later; similar instructions were sent to the Monarchy's ambassadors and ministers in other capitals, who would deliver the text, with appropriate explanations, on 24 July to the states' governments. Even Berlin was not shown the text until the eve of its delivery, probably for fear that the Germans might wish to tone it down.[31]

In the meantime, however, all Berchtold's precautions against a premature leak concerning the Monarchy's intentions had been undone – and partly by Berchtold himself. On 13 July, he allowed a retired former colleague, Heinrich von Lützow, to be present during a strategy meeting with the German ambassador and Ballplatz officials at which the proposed terms of the ultimatum and the timing of its delivery were discussed in some detail. Concerned by what he heard, Lützow shared his concerns over lunch two days later with his friend, the British ambassador, Maurice de Bunsen. De Bunsen reported the conversation to London; more importantly, he mentioned it to his Russian colleague, Nikolai Shebeko. Simultaneously, the German envoy in Rome warned the Italian Foreign Ministry about Austro-Hungarian intentions, and the Italians, whose ciphers were an open book to the other powers, disseminated this information to their missions overseas. Thus, well before Poincaré's visit to St Petersburg ended, the Russians, the French and the British were aware, in general terms, that Austria-Hungary intended to make harsh demands of Serbia which could lead to war.[32] The consequences of this shared knowledge in the capitals concerned are related in other chapters of this volume. It is worth noting that Berchtold himself had studiously avoided giving Italy, nominally the Monarchy's ally but also its rival for influence in the Balkans, any information whatsoever about his plans. Despite German advice to the contrary, the Italians were kept in the dark until the very last moment; one factor, among others, in Italy's decision to leave the Triple Alliance in 1915.[33]

In Serbia, an election campaign was in full swing and Prime Minister Nikola Pašić was away from Belgrade campaigning in the provinces. When, therefore, Baron Giesl presented the Monarchy's ultimatum at 6 pm on 23 July, the recipient was the Minister of Finance, Lazar Pacu. Giesl demanded the Serbian Government's reply within 48 hours, that is, by 6 pm on 25 July. There is some evidence[34] that if, as in 1909 and 1912, they had received no assurance of Russian support, the Serbs would have accepted the Monarchy's demands unconditionally, including clauses 5 and 6, thus robbing the Monarchy of a *casus belli* and, at least in the short term, averting a world war. But Serbia did receive, on 25 July, sufficiently supportive messages from St Petersburg to enable it to craft a response, well described by Christopher Clark as 'a masterpiece of diplomatic equivocation', offering only qualified acceptance of the two clauses most injurious to Serbian sovereignty. These qualifications sufficed for the Monarchy to regard the ultimatum as rejected. In anticipation, Giesl and his staff had already packed their bags. Giesl received the Serbian reply on the stroke of 6 pm, from Pašić (now back in Belgrade), and caught the 6.30 train to Budapest and onwards to Vienna. Diplomatic relations between Serbia and the Monarchy were thus broken off. Three hours earlier, Serbia had already mobilised for war.[35]

These concrete events – the closure of the Monarchy's legation in Belgrade, the rupture of relations with Serbia and Serbian mobilisation – gave Vienna cold feet. There were the beginnings of an appalled realisation that the road on which the Monarchy, with Germany's active encouragement, had embarked might actually lead to a European war. Both Berchtold and the Emperor were suddenly eager to tell themselves, each other and anybody who cared to listen that a rupture of diplomatic relations did not necessarily mean war. The Monarchy's ultimatum was now described in its diplomatic correspondence as merely 'a *démarche* with a time limit'. In Vienna, hopes were now pinned on the possibility that Austria-Hungary's cumbersome mobilisation process would take at least two weeks, offering plenty of time for the Serbs to change their minds and accede to all demands. Szögyény's telegram from Berlin on 26 July partially extinguished these wishful thoughts, making it clear that the Germans assumed that an unsatisfactory Serbian response to the ultimatum would be followed 'immediately' by a declaration of war and by military operations: 'Any delay in commencing military operations is regarded here [in Berlin] as a great danger because of the interference of other Powers. They [the Germans] urgently advise us to go ahead and confront the world with a *fait accompli*.' With the zeal of a recent convert, Tisza now urged Franz Josef to 'order mobilisation at once … The slightest delay would gravely injure the reputation of the Monarchy for boldness and initiative and would influence the attitude not only of our friends and foes but of the undecided elements and result in the most fatal consequences.'[36]

Berchtold now faced yet another dilemma. German pressure could not be ignored; but Conrad, on purely military grounds, wanted no declaration of war before 12 August at the earliest, when mobilisation was complete. Berchtold overruled Conrad's objections and accepted Berlin's advice. On 27 July, the Emperor approved a declaration of war on Serbia, dispatched by telegram to the Serbian Government the following day. Berchtold still hoped, despite the declaration of war, that the Monarchy's slow mobilisation would concentrate Serbian minds and make a peaceful resolution possible. The eight army corps deployed along the Monarchy's frontier with Serbia had already been mobilised as a precaution; under Conrad's 'Plan B [for Balkan]', they would be joined by the rest of the Monarchy's armies. Deployment in Galicia, 'Plan R [for Russia]' should, Conrad decided, await hard evidence of Russia's hostile intentions. In the meantime Berchtold rejected, with German encouragement, both the British offer of four-power mediation and the Russian offer of bilateral discussions. Berchtold realised that any form of negotiation was bound to lead to some degree of derogation from the terms of the Monarchy's ultimatum: he was determined that if war was to be averted, Serbian capitulation must be total and the terms of the ultimatum accepted in their entirety.[37]

In the meantime there had been developments in the capitals of the Triple Entente (described in other chapters of this volume), which – together with the German Kaiser's sudden conviction that the (deceptive) emollience of the Serbian response to the Monarchy's ultimatum removed the case for war – led to a change of heart in Berlin. Faced with the real threat of a world war, the Germans became overnight converts to the desirability of mediation and requested the Monarchy go no further in its military action against Serbia than the occupation of Belgrade. On 30 July, in a telegram to Ambassador Tschirschky in Vienna, the German Chancellor declared, 'We are, of course, prepared to fulfil our duty as allies, but must decline to let ourselves be dragged by Vienna, wantonly and without regard to our advice, into a world conflagration.'[38] Given that only 48 hours earlier Berlin had been advising Vienna to spurn Foreign Minister Sir Edward Grey's offer of mediation, this was outrageous hypocrisy.

Bethmann Hollweg's telegrams from Berlin were beginning to carry a whiff of panic. In a second message, received by Tschirschky at 12 noon on 30 July, he relayed a report from the German Ambassador in London of a conversation in which Grey had warned that Germany 'should not be misled into supposing that we [Great Britain] should stand aside' in the event of a war involving Britain's allies, France and Russia. Bethmann Hollweg added his own comment: 'Thus, if Austria rejects all mediation, we are on the brink of a conflagration in which England would be against us, Italy and Roumania [sic] by all appearances not with us, and we should be two against four Great Powers.' Within two hours, Tschirschky was reading the full text of this telegram, twice, to Berchtold, over lunch. Berchtold listened, 'pale and silent'.[39]

Berchtold nevertheless held firm against mediation or direct conversations with Russia. With all the obstinacy of a weak man, he refused to abandon the course on which the Monarchy had embarked, originally with German encouragement – indeed, at German insistence. Three factors may be adduced in Berchtold's defence. He was undoubtedly correct in believing that any eleventh hour softening of the terms of its ultimatum could irreparably damage its prestige and authority in the Balkans. Secondly, the German Ambassador, Tschirschky, from the outset a determined advocate of the destruction of Serbia, deliberately soft-pedalled Berlin's belated conversion to the merits of mediation, choosing not to convey to Berchtold the strength and urgency of Bethmann Hollweg's new policy until the very last moment.[40] Finally, Berlin on 30 July was speaking with two voices: while Bethmann Hollweg was urging Vienna to accept mediation and talks with Russia, General Moltke, the German Chief of Staff, was in direct contact with Conrad, his Austrian opposite number, insisting that the Monarchy should reject mediation and mobilise without delay – against Russia. The Monarchy's Military Attaché in Berlin telegraphed on 30 July:

> Moltke says he would regard the situation as critical unless the Austro-Hungarian Monarchy at once mobilises against Russia. Russian publication of the order to mobilise creates necessity for counter-measures on part of Austria-Hungary ... This would give the *casus foederis* for Germany. Bring about honourable arrangement with Italy by assurances of compensation to keep Italy in the war on side of Triple Alliance ... Reject renewed English *démarche* for maintenance of peace. Last means of preserving Austria-Hungary is to fight out a European war. Germany with you unconditionally.[41]

'Who rules in Berlin?', Berchtold cried in exasperation. The humiliation of Serbia and the restoration of the Monarchy's influence in the Balkans was no longer Germany's priority: as Wilhelm made brutally clear to Franz Josef on 31 July, Austria-Hungary's duty was now to protect Germany's south-east flank against Russia – 'in this gigantic struggle ...

Serbia plays a quite subordinate role which demands only ... defensive measures.'[42]

Moltke's injunctions were superfluous. Berchtold was determined not to venture into the quagmire of negotiation or mediation. He and Conrad were finally at one in their determination to bring Serbia to heel. On Friday 31 July, Berchtold authorised General Krobatin, the Minister for War, to submit the general mobilisation order to the Emperor for signature. He did so in the knowledge that Russia had already initiated a partial mobilisation; that Great Britain would almost certainly intervene in support of France and Russia if war broke out; and that, consequently, the full mobilisation of the armies of Austria-Hungary must inevitably lead to a European conflagration. With the exception of Tisza, the Emperor's ministers showed little awareness of the parlous condition of those armies. The Monarchy's defence budget was smaller than those of any of the Great Powers: 25 per cent of those of Germany and Russia, 33 per cent of those of Britain and France. In contrast with its dazzling uniforms, the imperial and royal armies were poorly equipped and badly led. The supply of ammunition was inadequate even for training, let alone combat. By the end of 1914, the Monarchy was to lose over 800,000 men killed, wounded or captured in Galicia and nearly 50,000 in the Balkans.[43]

The Emperor's mobilisation order was published on 1 August and mobilisation began on 4 August. Events elsewhere ensured that there could now be no going back. The first shots had, in fact, already been fired. On 29 July, the day following the Monarchy's declaration of war on Serbia, Austro-Hungarian river gunboats had shelled Belgrade, destroying a number of buildings; the Serbs, on their part, had blown up the bridge which linked their country to Hungary. On 10 August,

Austro-Hungarian troops based in Bosnia began to cross the river Drina into Serbia. The First World War had begun.[44]

§

It can be argued that if, at the beginning of July, Tisza had not vetoed Berchtold's and Conrad's plan for an immediate attack on Serbia, *'sans crier gare'* as he put it, the Monarchy might have got away with it. In the immediate aftermath of Sarajevo, Vienna could have counted on a degree of sympathy from other powers especially, perhaps, from the monarchies among them. A successful surprise attack would have confronted the powers with a *fait accompli* which they might have been reluctant to reverse by going to war. But would a surprise attack have been successful? On the evidence of the Monarchy's defeats by Serbian forces in August 1914 and subsequently, it would not.[45] A surprise attack on Serbia would almost certainly have resulted in a bloody stalemate in which Russia would eventually have intervened in support of her Orthodox client. The end result might not have been dissimilar from what actually happened in July/August 1914.

It is hard to escape the conclusion that the Dual Monarchy, in its determination to use Sarajevo as a pretext for the destruction of Serbia, and imperial Germany, in its reckless encouragement of its ally's lust for revenge – not just for Sarajevo but also for earlier humiliations – must together share prime responsibility for the onset of the conflagration which engulfed Europe in August 1914. It is tempting to speculate on the likely course of events had Tisza maintained his veto on the Monarchy's desire to annihilate Serbia. A more prolonged political stalemate in Vienna might have given the other powers time to appreciate more clearly the probable repercussions of another Balkan war and to take precautionary action. For allowing himself to be persuaded too easily to abandon his opposition to war, István Tisza must take his share of responsibility for the cataclysm.

4

1 August 1914: Germany declares war on Russia – part I

The Problem of Germany[1]
Alan Sharp

On 28 June 1914 Kaiser Wilhelm II was racing his yacht *Meteor* in the Kiel regatta when he was informed of the assassination of his friend Franz Ferdinand, on whom he was counting to make Austro-German ties even closer once the archduke became the Austro-Hungarian emperor. Wilhelm decided to go to Berlin immediately to 'take the situation in hand and preserve the peace of Europe'.[2]

Wilhelm's instinctive decision acknowledged the potentially pivotal part that Germany could play in determining the course of events and the importance of his own role in maintaining European peace. If peace was the objective then he, and his advisers, whether deliberately or through incompetence, were unsuccessful. Debate about responsibility for the outbreak of the First World War began in July 1914 and has continued ever since, with a particular longevity and political sensitivity in Germany, for reasons that have changed over time. In 1914 it was crucial that the Chancellor, Theobald von Bethmann Hollweg, could portray Germany as the victim of Russian aggression to ensure the support of the powerful German Social Democrat Party, the SPD. After 1919 Germany chose to interpret Article 231 of the Treaty of Versailles as attributing sole guilt to Germany (which it did not) and sought to undermine the credibility of the whole settlement by an extensive campaign to 'prove' German innocence. This resulted in the publication of a mass of carefully selected, edited and, if necessary, falsified documents, first by Germany, then, at varying intervals, by the other belligerents.[3]

Overwhelmed by such a quantity of evidence, the general consensus by the 1930s was that the First World War had been a terrible accident that no one had intended – in David Lloyd George's phrase, 'the nations slithered over the brink into the boiling cauldron of war'.[4] Such an interpretation, which was convenient in the era of the appeasement of Nazi Germany, survived the Second World War, which was interpreted as Hitler's responsibility. This suited West Germany, seeking rehabilitation and the restoration of its sovereignty, and America and its allies, for which German resources were important as the Cold War developed. Hitler and the Third Reich could be represented as an aberration (and one, for which the peacemakers in 1919, by their vindictive and unjust accusations and treatment which undermined the fledgling Weimar Republic, could be deemed partially responsible).[5]

This cosy consensus was shattered in 1961 when Professor Fritz Fischer published *Griff Nach der Weltmacht* ('Grasp for World Power' – though the title of the eventual English translation, 'Germany's Aims in the First World War' more accurately reflected its content). His claims, based on meticulous archival research and, in particular, upon Bethmann Hollweg's ambitious statement of war aims in September 1914, were that Germany had conducted an aggressive foreign policy in the 1900s, that it had deliberately risked a European war in 1914 and that its war aims were expansionist, presaging those of the Third Reich. This was political dynamite. Many West German politicians and historians saw Fischer's views as little short of treason, suggesting as they did continuity between Nazi aims and those of Wilhelmine Germany.[6]

In his second book, *Krieg der Illusionen* (War of Illusions) published in 1969, Fischer argued that Germany's course to war in 1914 had been set by the so-called 'War Council' of December 1912, when, against the backdrop of the First Balkan War and infuriated by Britain's insistence that it would not allow France to be eliminated as a major power, the Kaiser called his military and naval advisers (though not Bethmann Hollweg) for a Sunday morning consultation. All agreed that war was unavoidable in the near future and that steps should be taken to prepare German public opinion. The Chief of the General Staff, General Helmuth von Moltke (the Younger), wanted to act 'the sooner the better' but Admiral Alfred von Tirpitz claimed the navy would not be ready for a further 18 months – in the summer of 1914, when the Kiel canal, linking the Baltic and the North Sea, would be re-opened with the capacity to accommodate Dreadnoughts. As with Bethmann Hollweg's 'September Programme', historians have debated the significance of this meeting. Was it proof of a warlike intention as Fischer contended or merely the Kaiser engaging in a typical show of bombast from which he would later retreat? Both viewpoints have their advocates.[7]

Fischer's claims, undermining as they did Germany's preferred interpretation of its innocence in the origins of the war, the unjustified nature of the Versailles settlement and a sharp break between the Wilhelmine and Nazi periods, provoked huge political and historical controversy, resulting in far-ranging debate. While there was never a total consensus, most historians came to accept the centrality of Germany's role in the July crisis and that the primary responsibility for the First World War lay with Germany. German policy could be construed as deliberately seeking conflict in 1914, as stumbling ineptly into war or as located at various points within those parameters. The decisions of Germany's leaders, both positive and negative, determined the course of events at key stages in the interval between the assassination and the outbreak of war and provided the stimuli to which the other powers reacted or responded. Wilhelm and the other German decision-makers, far from achieving peace, provided the vital link that transformed yet another Balkan crisis into first a European, then a world war.[8] Why, and for what reasons, did this occur?

The German Empire of 1914 was very different to that proclaimed by Otto von Bismarck in the Hall of Mirrors at Versailles on 18 January 1871 following Prussia's victory in the 1870–1 war with France. The then mainly rural and agricultural country of some 40 million people, of whom 64 per cent lived in the country, was, by 1914, an urban and industrial giant with a young and vigorous population of 66 million of whom 60 per cent lived in towns and cities. Its annual production of coal had risen from 85 million tons to 277 million tons in 1913, only marginally behind Britain at 292 million tons, while its steel production, which in 1871 was half that of Britain, now stood at 17.6 million tons, more than the combined total for Britain, France and Russia. In the new electrical and chemical industries Germany was a world leader, it was a major international trader and it had a formidable army and a modern fleet of Dreadnought battleships.[9]

Yet a state which should have had supreme confidence in its

ability to cope with the challenges of a new century seemed strangely pessimistic about the future. Bethmann Hollweg, surveying his estate at Hohenfinow, north-east of Berlin, wondered 'if there was any purpose in planting new trees; in a few years the Russians would be here anyway'. 'The future', he said 'belongs to Russia which is growing and growing and is becoming an ever-increasing nightmare to us.'[10] Fear of Russia's mounting strength, an expectation of future conflict between the two empires, and the sense that the assassination of Franz Ferdinand offered an opportunity to deal with Russia before it became too powerful were recurring themes in the thoughts of Germany's leaders during the July 1914 crisis.

There was also concern that Germany's international position seemed destined to weaken. Bismarck's policy of allying Germany with both Austria-Hungary and Russia, the states he saw as most likely to upset European peace, lapsed when his successors failed to renew the Reinsurance Treaty with Russia in 1890. Faced with the Dual Alliance between France and Russia, dating from 1894, and Britain's closer relationship with both since the settlement of many mutual colonial and imperial difficulties in the 1904 Entente with France and the 1907 Anglo-Russian Convention, Germany's only reliable partner in the rival Triple Alliance was the Austro-Hungarian Empire. This was an asset of depreciating value, given its recurrent problems with its multi-national population – 'that ever increasingly disintegrating composition of nations beside the Danube' in the words of German Foreign Minister, Gottlieb von Jagow.[11] Austria-Hungary's reliability was uncertain in the case of an attack on Germany, which also harboured severe doubts about the loyalty of its other supposed allies, Italy and Romania. Germany's clumsy efforts to escape its perceived encirclement by Britain, France and Russia in the two Moroccan crises of 1905 and 1911 only encouraged greater consultation between the Entente partners about possible military and naval cooperation. Despite its apparent success in obtaining recognition of its rights, both episodes left Germany with a feeling of failure and isolation, encouraging a determination to avoid future humiliation. On 6 July 1914 Wilhelm repeatedly told Alfred Krupp, the armaments manufacturer, 'This time I shall not back down.'[12]

Germany's decision in 1898 to build a battle fleet strong enough to vie for supremacy in the North Sea offered attractive domestic advantages — investment possibilities for capitalists, profits and employment for the owners and workers in the mines, steelworks and shipyards, and enhanced promotion prospects for middle-class naval officers denied them in an army dominated in its upper ranks by the Junkers, the Prussian land-owning nobility. If the army was a Prussian institution, Tirpitz's navy symbolised the new unified Germany, technologically advanced, with the wealth and industrial skill to build the most prestigious weapon of its day, the Dreadnought battleship. Internationally this was a less successful initiative, creating a naval building race and ill-feeling with Britain before Germany ceded the competition after 1912. Not only was Britain alienated and driven closer to the Dual Alliance but resources which might have strengthened Germany's army were diverted to build ships which, unlike its submarines, would play no significant role in the First World War. The loss of the naval race increased Germany's determination not to lose the battle for military supremacy in Europe.[13]

France, whose population was stagnant compared to the enormous 19th-century demographic growth of the other powers, had recently increased the length of service for its army conscripts from two to three years and would undoubtedly take measures to remedy the deficiencies in equipment noted in Senator Humbert's report of July 1914. Largely financed by French loans, Russia was building more strategic railways which, by 1917, would considerably reduce the time it took to assemble its armies from across the expanses of its territory. Both developments threatened the timetable of Germany's contingency plan for dealing with a war on two fronts against the Dual Alliance based on the original conception of General Alfred von Schlieffen and modified by his successor as Chief of the General Staff, General Helmuth von Moltke. This envisaged a six-week offensive to defeat France, while standing on the defensive against Russia, before moving assets east to overcome Russia in six months. By 1914 Germany had no alternative plan B, thus ensuring that whatever the circumstances war against either France or Russia alone was an impossibility and the nightmare of a two-front war an inevitability. If this should happen, however, Germany's leaders perceived that war in 1914 seemed a better proposition than one fought later.[14]

Germany's industrial success had domestic consequences. Disputes between the land-owning Junker nobility and the leaders of industry over Germany's tariff policies divided the German elite. The former wanted protection for agricultural products to prevent cheap imports from abroad and to keep their grain prices high, together with low tariffs on machinery to reduce their equipment costs. The latter wanted a tariff wall to protect industry and the cheapest grain prices possible so that their workers could afford bread without the need for higher wages. The growth of an urbanised industrial workforce contributed to the expansion of the SPD to become the world's largest socialist party and the major single grouping in the pre-1914 German parliament, the Reichstag. Although theoretically Marxist and committed to revolution, its practice was evolutionary though its demand for greater parliamentary control was still perceived as a powerful challenge to the empire's political and constitutional framework. Its votes would be crucial in approving any government call for war finance.

There was mounting pressure to reform the Prussian constitution's three-tiered voting system constructed to preserve the dominance of the Junkers in whose favour it was heavily skewed. In addition to the challenge from below, Junker control was increasingly threatened by their inability to fill the growing number of military and civil leadership posts occasioned by Germany's changing demographic. This, Fischer suggested, opened another line of enquiry. Had Germany undertaken an aggressive foreign policy to divert domestic criticism of an out-moded form of government unsuited to the modern, industrial and urbanised state into which Germany had evolved? Alternatively, was the German elite too divided to coalesce in the evolution of such a consistent policy?[15]

One of the key questions was precisely who was making German policy under the Wilhemine system with its peculiar mixture of autocratic, parliamentary, federal and imperial elements. In theory foreign policy and the crucial decisions for war and peace lay with the Kaiser – as he boasted to the future Edward VII, 'I am the sole master of German policy and my country must follow me wherever I go.'[16] The reality was more complex as various competing civilian and military elements sought the Kaiser's backing for conflicting policies – Moltke argued, reasonably consistently, for war against

Russia (and hence France), whereas Bethmann Hollweg, though willing to risk war, hoped (however unrealistically) to avoid it. At a number of crucial moments in the crisis Wilhelm's interventions were decisive, but at other times they were ignored or sidelined. His eccentric interpretations of his role, his inconsistency, and his unhelpful intrusions and utterances led his advisers to develop skills in 'managing' him but his power and influence remained considerable. He appointed and dismissed the chancellor, who was normally also the minister-president of Prussia, without reference to parliamentary majorities or debates. Under Bismarck, though to a lesser extent under his successors, the chancellorship was the nodal point of German policy but this was undermined by the right of direct access to the Kaiser for the military and naval commanders, without the need for the chancellor's knowledge or permission.

Wilhelm's birth had been very difficult, leaving him with a permanently withered left arm, both of which circumstances may have contributed to the complexities and contradictions of his character. The grandson of Queen Victoria, Wilhelm had a schizophrenic relationship with Britain, a country that he at once admired and disliked. Frequently bellicose in his speech and in his indefatigable marginal comments on dispatches and government papers, he was, when matters reached crisis point, normally a force for peace, often to the exasperation of his military advisers.

His first reaction to the assassination was. 'Now or never. The Serbs must be disposed of and that right soon!'[17] It was therefore no surprise when, in the key episode of the crisis, he responded positively to the Austro-Hungarian request of 5 July to, in effect, transform their defensive pact into an offensive alliance. When the Austro-Hungarian Foreign Office's

Count Alek Hoyos came to Berlin with Emperor Franz Josef's plea for help, Wilhelm, without consulting Bethmann even though he recognised the European implications could be dramatic, told him 'if it should come to a war between Austria-Hungary and Russia, we should be confident that Germany would stand by our side with the customary loyalty of allies.'[18] Austria-Hungary could now discipline Serbia, confident of Germany's support even if this provoked Russia to respond with force.

Wilhelm knew Austria-Hungary would not dare to act without the reassurance of this 'blank cheque', which he hoped would never need to be cashed. Instead he urged Franz Josef to crush Serbia quickly and present Europe with a fait accompli while shock at the assassination and sympathy for the Emperor might discourage hostile reaction.[19] From the outset Wilhelm's attitude mirrored that of his advisers in a curious juxtaposition of ideas which reflected the dual nature of German policy. He hoped that Russia, no friend of regicides, would not intervene and an Austro-Serbian conflict could be contained, or, that if Russia did react, which he perceived to be less likely, this would ensure Austria-Hungary's commitment to any ensuing Russo-German war. Thus, if there was to be war, a Balkan crisis was preferable to a quarrel arising elsewhere. Either outcome could wreak havoc on the Franco-Russian alliance and the Ententes, and leave Germany as the continental hegemon. As Bethmann Hollweg's private secretary, Kurt Riezler, noted in his diary for 8 July, 'If the war comes from the East, so that we are marching to Austria-Hungary's aid instead of Austria-Hungary to ours, then we have a chance of winning it. If war does not come, if the Tsar does not want it or France, dismayed, counsels peace, then we still have a chance of manoeuvring the Entente apart over this action.'[20]

What upset the calculations of Bethmann and the Kaiser was Austria-Hungary's inability, for both military and political reasons, to take swift punitive action against Serbia. Much of the army was on harvest leave and the Hungarian Premier, István Tisza, refused, for over a fortnight, to sanction a war against Serbia which he feared, at best, would result in annexation of territory increasing the empire's Slav population and threatening even further Hungary's privileged constitutional position. Even when, on 14 July with reluctance, Tisza agreed to the drafting of an ultimatum to Serbia to be approved at a further meeting on 19 July, it was decided to delay its presentation until 23 July, when French President Raymond Poincaré and Premier René Viviani would be at sea and practically uncontactable after their state visit to Russia. By then the European powers were aware that Austria-Hungary intended to send an unacceptable ultimatum to Serbia, leaving little doubt that its annihilation, and not justice for Franz Ferdinand, was the real objective. The German hope that a fait accompli followed by a peace offensive towards the Entente powers would ward off retaliation now looked forlorn.[21]

Despite this Germany still sought to isolate any Austro-Serbian conflict and, to this end, the Kaiser and the military leadership departed on vacation to maintain a semblance of normality. On 21 July Bethmann Hollweg emphasised to his ambassadors in London, Rome and St Petersburg the restraint exercised by Austria-Hungary in the face of past and continuing Serbian provocation and the impossibility of the empire not reacting to this latest outrage, adding 'We urgently desire a localisation of the conflict, as the intervention of any other Power would, as a result of the various alliance obligations, bring about inestimable consequences.' The risks involved in Germany's policy were becoming more apparent. On 19

July Jagow wrote to Prince Lichnowsky, the ambassador in London, 'We must attempt to localise the conflict between Austria and Serbia. Whether we shall succeed in this will depend first on Russia, and secondly on the moderating influence of Russia's allies ... I desire no preventive war, but if war should come, we cannot hide behind the fence.'[22]

The presentation of the Austro-Hungarian ultimatum to Serbia on 23 July was a watershed, its content and 48-hour limit alerting foreign ministries across Europe to the imminent danger of war. 'C'est la guerre européenne' [It's European war], declared Sergei Sazanov, the Russian Foreign Minister, though the Kaiser remained confident that Serbia would not fight.[23] On 24 July the Russian Council of Ministers decided to seek an extension of Austria-Hungary's deadline but also to request the Tsar to be ready to mobilise the four military districts of Kiev, Odessa, Kazan and Moscow.[24] Nicholas II authorised preliminary steps towards this the next day. Like Austria-Hungary earlier, Russia considered that it could not remain supine in the face of any further challenge in the Balkans and still retain its status as a Great Power. Germany had miscalculated and the timetable of its military planning might now be disrupted by any Russian mobilisation, even though partial and directed at Austria-Hungary.

Sir Edward Grey, the British Foreign Secretary, still hoped to avoid disaster by invoking the Concert of Europe. This conference of the Great Powers had evolved from the more formal congress system after 1815 and had resolved peacefully many international problems in Europe, most recently in 1913 the aftermath of the Balkan wars. Over the weekend of 25/26 July Grey issued invitations to the governments of Berlin, Rome and Paris to authorise their ambassadors to consult with him in London in the hope of mediating a resolution to the conflict. Dismissed by some historians as an initiative without hope of success,[25] Grey's attempt to bring an international solution to the crisis represented the last realistic opportunity for a peaceful outcome, before the pressures of prestige and military timetables became inexorable. It was rejected by Germany which, despite Grey's sympathetic stance towards Austria-Hungary during the 1913 London conference, feared that, with Italy no friend of the Habsburgs, Germany would be the only power willing to defend its ally's interests. 'We could not take part in such a conference,' Bethmann told Lichnowsky on 27 July, 'as we would not be able to summon Austria before a European court of justice in her case with Serbia.'[26]

When Grey learned that day of the skilful Serbian response to the Austrian ultimatum he suggested to Lichnowsky 'that Serbia had agreed to the Austrian demands to an extent such as he would never have believed possible' and that Germany should urge its ally to accept the reply, or use it as the basis for a conference. The Kaiser agreed, writing to Jagow on 28 July, 'The few reservations that Serbia makes in regard to individual points could, according to my opinion, be settled by negotiation. But it contains the announcement *orbi et urbi* of a capitulation of the most humiliating kind, and as a result, *every cause for war* falls to the ground.' He offered to mediate and urged the Austrians to undertake a symbolic invasion of Serbia and then 'halt in Belgrade'.[27]

His ministers demurred and delayed telling Vienna of the Kaiser's advice, instead passing London's suggestion of a conference to Austria, while advising its rejection. 'The German Government', noted the Austrian ambassador in Berlin, Ladislaus Szögyény, 'assures us in the most *decided way that it does not identify itself* with these propositions, that on the contrary it advises to disregard them, but that it must pass them on to satisfy the English Government.' Bethmann Hollweg explained to the German Ambassador in Vienna, Heinrich von Tschirschky, the reason for this duplicity, 'If we rejected every mediation proposal the whole world would hold us responsible for the conflagration and we would be represented as the ones really driving towards war. That would also make our own position at home an impossible one, where we must appear as the ones being forced into war.'[28]

Shortly after this Bethmann Hollweg appears to have changed his mind and began urging caution on the Austro-Hungarian Chancellor, Leopold Berchtold, offering belated backing to the 'halt in Belgrade' option.[29] It was too late, the Austrians had already begun to mobilise, while Moltke, who contacted the Austrian commander, General Franz Conrad von Hötzendorff, behind Bethmann Hollweg's back, urged vigorous and punitive action. Confronted with this contradictory advice, Berchtold asked Conrad, 'Who actually rules in Berlin, Bethmann or Moltke?'[30] It was an extremely pertinent question.

Germany's rejection of a conference and the Austro-Hungarian partial mobilisation and declaration of war against Serbia on 28 July tipped the balance away from the diplomats and towards the military leadership. Russia's partial mobilisation on 29 July exposed as illusory German confidence that it would not intervene in the Austro-Serbian conflict. This news, which reached Berlin on 30 July, put great pressure on the German leadership to proclaim a State of Imminent Danger of War, the phase preparatory to mobilisation, but, anxious that Russia should be shown as the instigators of conflict, they resisted. On 31 July Germany learned that

Russia had ordered full mobilisation at midnight the previous day. A visitor to the Prussian War Ministry found 'Everywhere beaming faces, people shaking hands in the corridors, congratulating each other on having cleared the ditch.' Bethmann Hollweg had been handed a precious card in his successful attempts to persuade the SPD to back a defensive war against Russia. Müller noted triumphantly in his diary for 1 August, 'The mood is brilliant. The government has succeeded very well in making us appear as the attacked.'[31]

The Austro-Serbian conflict was now subsumed into something much larger. Wilhelm misleadingly claimed to Franz Josef on 31 July, 'I am prepared, in fulfilment of my alliance obligations, to go to war against Russia and France immediately ...'. The alliance obliged Germany and Austria-Hungary to support each other if either was attacked by Russia; war against France had not been mentioned. The 'blank cheque' of 5 July had promised Austria-Hungary support if Russia intervened in its local war against Serbia. Wilhelm's next demand has been described as 'monstrous in its wording, in its total disregard for the interests of an alliance partner, and in its complete misrepresentation of the situation.'[32] He stated:

In this hard struggle it is of the greatest importance that Austria directs her chief force against Russia and does not split it up by a simultaneous offensive against Serbia. This is all the more important as a great part of my army will be tied down by France. In this gigantic struggle on which we are embarking shoulder to shoulder, Serbia plays a quite subordinate role, which demands only the most absolutely necessary defensive measures.[33]

Franz Ferdinand had faded into oblivion and Austria-Hungary was no longer the prime mover, rather it had become a support player in Germany's attempt to crush the Dual Alliance.

On 31 July Germany mobilised. One of the striking features of the July crisis was the civilian politicians' ignorance of what mobilisation meant for their own state, let alone for other states. Germany's case was extreme in that mobilisation, under the terms of the Schlieffen/Moltke plan, meant war. In order to meet the timetable for the rapid defeat of France it was necessary to bypass the main French defences by infringing the neutrality of Luxembourg, to secure a vital railway link, and that of Belgium, where key fortresses such as Liège and Namur had to be seized rapidly. German mobilisation, therefore, did not just entail the assembly and concentration of its troops, it meant their immediate dispatch to fight. In the absence of any other plan (the Eastern Deployment Plan for a war against Russia alone was scrapped in 1913) it guaranteed a war on two fronts.

Thus when, for an illusory moment on 1 August, it appeared that Grey might deliver French and British neutrality if Germany did not attack France, and the Kaiser demanded a redeployment of his forces against Russia alone, Moltke refused. 'It is utterly impossible to advance except according to plan: strong in the west, weak in the east.' 'Your illustrious uncle [Helmuth von Moltke the Elder, the Prussian commander in the 1860s and 1870s] would not have given me such an answer' Wilhelm declared, but this rapidly became irrelevant when it emerged that no guarantees of Anglo-French neutrality were on the table. Moltke, badly shaken by what he interpreted as Wilhelm's underlying wish for peace, was allowed to proceed as planned. On 1 August Germany declared war on Russia when it refused to reverse its mobilisation. On 2 August German troops occupied Luxembourg. On 3 August Germany declared war on France, claiming a number of spurious provocations, and presented Belgium with an ultimatum, demanding passage to allow its forces to attack France. When Belgium rejected this, Germany invaded on 4 August, triggering an ultimatum from Britain demanding that it evacuate Belgium. When this expired without reply at 11 pm that night, Britain declared war on Germany.[34]

As war became increasingly likely in late July Bethmann Hollweg's new priority had been to try to persuade Britain to remain neutral. Lichnowsky in London warned on several occasions that if France became involved this was unlikely. On 29 July Bethmann Hollweg promised, in return for an undertaking of British neutrality, that Germany would make no demands upon the metropolitan territory of a defeated France, though he did not exclude colonial losses, and that it would respect the neutrality of Holland. He suggested that French actions might require Germany to undertake operations in Belgium, but he guaranteed respect for its integrity after the war. Sir Eyre Crowe, one of the key figures in the British Foreign Office, minuted, 'The only comment that need be made upon these astounding proposals is that they reflect discredit on the statesman who makes them.' Grey, enraged at the suggestion that Britain could permit France to cease to be a Great Power, rejected the proposition without even consulting his colleagues, declaring that, 'for us to make this bargain with Germany at the expense of France would be a disgrace from which the good name of this country would never recover.'[35] Given the problems that Grey faced from his colleagues in his support of France, the threat of a German invasion of Belgium became pivotal in the debates in the

British Cabinet, offering a cause around which most of those who had previously opposed a continental commitment could rally. The invasion itself brought a united Liberal government and country into the conflict, transforming a European war into a world conflict.

Germany's policies throughout the July crisis contained more than their share of wishful thinking: Austria could crush Serbia rapidly; there would be no Russian intervention; this would destroy Russia's credibility as an ally, demolishing both the Dual Alliance and the Triple Entente; German hegemony could be secured peacefully; if a European war did come Britain would remain neutral; 1914 was a better time to fight than later; and victory in that war would achieve German hegemony by other means. The risks involved in these gambles were obvious, and yet there does seem to have been an element of complacency in Berlin in the weeks after the issuing of the blank cheque. Having urged Austria to punish Serbia, Bethmann Hollweg was slow to realise the severity of the crisis as July unfolded, preferring to believe that all would be well. Germany's leaders did not shirk war in 1914 but whether they actively sought one, or, through incompetence, lost control of the diplomacy of the crisis and stumbled into conflict remains a hotly disputed topic which continues to exercise historians.

5

1 August 1914: Germany declares war on Russia – part II
From Steamroller to Empty Chair
Charlotte Alston

James Headlam-Morley was a junior member of the British delegation to the Paris Peace Conference in the spring of 1919. 'In the discussions, everything leads up to Russia', he complained in his diary. 'Then there is a discursive discussion; it is agreed that the point at issue cannot be determined until the general policy towards Russia has been settled; having agreed on this, instead of settling it, they pass on to some other subject'.[1] Likewise, Herbert Hoover, who accompanied the American peace delegation to Paris, described Russia as 'Banquo's ghost sitting at every council table' at the peace conference.[2]

Russia's contribution to the Allied war effort is often forgotten today. While popular understandings of the First World War are much focused on trench warfare in the West, studies of Russian history in this period have the revolutions of 1917 as the centrepiece. For contemporaries, however, Russia's contribution, her rights and responsibilities, and her absence at the peace were keenly felt. French Prime Minister Georges

Clemenceau saw the Russian withdrawal from the war in the spring of 1917 as an unforgiveable betrayal of its allies.[3] Anti-Bolshevik Russians in Paris, campaigning for intervention in the civil war and against recognition of the Bolsheviks, argued the opposite: Russia was still an ally, and needed help from the British, French and Americans now more than ever. *The Russian Outlook,* an Anglo-Russian periodical which argued relentlessly in favour of intervention, questioned in May 1919 whether it was possible to:

> forget what Russia did for us? It was she who, by that gallant hopeless advance on the Eastern Front, relieved the pressure on the west in the early autumn of 1914, and by that means saved Paris. And to save Paris was to save London. How often during the dreary years that followed did Russia come to our aid, how often has she saved us?[4]

In April 1919 the Russian Liberation Committee published the numbers of Russians mobilised, killed, wounded and captured during the war under the headline 'What Russia Has Done for the Common Cause'.[5]

This chapter explores Russia's trajectory from the country's entry into the war through to its absence at the peace; the reasons that Russia became involved in the conflict, and domestic responses to this; the country's relationship, both political and cultural, with its allies; the experience of war and revolution and the resulting fracturing of Russian representation at the peace settlement and in other negotiations with the Allies.

In comparison with the many volumes devoted to the origins of the First World War in Britain, France and Germany, there are relatively few treatments of Russia's entry into the conflict. Western historiographical debates about the causes of the First World War had little impact in Soviet Russia. Fritz Fischer's 1961 *Griff nach der Weltmacht* (Grasp for World Power),[6] so controversial in Western Europe, received little attention. This was in part because free and open discussion of historical events was so difficult (and, after all, Lenin himself had laid down his own judgments on the First World War, which were not to be questioned), but was also because Fischer's emphasis on German imperialism only confirmed the already established party line.[7] In addition, the Russian decision to go to war has been a subject of secondary concern precisely because of its catastrophic consequences: the revolution that followed has tended to occupy historians to a much greater extent. There are nevertheless several studies of this topic that give detailed and thoughtful accounts of the Russian decisions and the factors that influenced them.[8]

Russia's entry into the war: context

The assassination of Archduke Franz Ferdinand on 28 June 1914 was greeted in Russia as an unpleasant but hardly significant event. Tsar Nicholas II and his family were on a summer cruise along the Baltic coast. They would not return until 19 July, and were more disturbed by news of a vicious attack on the monk and healer Rasputin, on 29 June, than by the fate of Franz Ferdinand.[9] Vladimir Gurko, a member of the State Council, attended a dinner in Tver shortly after the news had broken, at which those present expressed amazement at the idea that Europe might be on the brink of some kind of crisis.[10] Indeed, in the following weeks it seemed to Foreign Minister Sergei Sazanov that Europe's horror at the assassination was subsiding. When it became clear that the Austrian government intended to regard the assassination as a plot on the part of the

Serbian government, Sazanov maintained that the innocence of the Serbs was 'so clear' that the Austro-Hungarian government would surely be obliged to withdraw its accusation.[11] Although we now know that Serbian military intelligence did sanction and support the assassination of the archduke, there is no evidence that officials in the Russian government knew anything about it.[12] The delivery of Austria-Hungary's ultimatum to Serbia therefore took Russia's statesmen by surprise, and posed them a genuine dilemma. Although the decisions that propelled Russia into the war were taken in the following days, at meetings of the Council of Ministers on 24 and 25 July, these decisions had deep roots and were a response to developments in Russia's foreign relations, defence, society, economy and empire over the preceding decades.

In the late 19th century Russia's ambitions had focused principally on expansion in the Far East, but defeat in the Russo-Japanese war and the Anglo-Russian Entente of 1907 curbed these efforts in the first years of the 20th century and brought the Russian government's attention back to Europe. The unfortunate collision of Russian and Austrian interests in the Balkans demanded careful negotiation between the two governments. Such negotiations were not made any easier by the rise of nationalist ambitions in the region, nor by the decline of the Ottoman Empire in this period. While Russia's statesmen acted cautiously for fear of upsetting Great Power relations in Europe, the feeling built in the years before 1914 that others perceived this caution as weakness, and that European powers were taking advantage of this to usurp Russia's rights and obligations as regarded the Balkans, Constantinople and the Straits.

Russia's relationship with other Slavic nations and nationalities had an important role to play in the country's imperial identity, as did its role as the leading Orthodox power. The Russian reading public fostered an enthusiastic pan-Slav sentiment; the desire for the independence (under Russian protection) of the smaller Slav nations that were not already part of the Russian Empire was manifested in newspaper articles, committees and literature. Aleksei Khomiakov's poem 'The Eagle', written in the 1830s but gaining in popularity later in the century, called on the Russian 'eagle of the north' to protect its 'younger brothers' on the Danube, in the Carpathians and in the Balkans, and to 'shatter the cruel chains that hold them captive'. Although often unpopular with Russia's statesmen because it caused unpredictable displays of popular feeling which did not always accord with their pragmatic aims, Pan-Slav sentiment was difficult to ignore.[13] Public opinion had driven Russia into war with Turkey in 1877; regardless of the Russian victory in that conflict, the Tsar had been obliged by the European powers (at the Congress of Berlin) to hand back many of the country's territorial gains. In 1908, when Austria-Hungary annexed the provinces of Bosnia and Herzegovina, liberated from the Ottoman Empire by the Russians in the 1870s, there had been public uproar. Aleksandr Izvolsky, Russia's Foreign Minister, thought he had negotiated concessions in return for the annexation (a re-opening of discussions around Russian warships using the Straits) but these were not honoured and the Russian government was left embarrassed. During the Balkan wars of 1912–13, Russian sympathy for the Balkan states was complicated by the fear that Bulgaria (rather than Russia) might gain control of Constantinople and the Straits.[14] In 1913, the appointment of German General Liman von Sanders as head of a military mission to the Turkish army was seen as both a threat and an affront.

Russia's relationships with the other European powers also shifted markedly in the late 19th and early 20th centuries. During the reign of Alexander III, Russia's alliance with Germany and Austria-Hungary in the League of the Three Emperors was formalized (in 1881) and renewed (in 1884). By the 1890s however, these agreements had lapsed. Tensions in the Balkans meant that Russia and Austria-Hungary were always awkward partners in the alliance, and the Tsar had come to distrust Bismarck's role in the partnership, particularly in the wake of his support for Bulgarian expansionist ambitions in 1886. The 'Reinsurance Treaty' signed by Russia and Germany in 1887 did not last beyond the accession of Wilhelm II in 1890. In 1894, the Russian and French governments concluded a military and political agreement which committed them to each other's defence in the case of a war with Germany (it included details about the number of troops to be deployed) and allowed for substantial French investment (both by the government and individuals) in Russia.[15] Izvolsky strengthened Russia's alliance with France, not least by concluding a hard-won complementary agreement with Great Britain in 1907. This agreement resolved tensions between the two countries, but by no means suggested that Britain, France and Russia would end up fighting a war against Germany together.[16] Rapprochement between Russia and Germany remained on the cards under Izvolsky and under Sergei Sazanov, Foreign Minister from 1910. When Nicholas II and Kaiser Wilhelm II met at Bjorko in 1905 and signed a secret agreement, the Tsar's ministers were horrified, and the treaty was quickly nullified.

Relations between France, Russia and Britain had also been momentarily threatened by the war that broke out between Russia and Japan in 1905. On the night of 21/22

October 1904 the Russian navy had attacked a group of British fishing trawlers in the Dogger Bank area of the North Sea. Russia and Britain had seemed dangerously close to war: with Britain allied with Japan and Russia with France Anglo-French relations were also threatened. Diplomatically, Russia's defeat by Japan was perhaps the best outcome for the fragile alliance system. In terms of Russian prestige, it was a disaster. The Japanese capture of Port Arthur, and the destruction of the Russian navy at the battle of Tsushima, showed up Russia's military weakness to rest of the world and also severely damaged Russia's armed forces. Nevertheless, in the years preceding the First World War, the Russian government invested heavily in defence, rebuilt its navy and attempted to reform the army.[17] Russia had a standing army of 1.3 million at the outbreak of the war: its numerical superiority earned it the epithets applied by its allies about 'steamrollers' and 'glaciers'. Despite previous military defeats, the country's vast population, agriculture and growing industry seemed to make it a formidable ally.

Russia's increasing economic and military strength also made a more assertive foreign policy possible by 1914. The history of caution and defeat in European diplomacy in the preceding years certainly informed the mood in the Council of Ministers in July 1914. From the Congress of Berlin to the Austrian annexation of Bosnia, it was felt that Russia had failed to act on too many occasions. The Tsar's ministers were aware of the domestic risks involved in entering the war, but they also warned Nicholas of the potential public backlash should he not do so. In the 24 July meeting, Sazonov pushed for a firm stand: the concessions Russia had made over the last ten years had only been interpreted by the German government as a sign of Russian weakness, he argued. In a speech which apparently swayed the Council considerably, The Minister for Agriculture, Aleksandr Krivoshein, concluded that remaining passive would not prevent a European war: Russia must now take an assertive stance. Russia's military chiefs concurred. The Council's decisions – to ask the Austrians to extend the deadline on the ultimatum, to advise the Serbs to comply with any terms which did not threaten the independence of their state, and to arrange, if required, for mobilisation of four military districts – were confirmed in a meeting chaired by Nicholas the following day.[18] After much discussion about the merits or otherwise of mobilising on the Austrian but not the German front, full mobilisation was ordered on 30 July. Just like statesmen in so many of the European capitals in the summer of 1914, Russian ministers were more prepared to take the risk of involvement in a European war than they were to be left out of it. The Russian mobilisation prompted a German declaration of war on Russia on 1 August.

Russia's entry into the war: reactions

Accounts of the outbreak of war in Russia have traditionally emphasized the surge of patriotic enthusiasm that gripped the Russian people in the summer of 1914. In St Petersburg around 250,000 people joined in a patriotic demonstration outside the Winter Palace. Similar events were organized across the country, at which patriotic songs were sung and portraits of the Tsar displayed. Duma members, including socialists and representatives of the empire's many nationalities, publicly reaffirmed their loyalty to the Tsar. However, Joshua Sanborn has challenged the idea that these demonstrations indicated widespread support for the war. Riots among reservists called up to fight occurred in many of the provinces of the Russian Empire. Just as there were vocal patriots across many social categories, Sanborn tells us there were also outspoken opponents of the war in all walks of life.[19] Vladimir Gurko recalled no 'patriotic exultation' amongst Russia's peasantry: their mood was rather one of 'muffled, submissive, sullen discontent'.[20] In February 1914 loyal monarchist Petr Durnovo had written a devastating critique of the potential consequences of war for Russia. This memorandum is famous because it now seems so prophetic – it predicted the disintegration of the Russian government and a tide of popular revolution – but it can also be seen to suggest right-wing dissatisfaction with Nicholas's government and foreign policy.[21] Russia's socialists, like their counterparts across Europe, adopted a 'defencist' position, prepared to support their government's prosecution of the war providing it was for the country's defence and not for imperialist or annexationist aims. Only the Bolshevik party took a different line. Lenin delighted at the war: a Russian defeat could only bring the revolution closer.[22]

Russia's liberals hoped that cooperation in the war effort would lead to a greater involvement on the part of civil society in the government of the empire. The declarations of loyalty made by representatives of Russia's minority nationalities were also founded on the assumption that they would be rewarded with greater control over their own affairs. The Lithuanian representative at the Duma, Martynas Ycas, spoke explicitly (while reaffirming his loyalty to the empire) about the establishment of a Lithuanian state within a Russian federation at the end of the war.[23] The hopes of neither nationalists nor liberals would be rewarded; at least not by the imperial government.

Russia and its allies

A rapprochement with autocratic Russia was not an easy sell to the democratic British and republican French publics. Vigorous efforts were nevertheless made to achieve this. In Britain this had begun even prior to the signature of the Anglo-Russian agreement of 1907, and encompassed efforts by establishment figures such as Donald Mackenzie Wallace (the 'father' of Russian studies and author of the two-volume *Russia*, published in 1877 and based on six years of travel and study in the Russian Empire) who had been encouraged by Edward VII to build Anglo-Russian understanding; and by a younger generation of Russophiles who sought to establish friendly relations with the liberal elements in the Duma.[24] Despite the humiliating defeat of the Russian army in the Russo-Japanese war of 1904–5, confidence in its ability was high. In the weeks following the outbreak of war the British press was full of images of the Russian army as a glacier, slow but irresistible, or a river in flood, passing onward with 'magnificent inevitability'; or as the familiar 'steam roller', which would crush everything in its path.[25] Books praising Russia and exploring Russia's psychology appeared: from *The Self-Discovery of Russia* to *Our Russian Ally*. One Russian writer observed that 'all England is flooded with books about Russia ... Here, for instance, we read of "Glorious Russia"; in another book about "Contemporary Russia"; elsewhere of "Armed Russia"; here is "Friendly Russia", and so on they go. No one in the world has ever been so infatuated with us as the English are at present'.[26] This was hardly universal, however: at the outbreak of war Morgan Philips Price, who went to Russia as the *Manchester Guardian* correspondent, complained that 'we were supposed to be crushing Prussian militarism and "making the world safe for democracy", and yet we were in alliance with the most reactionary and tyrannical power in Europe'.[27]

In fact, the extent of Russian engagement with the enemy in 1914–15 obliged the Allies to embark on propaganda efforts within Russia – to convince the Russian public of their compatibility as allies and their appreciation of the Russian contribution to the conflict, and to circulate information in Russia about Allied efforts on the Western Front. To this end a British Propaganda Bureau was established in Petrograd: its projects included placing items on the Allied war effort in national and regional newspapers, and circulating films about the Western Front.[28] In 1915, units of Belgian and British armoured cars, which had proved of little use in the entrenched conditions of the Western Front, sailed to Russia to join the war effort there. The British armoured car unit spent months stranded in Alexandrovsk, but eventually saw service on the Galician front before being shipped home upon the outbreak of revolution.[29] Despite the lack of a really coordinated joint strategy in the war, the importance of the Russian front to the Allies meant there was a substantial investment in loans and the supply and transport of war materiel to Russia.[30]

Fighting the war

Russia's role in the alliance was to divert significant numbers of German troops from the Western Front, and in this objective its war effort, while it lasted, was a success. When the Russians withdrew from the war in 1917, Allied commanders nervously counted the number of German divisions being moved to the Western Front each week. Yet, socially and politically, Russia's war effort was a disaster. More than 18 million men served in the Russian army between 1914 and

1917. Somewhere in the region of 2 million lost their lives.[31]

The Russian command opted for a two-pronged strategy, launching offensives against the Austrian army in Galicia and the Germans in East Prussia. The Russians achieved a series of victories in the south-west, capturing more than 220,000 Austrian troops by the spring of 1915. They proved unable to replicate these successes against the German army, however. They suffered an early and humiliating defeat at the battle of Tannenberg in August 1914. During 1915, the German army reinforced the Austrians on the Galician front, and steadily occupied the whole of Poland, Lithuania and parts of Belorussia.

Some of the responsibility for Russia's poor military performance lay with the army's leadership. At the highest level, there were frequent disagreements between factions led by the Minister of War, Vladimir Sukhomlinov, and the Supreme Commander, Grand Duke Nicholas. The incompetence of some of the army leadership (many of whom were appointed because of their relationship to the Tsar rather than on merit) was also glaringly apparent. V M Bezobrazov, a general in his sixties who had fought in the Russo-Turkish war, is a case in point. Dismissed from the command of a Guard division after a public fight with the corps commander, he was reappointed as commander of the whole Guard corps. After a quarrel with the commander of the Third Army, in which he refused, on grounds of honour, to allow the Guard to retreat, he was removed from that position, only later to be given command of the Guard Army.[32] Neither was innovation valued: a string of successes won by General Aleksei Brusilov on the Galician front was not followed up. Nicholas II's decision to put himself in charge of the armed forces in 1916 only associated him more closely with the army's military failures.

However, the country's economy and infrastructure were also the source of considerable problems. Within a month of the outbreak of war it was already clear that the quantity of munitions required would massively exceed expectations. Russia's industrial sector struggled rapidly to redress this shortfall. Despite improvements to the capacity of the country's railways, the pressure of transporting troops, munitions, equipment, food and refugees placed considerable strain on Russia's transport system and made supplying both the fronts and the cities with the requisite materials a daunting task. Conscription depleted the labour available in factories, mines and farms, and this further exacerbated the problems in supply of food, equipment and fuel. Not only were soldiers poorly fed and supplied, but there were severe shortages in the cities. The German occupation of Russia's borderlands also meant the loss (or relocation) of many industrial enterprises. Massive population displacement, and a flood of refugees pouring into central Russia, placed further pressure on both transport and resources.[33]

The tsarist regime remained suspicious of the participation of civil society in the war effort. Russia's commercial classes and liberal intelligentsia became involved in the supply of food, equipment and medical assistance. They hoped that the extension of their responsibilities in the public sphere would make it difficult for the government to avoid political and economic reforms after the war. The All-Russian Union of Zemstvos and the All-Russian Union of Towns, both formed at the outbreak of war, organised medical aid at the front and the resettlement and supply of food and other necessities to refugees in the interior. In 1915 these two organisations formed a supply committee, Zemgor, which supplied the army with munitions and uniforms. War industry committees sprang up across the country, seeking to fill military orders by going beyond the major industrial enterprises and using the full breadth of Russia's manufacturing capacity.[34] There was antagonism between these organisations and the state, however, and a growing sense developed that the war was being mismanaged. In the autumn of 1915, liberal politician Vasily Maklakov published an article in which he cast Nicholas in the role of a 'mad chauffeur' about to drive the Russian car off a cliff, while more capable individuals struggled over whether to grab the wheel from his hands.

Fortunately there are people in the automobile who know how to steer. One needs to take the wheel quickly. But changing seats while moving is difficult and dangerous. One second without anyone guiding the automobile and it goes into the abyss.

There is no choice though – you are headed into the breach. And the chauffeur won't budge. Perhaps he is blinded and cannot see, or is feeble-minded and doesn't grasp what is happening. Or it could be from professional conceit or obstinacy. But he clings to the wheel and won't let go for anyone. What can be done now? Force him to give up his place? That might work were this a rustic cart or if these were ordinary times along a flat, quiet road. Then perhaps it would seem like salvation. But could it be done on this steep slope, on this mountain road? Would you have the dexterity and strength? In fact *his* hands are on the wheel. He is driving the car now, and one wrong turn or awkward movement of his hands and the car is wrecked. You know this, but *he* knows it, too. And he is emboldened by your anxiety and your powerlessness: 'They won't dare touch me!'[35]

This perception that the war effort was being mismanaged was becoming increasingly widespread. It was not helped by the scandal that surrounded the imperial family's relationship with Grigorii Rasputin, whom the Tsarina relied upon for help with her son Alexei's illness, but increasingly also for political decisions. The Rasputin affair brought the imperial court into serious public disrepute. The Tsarina's German ancestry also prompted some critics to regard the mismanagement of the war 'not as stupidity, but as treason', as the Foreign Minister Pavel Miliukov put it.[36] By the close of 1916 there was increasing dissent within civil society, shortages in the cities and the war effort was disintegrating.

From war to civil war

The events of February to October 1917 changed the political landscape in Russia entirely. They also fundamentally altered Russia's relations with her former allies. While the Provisional Governments that governed from February to October pledged to keep Russia in the war, and even mounted a new offensive in June, public dissatisfaction with Russia's participation in the war and with the lack of visible social and political change increased by the week. Socialists in the soviets (workers' and soldiers' councils) held the liberal politicians to account, but failed to offer a credible alternative. The liberals in government saw themselves as caretakers who could take no decisive action until a Constituent Assembly, fully representative of the Russian people, had been elected. The moderate socialists saw this as the first, bourgeois stage of the revolution, which needed to run its course. After Lenin's return to Russia in April 1917, the Bolshevik party took a more assertive stance, distancing itself from other socialist parties and demanding an end to the war and the redistribution of land to the peasants. Through the summer and autumn it built a support base in the soviets that allowed it to launch a coup d'état in October.

Recent research on the revolutionary year has explored how very differently events played out in Russia's provinces from the familiar picture in Moscow and Petrograd.[37] In Transbaikalia, distant from the capital cities and with a relatively thriving economy, cooperation between liberal and socialist parties continued into 1918.[38] In Ivanovo-Kineshma, the heavily industrialised centre of Russia's textile industry, workers were chastising the Bolsheviks for failing to take action well before October.[39] In Russia's border states, the revolution and the end of the war in Europe allowed for the emergence of independent governments in, among other places, Estonia, Latvia, Lithuania, Georgia and Ukraine.

Russia's war officially ended with the signature of the Treaty of Brest-Litovsk in March 1918. Lenin faced opposition within his own party over the decision to negotiate with the Germans at all. The treaty gave up great swathes of territory that had been part of the Russian empire, including Ukraine and the Baltic States – and, more pertinently for many leading Bolsheviks, it gave up large revolutionary populations. The treaty was also, with the decision to close Russia's Constituent Assembly when it met in January 1918, one of the triggers for the organisation of serious military opposition to the Bolshevik regime. By the summer of 1918 centres of opposition were emerging in Samara, in Omsk and in the Don region. During 1919, as a backdrop to the Paris Peace Conference, major offensives were launched against the Bolsheviks by forces led by Admiral Kolchak (in the spring), General Denikin (in the summer) and General Iudenich (in October).[40] The British, French and American governments struggled first to find allies of any political shade who might restore an Eastern Front in the war against Germany, and then to know with which of these Russian generals and politicians they might deal in making the peace.

The Paris Peace Conference

Delegates from numerous new governments established on the territory of the former Russian Empire appeared in Paris in 1919. There were Estonians, Latvians, Lithuanians, Georgians, Ukrainians, Armenians, Azeris, Belorussians, Don Cossacks and Kuban Cossacks. Zourab Avalishvili, a Georgian representative, acknowledged his role as a 'switchman' who would transfer his country's orientation from Germany to the victorious Allies.[41]

The representatives of these new states shared information and tactics during their time in Paris. None of their delegations was officially recognized, but they were occasionally given a hearing: many had extensive contact with junior members of the Allied delegations, for what this was worth.[42] What was missing was a representative of the Russian government with whom the Allies were prepared to deal. Anti-Bolshevik Russians of all shades appeared in London, Paris and New York in 1918−19, campaigning against recognition of the Bolshevik government and in favour of intervention.[43] In Paris, Prince Lvov headed the Russian Political Conference, a body established to represent anti-Bolshevik interests at the Peace Conference. Its members included the former Foreign Minister Sergei Sazonov, liberal critic and member of the Provisional Government Vasili Maklakov, and revolutionary terrorist Boris Savinkov, who reportedly sat in cafés in Paris with his back to the wall for fear of assassination.[44] They had the tacit support of Admiral Kolchak and General Denikin, who had few other options in terms of representation of their interests in Paris.[45] The principal aims of the Russian Political Conference were to muster support for intervention against the Bolsheviks; to prevent any recognition of or negotiation with the Bolshevik government; and to protect what its members saw as Russia's vital interests. They were particularly concerned by Allied interest in the independence of the Baltic States – Estonia, Latvia and Lithuania. The commerce of these provinces had been developed by Russia, they argued, and the region was also vital for Russia's defence – Russia would never consent to give them up.[46]

There were several early initiatives to resolve the 'Russian Question' in Paris. The first was a proposal put forward on 22 January 1919 that all parties in the Russian conflict, including the Soviet government, be invited to a separate peace conference, with Allied representation, on the island of Prinkipo in the Sea of Marmara. The Soviet government and the representatives of Estonia, Latvia and Lithuania all agreed to attend, but the anti-Bolshevik Russians refused, and the proposal was allowed to slide. A second initiative was the mission sent to Russia under the American diplomat William Bullitt in February to ascertain the conditions on which peace with the Bolsheviks could be secured. Bullitt returned with a proposal, approved by Lenin, that all existing de facto governments on the territory of the former Russian Empire should remain in possession of the territory they currently controlled, until the peoples of those territories decided otherwise. No action was taken at the Peace Conference in response to this proposal.[47] At the same time, high-profile figures such as Winston Churchill and Marshal Foch were still advocating more substantial military assistance to the anti-Bolshevik forces in the Russian Civil War. Kolchak's victories in the spring of 1919, which brought his troops to within 75 miles of the Volga, prompted the Council of Four (Prime Minister David Lloyd George of Britain, French Premier Georges Clemenceau, the Italian leader Vittorio Orlando and America's President Woodrow Wilson) to dispatch a note setting out the terms on which they would support Kolchak's government to 'establish themselves as the government of all Russia', and implying that, if certain guarantees about democracy and the independence of the border states were met, then recognition would follow.[48]

The ebb and flow of the military situation in Russia was just one of the problems that confounded decision-making on Russia at the Paris Peace Conference. The contradictory policies followed by the Allies when dealing with the anti-Bolshevik Russians and the representatives of the border states were another. While many Allied delegates were impressed with the efforts of the Estonians and Latvians, for example, and supported their claims to national self-determination, there was little chance that a restored anti-Bolshevik Russia would allow the continued existence of these independent states. In addition, as with so many questions in Paris, there seemed to be little coordinated policy within national delegations, let alone among the victorious powers as a whole. Esme Howard, in charge of Russian affairs for the British delegation, noted that relations between the Allied delegations were 'so bitter that they might have been engaged before the armistice in fighting each other instead of fighting side by side'.[49]

The Treaty of Brest Litovsk in 1918, the Treaties of Tartu, Riga and Moscow, which established Soviet Russia's recognition of its Baltic neighbours in 1920, and the Polish-Soviet Peace in 1921 did more to determine the future of Russia and its former empire than those negotiated in Paris in 1919. Some of the former territories of the Russian Empire would be reincorporated militarily into the Soviet Union – the Ukraine for example – in the next couple of years. The Baltic states of Estonia, Latvia and Lithuania on the other hand would remain independent for the inter-war period. The Soviet Union would embark in the 1920s on a dual strategy of revolutionary internationalism and pragmatic diplomacy. Russia's experience in the 20th century was nevertheless definitively shaped by the trajectory between 28 June 1914 and 28 June 1919.

6

3 August 1914: Germany declares war on France

How France Entered the First World War

David Robin Watson

In France, as in all the states to be in engulfed in war only five weeks later, the assassination at Sarajevo on 28 June 1914 produced a very limited public reaction. The Great Powers had settled two Balkan wars only a year earlier, just as previous international crises since 1905 had ended without war. The general view was that international relations had entered a phase of stability and détente. Few foresaw that Austria-Hungary would use the incident to seek to overturn the gains made by Serbia in 1912–13, nor that its ally Germany would give it complete support. Although it was clear that there would be some response to this outrage on the part of Austria-Hungary, there was no reason to think in France, Russia or Britain that it would be of such a nature as to provoke a European war. The calculation in Vienna and Berlin, however, was that the assassination appeared a golden opportunity to crush Serbia, reversing the 1913 Balkan settlement, without another general conference of all the powers which might have limited its 'punishment'.

France's role in the diplomacy of July 1914 was more limited than that of any other of the Great Powers. There are two reasons for this. The first, and most important, is that the alliance systems of pre-1914 Europe interacted with German military planning. German military command had long before 1914 decided to begin any war against the country's Franco-Russian enemies with a massive and immediate attack on France through Belgium, while remaining in the first instance on the defensive in the east. Whoever devised the details of the final strategy, and whether this should be called the Schlieffen Plan or not, it was the plan followed by Chief of the General Staff Helmuth von Moltke in 1914, ensuring that the German nightmare of a two-front war became a reality. In the circumstances of the July crisis France would almost certainly have supported its Russian ally, but the question did not arise, as the war began with the German invasion of France. This ensured that any opposition to a war arising out of a Russo-German quarrel about Serbia became irrelevant. The second reason for the limited scope for French diplomacy during the July crisis is that it was deliberately organised in that way by Germany and Austria. They knew that the French decision-makers, the President of the Republic, the Prime and Foreign Minister, and the chief permanent official of the Foreign Office would all be absent from Paris on a long-planned state visit to Russia and Scandinavia. They were to travel on a French warship, and be absent from Paris from 16 to 31 July. Accordingly the Austrian ultimatum to Serbia was delayed until the French leaders had left St Petersburg in order to prevent them co-ordinating policy with their Russian ally.

News of the assassination reached France late in the afternoon of 28 June, when President Raymond Poincaré was watching horse racing at Longchamps, one of the highlights of the social season. He did not think it necessary to make any change in his plans that day or later. No signs of impending disaster are to be found in either Poincaré's diary or the French diplomatic correspondence of those days, long examined by historians in minute detail.[1] For France, the crisis only really began with news of the Austro-Hungarian ultimatum to Serbia on 24 July. Until then political life in the country followed the course it was already on, including the long-planned ceremonial visit of Poincaré and the Prime and Foreign Minister, René Viviani, to Russia and the Scandinavian countries. This involved stops in Sweden, Denmark and Norway as well as St Petersburg. As a result of the international crisis, the trip was curtailed after Stockholm, and the French leaders arrived back at Dunkirk on 29 July, already too late to play much of a role in the final act of the drama.

The other issues dominating the political stage in July 1914 were a parliamentary debate inspired by a critical report by Senator Humbert about the inadequacies of military supplies and, above all, the sensational affair of the murder of Gaston Calmette, editor of *Le Figaro*, then as now a leading daily newspaper. Calmette was conducting a campaign in *Le Figaro* against the Radical politician Joseph Caillaux, the Prime Minister in 1911 who had achieved a compromise settlement with Germany over Morocco. Calmette attacked Caillaux for this, threatening also to tackle his role in a financial scandal, the Rochette affair. *Le Figaro* published a passage from a love letter Caillaux had written to his then mistress, now second wife, in 1901. Fearing Calmette would publish other intimate letters, Caillaux's wife, Henriette, went to the newspaper's office and shot him dead.[2] Her trial took place from 20 to 29 July, when the jury acquitted her in the face of all evidence.

Naturally such a sensational affair, involving leading political figures, filled the columns of all the French newspapers throughout July.

Although eclipsed by the Calmette affair, the Humbert report into the supposed inadequacy of French armaments was also a matter of great concern, producing a parliamentary debate that continued over the national holiday on 14 July. This seemed so serious that Poincaré considered postponing the Russian state visit – as he had not done over the news from Sarajevo – but it went ahead as scheduled. This meant most of the key foreign policy decision-makers – Poincaré, Viviani and the top permanent official of the Foreign Office, Political Director Pierre de Margerie – would be absent from Paris almost a fortnight. Both the Minister of Justice, Jean-Baptiste Bienvenu-Martin, who became interim Foreign Minister, and Abel Ferry, who acted as Under-Secretary of State for Foreign Affairs, were completely unversed in such matters. Philippe Berthelot, de Margerie's deputy, was the senior permanent official: although he was soon to be an authoritative figure, at this point he was too junior to be able to take any decisive role, in the absence of his superiors.[3]

Poincaré's political dominance as president was totally abnormal. For nearly the whole of the Third Republic, after 1879, the president was a ceremonial figurehead. The period from Poincaré's election in 1913, until 1924, when his successor Alexandre Millerand was forced to resign, was the only time when the president sought to play a major role. Poincaré became President having been both Prime and Foreign Minister for the preceding twelve months. He hoped to change the system, arguing that France needed a president who could provide continuity and stability when governments and prime ministers rarely lasted more than a few months. This was a controversial move, bitterly resisted by his rival Georges Clemenceau, among others. Eventually it failed as Poincaré found himself eclipsed by Clemenceau, Prime Minister from 1917 to 1920, while Millerand was forced to resign in 1924, when his supporters lost control of parliament.

During the Briand and Barthou cabinets of 1913, Poincaré exercised considerable influence, less so when Doumergue combined the premiership and foreign ministry between December 1913 and June 1914. But with the totally inexperienced Viviani, from June to 3 August 1914, Poincaré was in charge. Viviani was one of the most mediocre of the politicians to become Prime Minister under the Third Republic. His value to Poincaré was as a left-winger who could command a parliamentary majority to uphold the military reforms of 1913, the Three Year Law, increasing the term of conscripts' service. This had been the central issue in French politics in 1913, and in the elections of April–May 1914.[4] He was inexperienced, completely ignorant of foreign affairs and psychologically unstable. Even before the crisis really developed, his behaviour during the visit to St Petersburg was decidedly odd. There can be no doubt that the diplomatic telegrams and dispatches sent under his signature were in fact the work of Poincaré. On 3 August Gaston Doumergue replaced him as Foreign Minister, although he remained Prime Minister until October 1915.

On 16 July the French leaders embarked, arriving in Russia on 20 July. Poincaré, who was appalled by Viviani's ignorance of foreign affairs, tried to give him a crash course in European politics, without much success. The following three days, 20–23 July, were mainly occupied with ceremonial, parades, receptions and gala dinners, but there was also time for discussions between the French team and the Tsar and his advisers.

Unfortunately, in spite of all attempts, no official minutes of these talks have ever been found. This allowed the development in the 1920s of a myth that the French and Russians had used this occasion to coordinate diplomatic activity so that the Serbian crisis would produce a European war. Poincaré's enemies in post-war France, some of them financed by Germany, developed a campaign centred on Poincaré, whom they attacked as 'Poincaré la guerre', claiming that he had manipulated the Tsar into the bellicose stance that led to the war.[5] In reality, until the Austrian ultimatum to Serbia was issued, deliberately timed to be after the French had left St Petersburg, there was no reason to expect a diplomatic crisis that would produce war in a matter of days.

The main sources available for their discussions are the memoirs of Poincaré and of Maurice Paléologue, the French Ambassador to the Tsarist court, and Poincaré's diary. They reveal that matters discussed included the French Three Year Law, Russia's relations with Britain, and the Austria-Serbian dispute, which was seen as posing a threat to peace, but not yet an imminent one. Poincaré also met the Austrian Ambassador and advocated caution, pointing out that Russia was likely to give support to Serbia, and that Russia and France were allies. This, as Poincaré later said, was not a threat but simply a reminder of realities, while silence could have been seen as approval of any Austrian action.[6]

After their departure from Russia just before midnight on 23 July, the French statesmen had only limited contact with events through garbled radio-telegram messages. On 24 July a telegram from their ship, via St Petersburg, recommended that Serbia accept as many of the Austrian terms as possible, while suggesting an international enquiry into the assassination, instead of an Austro-Serbian one. On reaching

Stockholm on 25 July they were informed of the visit of the German Ambassador to Paris, Wilhelm von Schön, to Bienvenu-Martin, the acting Foreign Minister. The German insistence that there should be no intervention by other powers alerted Poincaré to the gravity of the situation, and he wondered whether to return directly to Paris. This decision was taken the next day, 27 July. By that point, with news of the Austrian ultimatum, and the first Russian response of an announcement of 'a period preparatory to war', it was clear that Europe was moving rapidly to the edge of the abyss.

A telegram to the Russian Foreign Minister, Sazonov, signed by Viviani, confirmed that France would support Russia, according to the terms of the alliance, and in the interest of general peace. It was actually drafted by de Margerie in consultation with Poincaré. Not knowing this, the Italian historian, Luigi Albertini, singled it out as demonstrating Viviani's level-headed pacific attitude in contrast to the supposedly more aggressive Poincaré.[7] In reality, Poincaré believed that peace could only be served by facing the German-Austrian moves with firmness. He was concerned that Bienvenu-Martin in Paris and Viviani might, in their desire to preserve peace, show weakness and vacillation that would encourage the Germanic allies to take unacceptable and irrevocable steps. As did indeed happen. However, Paléologue in St Petersburg, without detailed instructions, was promising support to France's ally.[8]

It was only on the afternoon of 29 July that the French delegation got back to Paris. By now it was evident that Viviani was clearly incapable of controlling French policy and Poincaré took over. His first task was to discover what diplomatic moves had taken place while he had been at sea. He discovered, as he had feared, that Bienvenu-Martin had given the

German government the impression that France would not support Russia in any moves to counter the Austrian attack on Serbia. At that stage there had seemed little possibility of British support against the Central Powers. George Buchanan, British Ambassador to Russia, had informed Sazonov and Paléologue on 24 July that the British public would not support a war for Serbia. On the same day the British Cabinet, after hours of discussion of the Irish/Ulster situation, was asked by the Foreign Minister Sir Edward Grey to give some time to Europe. He proposed, with little sense of urgency, international mediation between Austria-Hungary and Serbia, and departed for his usual weekend fishing in the country. British proposals for an international conference such as the one that had followed the Balkan wars were, of course, directly opposed to the German-Austrian determination to crush Serbia without intervention by other powers. They were ignored as the plan launched by the 'blank cheque' of support from Germany to Austria on 5 July unrolled from the ultimatum of 23 July to the declaration of war by Austria on Serbia of 28 July, producing the Russian order for partial mobilisation on 29 July followed by general mobilisation ordered on 30 July for 31 July.[9]

Even back in Paris, Poincaré was not kept well-informed of the critical decisions taken in St Petersburg. Paléologue exaggerated his own importance by delaying reports to Paris, so that news of the Russian general mobilisation only reached Paris at 8.30 pm on 31 July. From that day to this some have argued that the Russian mobilisation was the crucial step from diplomacy to military engagement, and that therefore Russia bears as much, if not more, guilt than Germany for causing the war. By the same argument France is saddled with a share of the blame for not restraining its ally. As J V F Keiger has demonstrated, these arguments are certainly unfounded as far as France is concerned. French policy, as defined by Poincaré, was certainly not to allow the alliance with Russia to be sidelined, as had happened in 1908 and 1911. But equally it was not designed to encourage rash actions by Russia or Serbia. The timing of the ultimatum meant that Poincaré had small opportunity to influence events during the crucial days between 23 and 29 July. To some extent this produced the worst outcome: Paléologue had a free hand to encourage the Russian government to react strongly, while the conciliatory tone in Paris led the German authorities to believe that the plan of unilateral action against Serbia would not be resisted by France and its ally.[10]

As the real likelihood of war confronted minds during the last days of July, the part to be played by Britain became crucial. The French were convinced that if Britain declared its support for France and Russia, it would deter Germany from continuing with a policy that would involve war with all three of the Entente powers. But Grey found it impossible to make any such declaration of support as long as the impending war seemed to be about an incident in the Balkans. In vain did Paul Cambon, French Ambassador in London, remind the British of the military staff talks between the two powers, and of the 1912 naval agreement by which France had concentrated its fleet in the Mediterranean while Britain promised to safeguard the Channel for both. Grey insisted that Britain had no obligation to fight, to which Cambon retorted that, if so, the word 'honour' would have to be deleted from the English language.[11]

However, the last efforts of German diplomacy were preparing the way for a united response from the three Entente powers. On 30 July Germany offered not to annexe any French territory in Europe if Britain remained neutral, thus suggest-ing possible annexations of colonies. On 1 August France was told that even if it did not come to the aid of Russia and remained neutral, it would have to surrender its eastern for-tresses as a guarantee. In order to avoid any possible German claims of aggressive action, the political authorities in France ordered their armies to retire from the frontier zone, much to the annoyance of their commander, General Joffre. On 3 August Germany declared war on France, having made false claims of French attacks from the air. In France, opposition to war, which had surfaced in anti-war demonstrations on 28–29 July, disappeared completely when it came to resisting yet another German invasion of France itself.

Before 1914 many people thought a major war between the European powers to be inconceivable and impossible. Some believed that economic and financial interpenetration, the ele-ments referred to today as globalisation, had created a world in which war would be so much of an economic disaster as to be impossible. Many argued that the bankers and financi-ers would stop the political rulers from being so stupid. This proved not to be so: the captains of finance and industry did not seriously try to avert war. Others believed, as the French Socialist leader Jean Jaurès put it, that capitalism bore the seeds of war as clouds foretell the thunderstorm. Left-wing intellectuals such as J A Hobson, Rosa Luxemburg, Hild-ferding and Lenin argued that capitalist rivalries governed the political conflicts of the powers; but that the organised working class could either stop the outbreak of war (Jaurès) or turn the war into a revolutionary one against the bourgeoi-sie (Lenin).

Both France and Germany had important Socialist and trade union movements, which made resistance to 'capitalist' war a major element of their political programmes. They were supposedly united in the Second Socialist International, which had proclaimed at its Stuttgart Congress in 1907 that the working class would meet the threat of war with a general strike. This also did not happen. In Germany the powerful Socialist party unanimously voted war credits in 1914. In France, a much more rural society, the industrial working class was both smaller and less tightly organised. French trade unions had developed an ideology, syndicalism, based on independence from parliamentary socialism, but the syndicalist leadership had very limited support either among the working class or among the French population as a whole. Even so the authorities were sufficiently worried to prepare lists of anti-war militants – known as Carnet B – to be arrested in the event of war. In the event, the Radical Minister of the Interior, Louis Malvy, decided on 1 August 1914 not to go through with the arrests. Later, when this became public knowledge, it was part of the case against Malvy that led to his being tried for treason in 1918.[12]

The Socialist Party pursued an independent line of resistance to militarism and warmongering, under the leadership of Jean Jaurès. A large part of Jaurès' activity from 1905 to 1914 was concerned with problems of war and peace. He attracted much hostility, including the poet and philosopher Péguy's rhetorical call for him to be guillotined, as a result of his support for the anti-war declarations of the International. Jaurès was able to lay out a policy in which self-defence against foreign attack was not rejected, but which nevertheless positioned the Socialist movement as a bulwark against war.[13] He sought to put this into operation in late July 1914. Anti-war demonstrations were organised and well supported in both countries in the few days between the danger of war becoming public and the actual outbreak of hostilities. At the same time the members of the bureau of the International held an emergency meeting in Brussels on 29 and 30 July. They proclaimed that the proletariat in each country would put the utmost pressure on their governments to prevent war: however Jaurès stated, 'We [French Socialists] do not need to impose a policy of peace on our government; it is practising it.'[14] No precise steps were laid down except advancing the date of the forthcoming Congress of the International from September to 9 August, and changing its place from Vienna to Paris. These decisions were taken without awareness that the time left was to be counted in hours, not days or weeks.

By the time Jaurès had returned to Paris on the evening of 30 July, he had learnt of the Russian mobilisation, and thus of the imminent danger of war. He still hoped for peace, and asked to meet the Prime Minister on 31 July. However, Viviani was too busy to see him. He was at that very moment receiving from the German Ambassador the final ultimatum demanding French neutrality, and the surrender of the fortresses of Toul and Verdun as guarantees. Jaurès returned to the offices of the party newspaper *L'Humanité*, where he had to write a leading article for the next day's edition. He then went with a group of his party colleagues to dine at a local restaurant, where he fell victim to an assassin's bullet; it was a hot night and he was sitting by an open window, an easy target for Raoul Villain.

Villain was an adherent of the nationalist Right, whose literary and journalistic spokesmen, Maurras, Daudet, Barrès and others, had been calling for Jaurès' death. But a veil was drawn over this vicious polemic as both Left and Right declared that Jaurès, if he had lived, would have supported the patriotic call to defend France against German attack. There can of course be no certainty, but it does seem extremely probable that this would have been the case.

The anti-war demonstrations of late July did not continue once mobilisation was proclaimed and war began. This was marked in France by a special convocation of parliament when a presidential message was read out by the Prime Minister. The main points were that France had over the last 40 years not sought reparation for the wrongs it had suffered, and that during the crisis opened by the ultimatum to Serbia it had pursued a policy of prudence and moderation. So, overwhelming responsibility for the war which had broken out was borne by the German Empire. France had right on its side, and would be heroically defended by all its sons, whose sacred union in the face of the enemy would not be broken. This term of sacred union, Union Sacrée, became the title which characterised French political life for the duration of the war, although in reality conflict eventually reappeared.

When France found itself at war on 3 August 1914, for nearly everyone it came as a bolt from the blue, as it did, of course, in other countries. Only three or four days before, very few had thought that war was more likely than it had been for the past 20 or 30 years. The fact that there had been several international crises since 1905 only encouraged the idea that this time too diplomatic negotiations would fend off war. In France and Belgium, realisation that they had been invaded strengthened feelings of patriotic indignation. For the great majority however, there was no question of eager anticipation of triumph and victory. The mood can rather be characterised as one of indignant resolution to combat another German invasion.

We know a great deal about public opinion in France in the first weeks of the war, as primary school teachers everywhere were asked to report on the reaction to the mobilisation of conscript reservists. Although not all of these reports have survived, enough have done so to allow J J Becker, along with other sources, to provide a remarkably detailed and reliable survey. His conclusion is that opinion moved from total surprise to the indignation of a people convinced of its own pacifism, and certain that it had been attacked. The idea of recovering Alsace-Lorraine was rarely evoked. The reports echoed that from a village teacher in the Charente department. 'France did not want war: we were attacked: we will do our duty.'[15]

7

4 August 1914: Germany invades Belgium
Belgium: the Victim
Sally Marks

Historians have long debated the origins of the First World War. One or another has assigned at least partial responsibility for what it did or did not do to every state involved except one. Only strategic little Belgium has escaped responsibility, primarily because it adhered through the pre-war decade and the crisis itself determinedly and precisely to its unique legal status, which policy secured its honour if not its safety.

Belgium had long been known as the crossroads of Europe, where merchants and armies marched over the centuries. Thus, to insulate a potential flashpoint, when the Great Powers officially sanctioned the birth of the Belgian Kingdom in the 1839 treaties,[1] they imposed on it a state of perpetual neutrality and an obligation to defend that neutrality. Further, in their treaty with Belgium, the five powers guaranteed its independence, territorial integrity and neutrality, a commitment later assumed formally from Prussia by the North German Confederation and informally by the German Empire, of which the Prussian king was emperor. But nothing indicated whether this guarantee was individual or collective (variously, several and joint), that is, whether a power was obligated to defend Belgium against violation by another signatory or merely not to participate in the violation.

In 1867, Luxembourg's neutrality was also guaranteed, but British reluctance ensured that the guarantee was only collective. Then and in 1870, although the British government carefully retained a loophole, oratory in its Parliament distinguished sharply between the two guarantees. The impression conveyed was that the Belgian guarantee was a firm commitment whereas that of the Grand Duchy was not.

One of the causes of the Franco-Prussian War of 1870 was the desire of Napoleon III to absorb Belgium. When the war began, Britain, on its own initiative, signed treaties with both parties pledging to protect the kingdom from either. But France collapsed so quickly that Belgium was spared. It was not again threatened before 1914, and popular opinion assumed that, if it were, the 'miracle of 1870' would repeat itself. Attention focused on domestic issues and making money. German investment increased sharply in the pre-war years. Belgium remained outside the diplomatic mainstream and its uglier aspects.

After 1870, Belgium neglected its defences. The Catholic Party, which governed without cease from 1884 to 1914, opposed military expense. Bright young men were rarely eager to serve in an army that would never fight. Conscription was by lottery, but substitutes could be and were bought. King Leopold II campaigned for reform and, in 1909, simply refused to die until an army reform passed the Parliament for his signature. It abolished both lottery and substitutions and decreed that one son must serve from each family, but shortened the term of service.

From 1904 on, Leopold and his Cabinets had been

increasingly alarmed about the deteriorating European diplomatic situation. From Belgium's viewpoint, the Entente Cordiale of 1904 indicated that Britain had abandoned the role of independent mediator, as in 1870, in favour of attachment to France, of which there was considerable historic distrust, especially among Dutch-speaking Flemings in the north.[2] After 1904, some distrust adhered to Britain as well, reinforced by its campaign against King Leopold's Congo abuses. The two Moroccan crises of 1905–6 and 1911 raised the prospect of a Franco-German war. Belgian statesmen did not share the public faith in a recurrence of the 'miracle of 1870'. While consistently responding to enquiries that Belgium had complete trust in the integrity of all of its neighbours and that it would defend itself against any invasion, the Foreign Ministry studied every conceivable possibility, including the vexing one of a tiny incursion, probably by Germany, across Belgium's southernmost corner, which it could not defend.

Also in 1904, Leopold paid a visit to Emperor Wilhelm II of Germany, who informed him that a war between France and Germany was imminent, and that Belgium should join the German side, which would win. The irrepressible Kaiser sought an alliance and transit rights, urged an increase of the Belgian army and offered the startled king re-creation of the old Duchy of Burgundy out of three French provinces. Leopold declined and doubled his efforts toward the 1909 military reform. He and his government had known since 1904 of the Schlieffen Plan, each revision of which encompassed transit of more of Belgium, the easiest route to France's least defended frontier. Ultimately, Germany planned on 34 divisions and in fact sent an unprecedented million men against Belgium's six divisions of infantry and one of cavalry.

Britain, equally aware of the Schlieffen Plan, also worried.

In 1906 its Military Attaché in Brussels, Lieutenant-Colonel Nathaniel Barnardiston, gained limited military talks with Major-General G E V Ducarne, Chief of the Belgian General Staff. Nothing came of these, but during the wartime occupation the Germans found Ducarne's notes in a folder on which he had scribbled 'conventions anglo-belges'.[3] As Germany sought to blame any other state for the war's outbreak, this was trumpeted as proof of Belgium's un-neutral conduct, but in fact there were no conventions, only conversations.

Leopold's successor, Albert I, faced the same international problems as his uncle and repeats of many episodes, including the second Moroccan crisis in 1911, which heightened tensions considerably. Albert saw clearly what needed to be done but encountered difficulty in doing it, mainly because under the Belgian constitution he was commander-in-chief in wartime but had no military authority in peacetime. Thus there existed two rival military staffs, his and that of the army. His request for defensive plans against invasions from east, west and south went unmet, whereas other sensible proposals encountered bureaucratic obstruction. Albert wished to defend his kingdom near its frontiers, on the Meuse (Maas) River at the Liège (Luik) forts. Many generals and some politicians preferred a mid-country defence in front of the Antwerp national redoubt, abandoning much of francophone Wallonia.

Throughout, Berlin assumed that Belgium would either submit or merely make a symbolic gesture, ensuring unimpeded rapid German transit. Britain and France both questioned whether Belgium could or would engage in real resistance. Would there even be an appeal to the guarantors, especially if only a corner were violated? The uncertainty despite ritual Belgian assurances led to another British probe in 1911, when the Military Attaché, Lieutenant-Colonel G T M Bridges, sought new talks, and indicated that if the second Moroccan crisis had led to war, Britain would have landed troops without waiting for an appeal from Belgium since it was incapable of defending itself. This statement only heightened distrust. There were talks as well with France, which considered a preemptive strike into Belgium but decided to retain the moral high ground and let Germany violate the 1839 treaties first.

One reason for Entente concern was that the Catholic Party in power was deemed to favour Germany and resisted army increases. The burgeoning Socialist Party was pacifist. Even so, the king and the Cabinet head[4] Baron (later Count) Charles de Broqueville, aware that Leopold's military reform was important but insufficient, sought further measures, finally achieving a law on 30 August 1913. Though ten years would be required to achieve full effect, it imposed general conscription, sharply increased both expenditure and the size of the army and reinforced Liège's great fortress, indicating Belgium's true concern.[5]

Since Germany had built a surprising number of railway lines to the Belgian border and a large military camp as well, Albert contrived a visit to the Kaiser in November 1913. Citing minor incidents, Wilhelm insisted that French bellicosity would force war shortly. Albert disagreed about France, but Wilhelm persisted, saying Germany would win. The Chief of the German General Staff took the same line with both the king and the Belgian Military Attaché, telling the latter that Belgium should join Germany if it wished to retain its independence. Albert passed a warning to France. Upon his return home, an aide prepared a statement of his policy: 'We are resolved:– (1) to declare war at once upon any power that deliberately violates our territory, (2) to wage war with the utmost energy and with the whole of our military resources.'[6] As 1914 arrived, Broqueville told an aide, 'I am very much afraid about this year, that this war which I anticipate, which I dread, will break out while we are not prepared.'[7] Clearly those who then or later assumed that Belgian leaders still trusted all their neighbours, would not fight and were astonished at what transpired, underestimated them.

What transpired was the assassination of Franz Ferdinand on 28 June 1914, followed by the July crisis culminating in general war. Initially, the Belgian people and government were not greatly disturbed by events in Sarajevo, for neither had much interest in the Balkans. News on 24 July of Austria's ultimatum to Serbia first forced realisation in Brussels (and London) that a crisis existed. Belgium's interests were not affected, but its Berlin envoy warned that Germany might be behind Austria's actions. The Foreign Ministry began intensively to examine all documents and studies relevant to Belgium's situation, and the Cabinet started to meet daily. The Foreign Minister, (H F) Julien Davignon (later Viscount), continued to assure all who enquired that Belgium had no reason to distrust Germany (so as to offer no pretext), but three army classes were called up on 29 July when news arrived that Austria had declared war on Serbia. On 31 July word that Germany had proclaimed a state of imminent war (*drohende Kriegsgefahr*) brought first Dutch general mobilisation[8] and then a Belgian decision to commence general mobilisation at midnight. Thus, Belgium mobilised one day before Germany, which proved vital to the defence of Liège.

As the danger of general war became apparent, Britain asked France and Germany on 31 July whether they would respect Belgian neutrality if no other power violated it and enquired whether Belgium would defend its neutrality. Assurances immediately arrived from Paris and Brussels. Berlin stalled, suggesting it might not reply at all because doing so would reveal military plans. London noted the implications. In the absence of official word, late on 1 August Albert wrote a letter to his 'dear cousin' (the Kaiser)[9] seeking private assurances, with no immediate reply.

On 2 August, German troops occupied Luxembourg. Belgium hoped that interest was limited to its railways, segments of the main routes south, but a land exit was more likely, probably through Belgium. At 7.00 pm the German envoy presented Davignon with an ultimatum. Berlin had made matters as difficult as possible. The rather lengthy text was in German (which Davignon could not read), was presented on a gorgeous Sunday evening of the holiday month of August and required a reply within 12 hours. Blaming France for imminent hostilities, it promised to guarantee Belgian independence and repay any damage if Belgium permitted German troop transit; refusal meant war.[10] Assuming Belgian consent, Berlin aimed to ensure British neutrality.[11]

While translation was in progress, Broqueville arrived. He and Davignon both expected war. Once the full document was available, Broqueville took it to the king, while officials started drafting a rejection. Albert agreed that war had arrived and asked Broqueville if Belgium was ready. Broqueville said it was, though the heavy artillery, ordered from Krupp, had not arrived. This was optimistic considering the lack of a plan, coordination with the state railways, machine guns and other basic equipment and officers who had seen combat.

A Cabinet was called for 9.00 pm, to be followed by a Crown Council at 10.00. The latter consisted of the Cabinet plus a number of elder statesmen. As one party had ruled for 30 years, diversity was needed, so two Liberals were added on the spot, including Paul Hymans, the party leader. The Socialist leader, Emile Vandervelde, was out of town, as were many notables, and so did not become a Minister of State until 4 August. Though Albert, presiding, opened the Cabinet by saying, '… our answer must be "no", whatever the consequences. Our duty is to defend our territorial integrity',[12] the meeting was largely consumed by a quarrel about strategy between the two military camps and provided no guidance to the king. At the Crown Council, however, after brief mention of token resistance, unanimity was quickly reached on rejection of the ultimatum, and a committee chosen at midnight to draft a reply with Foreign Ministry officials. At 3.00 am they returned to the palace with a text, citing the 1839 and 1870 treaties and Belgian honour. It was unanimously approved without discussion or alteration. The Council ended at dawn, and a ministry diplomat delivered Belgium's rejection to the German legation at exactly 7.00 am.[13]

By then the ultimatum had become publicly known. Belgium was a kingdom transformed. It exploded in patriotic outrage at the insult to national honour.[14] Domestic quarrels disappeared, as did sympathy for Germany, so evident shortly before. Military morale soared. A divided nation and its Parliament were now completely unified, and flags appeared everywhere. Clearly, the decision conformed precisely to the national will.

At 8.00 am, the British, French, and Russian Ministers in Brussels were informed of the ultimatum and the Belgian decision, but no appeal for aid was made since no invasion had yet occurred. Russia could be of no practical help to Belgium, and the French response had never been in doubt.

Britain was another matter. For it, the crisis was domestic as well as foreign. Although Germany and Russia were now at war and France had mobilised, a sharply divided Liberal Cabinet in London was hesitating whereas a more assertive Conservative Party was eager to take power. News of the ultimatum early on 3 August solidified most of the Cabinet, and it was able to reach a decision for war with only a few resignations but no Cabinet crisis. The 1839 treaties were a factor, as well as a partial commitment to France. More important was British national interest which dictated that no Great Power dominate the Low Countries directly across the Channel – or the continent itself. In any event, the German ultimatum to Belgium took on a wider significance in that it considerably facilitated the British military participation that Germany's civilian leaders had hoped to prevent. Moreover, the two days between the ultimatum and the 5 August attack on Liège afforded Albert time to rally his people and foreign opinion and to prepare Belgian defences.[15]

Britain and France remained unclear about to what degree Belgium would fight, whereas Brussels did not yet know whether the violation would be massive or minor. On 3 August, the Belgian Cabinet sought only diplomatic support from the Entente guarantors. That evening, as Germany declared war on France, Albert telegraphed his English cousin, King George V, seeking diplomatic intervention. He also received the Kaiser's reply to his appeal of two days earlier. To Albert's disgust, it amounted to another effort to persuade Belgium to allow transit, for Germany never ceased trying to the last minute (and beyond) to ensure Belgian and British neutrality. Repeated German statements that transit 'was a matter of life and death' and that 'necessity knows no law'[16] are curious inasmuch as no power had shown any

interest in attacking Germany. In Brussels, a German diplomat, with tears streaming down his face, said, 'Oh, these
poor stupid Belgians! Why don't they get out of the way! ...
I know the German army. It will be like laying a baby on the
track before a locomotive!'[17]

The next morning clarified matters for all concerned. At
6.00 am on 4 August a German note informed Belgium that
since it had not complied, Germany would use force. At 8.00
am it did so, massively crossing the Belgian frontier 30 miles
(50 kilometres) from Liège, which led to general war. Once the
shock of the event actually occurring had worn off, Belgian
diplomats were relieved that the issue was absolutely clear,
without awkward questions about small corners or token
resistance. At 9.00 am Belgium broke diplomatic relations
with Germany. An hour later Albert, in uniform, addressed
a cheering parliament, proud that Belgium was honourably
doing its duty and vowing to fight unto death. Making no
mention of Germany or the ultimatum, he called for unity
and then left to command his army. In the afternoon, Brussels officially notified the Entente guarantors[18] of the invasion
but refrained from an appeal for military aid because Britain,
having offered support, decided instead on an ultimatum to
Germany to desist in Belgium. That expired at midnight, and
Belgium requested military aid at 8.00 am on 5 August.

That day the Brussels newspaper *l'Étoile belge,* reflecting
public opinion, declared: 'Whatever happens, honour is saved.
And as long as honour is saved, nothing is lost.'[19]Albert,
who had also cited honour, was more realistic, but knew
that Entente aid, which did not arrive until much too late,
was vital. Still, though crucial demolitions ordered at Liège
were not accomplished, the Kaiser's expectation of reaching France in three days was not met; only on 25 August

did the Namur (Namen) forts fall, opening the way south for exhausted German troops. Belgian resistance had shattered the tight timing of the Schlieffen Plan. In addition, the invasion afforded Italy an excuse to remain neutral. Belgium became the Entente's moral cause for lack of any other, especially after the German Chancellor referred to the 1839 Great Power treaty with Belgium as 'a scrap of paper'[20] while openly admitting that the invasion violated international law.

Belgian efforts to remain neutral and peaceful had failed, through no fault of its own. It equally tried to maintain the neutrality of the Belgian Congo, but German attacks on the harbour at Albertville (Kalemie) on Lake Tanganyika prevented that. Thereafter African troops under Belgian command conquered much of German East Africa, transferring part to Britain and retaining the rest until the war's end. In Belgium itself, troops from Antwerp repeatedly attacked the German flank, weakening its thrust into France, but the Belgian front soon settled into four muddy years on the Yser (IJzer) River. Honour, which mattered so much to Belgians, was indeed satisfied, though the price was very high, but security remained elusive until a new constellation of powers developed after another Great War.

8

4 August 1914: Britain (and its empire) declare war on
Germany – part I

Britain and the Outbreak of War
Alan Sharp

On 17 July 1914, 19 days after Franz Ferdinand and his wife
were assassinated at Sarajevo, David Lloyd George, the
Chancellor of the Exchequer, warned his Mansion House
audience that Britain faced the gravest situation 'with which
any Government in this country had had to deal for centuries'. He meant the Irish crisis over whether all, or parts, of
Ulster should be excluded from the provisions of the Home
Rule Act and the impending Triple Alliance strike by trade
unions representing railwaymen, miners, dock workers and
seamen. Although slightly less optimistic about international
relations than on 9 July when he had declared 'the sky has
never been so perfectly blue', he remained sanguine.[1] 'There
are,' he stated,

> always clouds in the international sky. You never get a
> perfectly blue sky in foreign affairs. There are clouds even
> now; but, having got out of the greater difficulties last year,

we feel confident that the common sense, the patience, the goodwill, the forbearance, which enabled us to solve greater and more urgent problems last year, will enable us to pull through these problems at the present moment.[2]

He was mistaken, 18 days later Britain declared war on Germany.

Lloyd George's emphasis on domestic rather than international concerns is echoed in the remarkable letters sent by the Prime Minister, Herbert Henry Asquith, to his 'darling', Venetia Stanley, a friend of his daughter, Violet. She was a woman less than half his age, with whom he was besotted and with whom he corresponded frequently between 1912 and 1915, when, to his great distress, she married Edwin Montagu, his former private secretary. After a brief reference to 'an "obituary" on the Austrian royalties' in his 30 June letter there is no further mention of international affairs in the next 16 until that of 24 July. Instead the Ulster crisis, together with political and social chit-chat, bridge and dinner parties dominated his correspondence, which often disclosed Cabinet secrets and confidential material.[3]

Only on 24 July did the Cabinet discuss the deteriorating European situation. Until then Sir Edward Grey, the Foreign Secretary, had consulted only Asquith, Lord Haldane, the Chancellor of the Duchy of Lancaster, who had earlier overseen much needed reforms to the Army, and Winston Churchill, the First Lord of the Admiralty, but, from the outset, he had recognised the potentially disastrous consequences of Gavrilo Princip's action. He feared Austria would use the assassinations as an excuse to destroy Serbia and that this would be intolerable to Russia, whose pretensions to be the protector of the Slavs had been severely jolted by the annexation of Bosnia-Herzegovina in 1908 and the series of Balkan wars. Any such Austro-Russian confrontation had little chance of remaining isolated, whatever the formal obligations of their respective alliances with Germany and France. He hoped to use the Concert of Europe, the informal arrangement which had evolved from the 1815 Congress system in which the Great Powers consulted on matters of mutual concern, to encourage France to curb Russia, but especially Germany to restrain Austria. In 1913 Grey had worked closely with Germany to resolve the Balkan conflicts. Perhaps overestimating the importance of this collaboration and possibly inadvertently misled by the German Ambassador, Prince Lichnowsky, who was himself deliberately misinformed by Berlin, he believed that this partnership could work again to avert conflict. These hopes were dashed by the Austrian ultimatum to Serbia, received that day and described by Grey as 'the most formidable document I had ever seen addressed by one State to another that was independent'.[4]

Asquith's report to Venetia of Friday 24 July's Cabinet is interesting both for its analysis of impending conflict in Europe and his belief that Britain could remain neutral:

Austria has sent a bullying and humiliating Ultimatum to Servia, who cannot possibly comply with it, and demanded an answer within 48 hours – failing which she will march. This means, almost inevitably, that Russia will come on the scene in defence of Servia & in defiance of Austria; and if so, it is difficult both for Germany & France to refrain from lending a hand to one side or the other. So that we are within measurable, or imaginable, distance of a real Armageddon ... Happily there seems to be no reason why we should be anything more that spectators.[5]

Grey and the Foreign Office believed otherwise. Although he maintained to the very end, as did Asquith, that Britain retained a free hand in its decision-making, he was also convinced that, despite the lack of any formal obligations, Britain should intervene on behalf of France and Russia for moral and strategic reasons, but he faced a deeply divided Liberal Cabinet in which the majority did not agree with him.

Grey maintained the previous Conservative government's 1904 Entente with France when the Liberals took power in 1905. Centred on a mutual recognition of Britain's predominance in Egypt and that of France in Morocco, this was essentially a settlement of long-standing worldwide colonial differences which had no direct link to European affairs. It did form, however, part of a wider attempt to redress the imbalance between Britain's resources and liabilities in the context of a changing international power balance and the growth of long-term peacetime alliances. When Japan's victory in the 1894–5 Sino-Japanese war had threatened to precipitate a new scramble for China following the earlier imperial division of Africa, and the Boer War had revealed a number of deficiencies in the nation's health and military preparedness, Britain began a painful reappraisal of its armed forces and international position.

The Navy remained Britain's paramount defence, though maintaining its supremacy against a growing number of rivals was increasingly difficult in an era of rapid – and expensive – technological advances. Richard Haldane, the War Minister, acknowledged in 1906, 'The first purpose for which we want any army is for oversea war. The Fleet defends our coast'. The government established a British Expeditionary Force (BEF) of six divisions, initially designed to deal with any potential threat to India, though the General Staff also had a European role in mind. Internationally, Britain twice, in 1898 and 1901, sought an alliance with Germany to bolster its position in Asia – a controversial policy which would have reversed the traditional stance of avoiding engagements that would commit Britain to future action.[6]

Quite apart from contemporary notions of common Anglo-Saxon blood ties, Germany seemed a natural choice as an ally. Together with Austria-Hungary and Italy, it constituted the 1882 Triple Alliance, the conservative bloc with which Britain had tended to cooperate through the 1890s, to counter the rival 1894 Dual Alliance of France and Russia, its main imperial and naval competitors. Germany would consider an alliance, but, understandably, given its common frontier with Russia, the state which constituted Britain's main Asian cause of concern, sought reassurances of British support in Europe, which were not forthcoming. It is interesting to speculate, in the light of developments in 1914, what might have happened if Germany had gambled on a purely Asian alliance. Instead, Britain turned to Japan in 1902 to conclude its only modern alliance before hostilities in 1914, settled a number of outstanding difficulties with the United States and drifted away from Germany, a process speeded by the realisation that its new fleet was targeted at Britain.[7]

It was, in part, the wish to avoid a quarrel between Russia and Japan precipitating a conflict between their allies, France and Britain, that motivated the French Foreign Minister, Théophile Delcassé, to seek a colonial accommodation with Britain. Three years later, to the disgust and alarm of many of the government's radical supporters, Britain concluded a similar agreement with Tsarist Russia, the only power that could threaten India, the heart of the British Empire. This Convention established spheres of influence in the contested territory of Persia (Iran) and relaxed tension on the Indian borders, particularly in Tibet and Afghanistan. Both arrangements fell far short of alliances – formal agreements to go to war on behalf of a partner in specified circumstances – and had no military implications. Germany's perception, however, was of a hostile coalition seeking to encircle it. Ironically it would be Germany's attempts at Algeciras in 1905 and Agadir in 1911 to escape this perceived noose that encouraged Anglo-French military conversations about potential cooperation in the event of a war with Germany in which both were involved. These talks did not commit Britain to fight for France but they did constitute a strong indication that the Entente was becoming more than a colonial bargain.[8]

Grey was later castigated for not informing his Cabinet colleagues of these conversations and for not indicating clearly to Germany that Britain would fight alongside France in any Franco-German conflict, the argument being that this would have deterred Germany. The first charge has some substance but the second fails on two grounds: first, the Cabinet would never have sanctioned such a categorical commitment; secondly, any British intervention in the early stages of a war, which Germany expected to win within six weeks, could have no serious influence on Germany's actions. Kaiser Wilhelm II himself had pointed out in March 1911, 'Excuse me saying so, but the few divisions you could put into the field could make no appreciable difference.'[9] Germany had received clear warnings long before July 1914 that Britain would not tolerate the destruction of France – indeed it was Haldane's message to that effect which triggered the so-called 'War Council' of 8 December 1912 in Berlin. During the crisis Grey stretched his Cabinet brief to alert Lichnowsky that Britain might intervene. In 1916 Lichnowsky acknowledged that he had warned

Berlin that Britain would not remain neutral, but had been ignored. Lloyd George's claim that 'Had he [Grey] warned Germany in time of the point at which Britain would declare war – and wage it with her full strength – the issue would have been different' was characteristically cavalier with the truth.[10]

Grey did consult a select group of colleagues after the talks between the countries' General Staffs began in 1905 and before the Cabinet debated them in November 1911. However, at the time of the Agadir crisis in the summer of 1911 most of the Cabinet were ignorant of the Anglo-French plan, approved by a carefully picked Committee of Imperial Defence on 23 August 1911, that, in the event of a Franco-German war over Morocco, the BEF should be sent to France. The November Cabinet meetings revealed the strength of opposition to any such continental commitment. Asquith, Grey, Haldane, Churchill and Lloyd George defended the plan but were decisively out-voted by their 15 colleagues, led by Lord Morley, the Lord President of the Council, and Reginald McKenna, the Home Secretary, who were opposed with various degrees of intensity but could not agree on a coherent alternative strategy beyond passing resolutions that there should no communications between Britain's General Staff and those of other countries that could commit Britain to war, and that such communications should be subject to previous approval by the Cabinet.[11]

In 1912 Britain and France decided to reposition their fleets, such that the main French disposition was in the Mediterranean, whence Britain withdrew some of its assets, completing a process of concentrating its ships in home waters. In an exchange of letters in November 1912 between Grey and Paul Cambon, the French Ambassador, the two countries agreed to consult in time of crisis but, crucially, each acknowledged that these naval realignments did not commit either to defend the positions of the other, nor did the staff talks restrict each other's freedom of action.[12]

The July crisis thus confronted a government which was deeply divided over Britain's commitment to France and Russia. John Burns, the Labour Minister of Local Government, epitomised the views of the radical majority: 'Splendid Isolation; No Balance of Power; No incorporation in the Continental System'.[13] Whilst anxious to avoid any suggestion that British policy might embolden them into taking intemperate action, Grey and his officials believed that Britain's security and prestige required it to support its Entente partners, not least because they, and other powers, perceived this to be a test of the value of Britain's friendship. Asquith told King George V on 28 July, 'Russia says to us, "if you won't say you are ready to side with us now, your friendship is valueless, and we shall act on that assumption in the future".'[14] Sir Eyre Crowe, one of the key Foreign Office advisers, widened this concern, writing on 25 July, 'Should the war come, and England stand aside, one of two things must happen; (a) Either Germany and Austria win, crush France, and humiliate Russia … what will be the position of friendless England? (b) Or France and Russia win. What would then be their attitude towards England? What about India and the Mediterranean?'[15] Even more alarming was the possibility that Russia and France, disillusioned with Britain, might seek an accommodation with Germany and Austria.

The political situation was very delicate. The Conservative opposition largely supported Grey's policy and was firmly committed to the Entente, though the bitter divisions over Ulster had rather muddied these waters and indeed soured relations between Grey and Sir Arthur Nicolson,

the Permanent Under-Secretary at the Foreign Office, a firm
Unionist. Asquith knew Grey would resign if the Entente was
abandoned, as would he and, probably, other key ministers.
Too firm a declaration of support for France would precipitate the resignation of the radicals. Either option would spell
the end of the Liberal government and bring in either a coalition or a Conservative ministry. Asquith's efforts to keep his
government together played a major role in the events of July
1914.

On Sunday 26 July Asquith reported that 'The news this
morning is that Servia has capitulated on the main points,
but it is very doubtful if any reservations will be accepted by
Austria, who is resolved upon a complete & final humiliation.'[16] Nonetheless, Nicolson still pursued Grey's policy of
seeking an ambassadors' conference in London of Britain,
France, Germany and Italy, to try to defuse the Austro-Russian confrontation. To warn that Britain should not be disre-
garded, Grey publicised Churchill's decision not to disperse
the fleet after the Spithead naval review, but he remained
hopeful that those he perceived to constitute a peace party in
Berlin would prevail.[17]

Such hopes were destroyed when Germany rejected a conference on 27 July and Austria declared war on Serbia on 28
July. Grey was now convinced that there would be a major
war involving all the continental powers with the possible
exception of Italy, whose allegiance to the Triple Alliance
was doubtful. At the Cabinet on Wednesday 29 July Grey
advocated support for France and was backed by Churchill,
Haldane, Crewe and Asquith but none of the other ministers. As Asquith wrote to the king on 30 July, 'After much
discussion it was agreed that Sir E. Grey should be author-
ized to inform the German and French Ambassadors that

at this stage we are unable to pledge ourselves in advance, either under all conditions to stand aside, or in any conditions to join in.' Grey also asked what Britain should do if, as he expected, Germany attacked France through Belgium, whose neutrality all the Powers, including Prussia, had guaranteed in 1839. The Cabinet refused to make any firm commitments. Asquith reported, 'It is a doubtful point how far a single guaranteeing State is bound under the Treaty of 1839 to maintain Belgian neutrality if the remainder abstain or refuse. The Cabinet consider that the matter if it arises will be rather one of policy than of legal obligation.' Burns recorded in his diary: 'critical Cabinet at 11.30. The discussion ensued. Situation seriously reviewed from all points of view. It was decided not to decide.' The Cabinet did sanction preliminary steps towards mobilisation and Asquith later that day approved sending the fleet to its war stations.[18]

The Cabinet did not meet again until Friday 31 July but there were critical developments at home and abroad. Perhaps with Asquith and Grey's approval, and certainly with Lloyd George's knowledge, Churchill approached the Conservative leadership through his friend F E Smith about a possible coalition. Whilst offering Cambon no firm support in the event of a Franco-German war, telling him 'we had not made up our minds what we should do, it was a case that we should have to consider', Grey warned Lichnowsky that, although Britain could stand aloof even from an Austro-Russian war over Serbia, he could offer no such assurance if France and Germany became involved. He was enraged that evening by a clumsy German attempt to buy British neutrality with an assurance that Germany would repair any damage caused by a violation of Belgian neutrality and that a defeated France would lose only colonies. He rejected this without consulting his colleagues. Meanwhile, on 29 July the Austrians shelled Belgrade and Russia ordered the mobilisation of its southern armies. After a brief moment of hope when it seemed that Germany would press Austria to 'halt in Belgrade', Russia, Austria-Hungary and Germany all ordered general mobilisation on 31 July.[19]

On 31 July the Cabinet authorised Grey to seek assurances from France and Germany of respect for Belgian neutrality. France's reply was affirmative, Germany's evasive but illuminating. Gottlieb von Jagow, the Foreign Minister, stated that anything he said 'could not fail, in the event of war, to have the undesirable effect of disclosing to a certain extent part of their plan of campaign'. Beyond that, recorded Jack Pease, the President of the Board of Trade, the Cabinet would only declare that, 'British opinion would not now allow us to support France – a violation of Belgium might alter public opinion but we could say nothing to commit ourselves.' Lewis 'Lulu' Harcourt, the Colonial Secretary, recorded 'It is now clear that *this* Cabinet will not join the war.'[20]

In the early hours of Saturday 1 August Asquith and William Tyrrell, Grey's private secretary, went by taxi to Buckingham Place with an appeal to the king's cousin, Tsar Nicholas II of Russia. Awakened in his nightshirt and dressing gown George signed it, but matters were moving beyond the reach of family ties. Germany declared war on Russia and France mobilised. Later the Cabinet authorised Grey to tell Lichnowsky that 'if there were a violation of the neutrality of Belgium by one combatant while the other respected it, it would be extremely difficult to restrain public feeling in this country.' The Cabinet refused to agree to send the BEF to help France or to mobilise the fleet, though Churchill, with Asquith's support, did so.[21]

Asquith noted, 'We came, every now & again, near to the parting of the ways.' Morley and John Simon, the Attorney General, favoured a clear declaration of British neutrality. 'This no doubt is the view for the moment of the bulk of the party.' Grey would resign if the government adopted such a policy. 'Ll. George – all for peace – is more sensible & statesmanlike, for keeping the position still open... . Winston very bellicose & demanding immediate mobilisation. Haldane diffuse (how clever of you to retrieve the second "f")' Asquith complimented Venetia, 'and nebulous.' He was not hopeful and confided, 'But if it comes to war I feel sure (this is entirely between you & me) that we shall have *some* split in the Cabinet. Of course, if Grey went I should go, & the whole thing would break up.'[22]

Grey told Cambon that afternoon that the government would not, at the moment, dispatch the BEF. He did, however, reveal his refusal, in response to Lichnowsky's request to guarantee British neutrality if Germany undertook to respect that of Belgium. Cambon raised the stakes by lamenting to Nicolson, 'Ils vont nous lâcher, ils vont nous lâcher' (They are going to desert us) and enquiring of Henry Wickham Steed, the foreign editor of *The Times*, 'J'attends de savoir si le mot honeur doit être rayé du vocabulaire anglais.' (Should the word honour be removed from the English language?). Nicolson sought out Grey: '...you have over and over promised M. Cambon that if Germany was the aggressor, you would stand by France.' All Grey could reply was, 'Yes, but he has nothing in writing.' Nicolson, who was not sufficiently appreciative of Grey's political difficulties, remarked bitterly, 'You will render us a by-word among nations.' In what proved a more effective intervention he wrote to Grey: 'M. Cambon pointed out to me this afternoon that it was at our request that France had moved her fleets to the Mediterranean on the understanding that we undertook the protection of her Northern and Western coasts'. This was not true, but, determined to bring the next day's Cabinet to a decision, Grey presented it as such.[23]

Sunday 2 August proved crucial. Before the first of two Cabinet meetings, Asquith received a message of unconditional support for assistance to France and Russia from the Conservative leadership, but his own party remained divided. He told Venetia, '... we are on the brink of a split. We agreed at last (with much difficulty) that Grey should be authorised to tell Cambon that our fleet would not allow the German fleet to make the Channel the base of hostile operations.' Burns resigned immediately and 'the Beagles' (Asquith's term for the minor members of the government), backed by Morley, Harcourt and Lloyd George and probably three-quarters of the parliamentary party, remained opposed to intervention. 'Grey of course will never consent to this, & I shall not separate myself from him ... It will be a shocking thing if at such a moment we break up – with no one to take our place.'[24]

It was now less a question of whether Britain would go to war, but of which government would lead it. Although Burns was persuaded to delay until the Cabinet met again that evening, the expectation was that perhaps seven ministers might resign, a fatal blow, but gradually Grey and Asquith's position improved. Before the morning meeting Harcourt, Lloyd George, Pease, Simon, Earl Beauchamp, the First Commissioner of Works, and Walter Runciman, the President of the Board of Agriculture, had agreed, 'we were not prepared to go into war now, but that in certain events we might reconsider [the] position such as the invasion wholesale of Belgium.' Crewe seemed persuaded by the threat to the

Channel, others, like Haldane and McKenna seemed to be wavering.[25]

At its second meeting the Cabinet agreed that a substantial violation of Belgian neutrality would constitute a *casus belli*. Herbert Samuel, the Postmaster General, carefully drafted two resolutions which placed the onus for any war upon Germany, either for bombarding the French coast or attacking Belgium. Burns and Morley resigned, with Simon and Beauchamp expected to follow, but Lloyd George did not. Characteristically, his motivation was opaque. He wrote to his wife on 3 August, 'I am moving through a nightmare world these days. I have fought hard for peace and I have succeeded so far in keeping the Cabinet out of it but I am driven to the conclusion that if the small nationality of Belgium is attacked by Germany all my traditions and prejudices will be engaged on the side of war.' His secretary, mistress and second wife, Frances Stevenson, later reflected, 'My own opinion is that L.G.'s mind was made up from the first, that he knew we would have to go in, and that the invasion of Belgium was, to be cynical, a heaven-sent excuse for supporting a declaration of war.' If so, he had very successfully hidden that conviction from his colleagues, but his decision was extremely important in maintaining the unity of the Asquith government.[26]

On Monday 3 August Germany declared war on France. The Cabinet learned of the German ultimatum to Belgium and the subsequent invasion. The Army was mobilised. Simon and Beauchamp resigned, though Lloyd George persuaded them to remain in place for the parliamentary debate that afternoon, during which Grey made a moving speech, transforming the political balance in favour of intervention. Asquith could report the following day, 'You will be relieved to hear that there is a slump in resignations.' Simon and

Beauchamp withdrew theirs, Burns and Morley persisted, but the government could survive – Runciman told Charles Trevelyan, one of the junior ministerial resignations, 'That one is miserable beyond measure is natural enough but in our view that is not in itself sufficient to justify us in handing over policy and control to the Tories'. At 2 pm on 4 August Grey sent an ultimatum to Germany, requiring an assurance of respect for Belgian neutrality by midnight German time, 11 pm in Britain. Theobald von Bethmann Hollweg, the German Chancellor, refused to do so, handing the Entente a propaganda coup by saying Britain was fighting for 'a scrap of paper'. After the hasty retrieval of an inaccurately worded document Britain declared war on Germany as the ultimatum expired. The continental conflict had become a world war.[27]

Preventing a major power controlling the Low Countries was traditional British policy, but Belgium was more important as a moral crusade that allowed colleagues opposed to Grey's commitment to the Entente to rally to the government. Grey's concern was to avoid Germany dominating the continent or Britain being left isolated by a Franco-Russian victory achieved without British support. Only with the greatest difficulty could he persuade his colleagues to share his not unreasonable concern about German ambitions and to support France and Russia. Where he was culpable was in his unwillingness to grasp the strategic requirements or the political nettles of a policy of continental commitment. 'The naval war will be cheap' Churchill promised, as he sought Lloyd George's support, and the expectation was that this, together with finance, would be Britain's main contributions. Britain did not have an army on the scale of those in Europe; to raise one in peacetime would have required conscription, a completely unacceptable proposition for Liberals and indeed many Conservatives, quite apart from the expense it would involve.

During their pre-war conversations Ferdinand Foch, one of France's leading generals, had told his friend, Henry Wilson, Britain's Director of Military Operations, 'After all it doesn't matter what you send us, we only ask for one corporal and four men, but they must be there right at the start. You will give them to me and I promise to do my utmost to get them killed. From that moment I will be at ease since I know that England will follow them as one man.'[28] The BEF was rather larger but its fate was very similar and it is certainly debateable whether its sacrifice was the key to the failure of Germany's plan to defeat France.[29] Nonetheless Foch was right; Britain would make a substantial contribution to the long war that was necessary to defeat Germany and its allies and would take Lloyd George, now its Prime Minister, to negotiate the peace settlement in Paris in 1919. More immediately the continental crisis overtook those other issues of which he had warned – the Ulster problem was shelved for the duration and the Triple Alliance strike never occurred.

9

4 August 1914: Britain (and its empire) declare war on
Germany – part II

How the Empire Went to War[1]

Antony Lentin

It was 10.45 on the evening of Tuesday, 4 August 1914. Fifteen
minutes remained before the expiry of Britain's ultimatum
calling upon Germany to respect the neutrality of Belgium. At
a special meeting of the Privy Council at Buckingham Palace,
King George V formally signed the declaration of war. When
Big Ben struck 11, the crowds outside the Palace responded
'with tremendous cheering, which grew into a deafening roar
when King George ... appeared on the balcony'.[2]

Constitutionally, the king's signature committed not just
Great Britain but the entire British Empire to enter the war.
How would the Empire respond in practice to the summons to
enlist in what was for most of its members a faraway quarrel?
In the most recent British Dominion, the Union of South
Africa, Barry Hertzog, leader of the opposition Afrikaner
National Party, was for neutrality. 'We are not pro-German
but anti-British',[3] he said. Closer to home, Ireland, constitu-
tionally an integral part of the United Kingdom, was at the

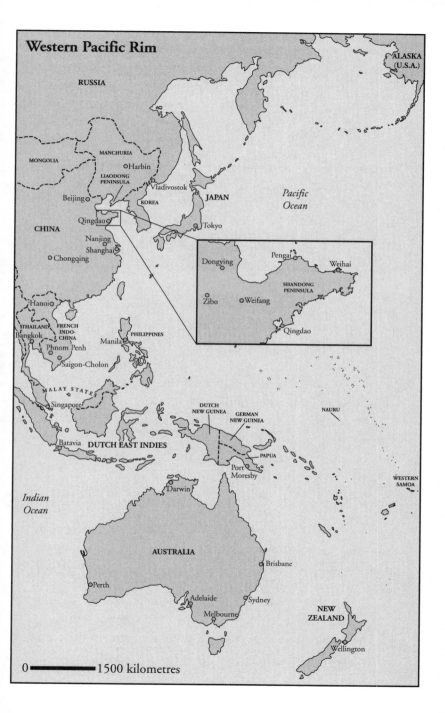

centre of a deep political crisis in London on the convulsive issue of Home Rule, a crisis which threatened to erupt in civil war just as Britain was on the eve of hostilities with Germany. Ostensibly Ireland fell into line –'the one bright spot', said the Foreign Secretary, Sir Edward Grey, 'in the very dreadful situation'. John Redmond, the Irish Nationalist leader in the House of Commons, declared that British troops could safely be withdrawn from Ireland, adding the somewhat ambiguous and qualified assurance that Irishmen North and South –'if it is allowed to us' – would 'defend the coasts of our country'.[4]

The British Empire in 1914 covered one-fifth of the earth's land mass and contained some 400 million people, of whom nine-tenths lived outside the British Isles. All were nominally British subjects under the British Nationality Act, 1914. They included 15½ million whites of British and European stock in Australia, New Zealand, Canada and South Africa and 366 million non-whites, of whom 300 million lived in India and who alone constituted one-fifth of the human race. Britain ruled over more than 90 million Muslims.[5]

The sea routes from Britain to the various parts of the empire were patrolled by the Royal Navy, still the world's biggest navy, and criss-crossed by the British Merchant Navy, which carried more than half the world's cargoes. Rudyard Kipling, virtual poet laureate of the empire, wrote in 1911 of the 'big steamers' on which Britain depended for raw materials and foodstuffs: 'We fetch it from Melbourne, Quebec and Vancouver. / Address us at Hobart, Hong-kong, and Bombay.' A worldwide network of undersea cables, supplemented in 1911 by a chain of imperial wireless stations, connected London with every corner of the far-flung empire. A penny stamp guaranteed delivery of a letter to the remotest outpost.

The empire was avowedly white-dominated. In his poem

'The White Man's burden' (1899), Kipling proclaimed Britain's imperial mission to send forth her 'best' in the thankless task of serving her non-white subjects overseas, 'the silent, sullen peoples', 'half devil and half child'. The strenuous paternalistic rule of imperialists like Rhodes in Southern Africa, Lugard in Nigeria and Curzon in India, though they ultimately governed in British interests, left everywhere the undeniable marks of Western civilisation. Railways joined sea ports to the interior of Africa and notably India (with 35,000 miles of track in 1914). District officers held sway over vast tracts 'in darkest Africa'[6] and such undeveloped spots as Borneo and New Guinea. Christian missionaries and British officialdom helped to curb slavery and to promote European-style progress, advances in agriculture, public hygiene and medicine. India boasted public schools and universities on the British model, to which increasing numbers flocked, while educated colonials gravitated to the imperial capital: Gandhi was not untypical in reading for the Bar in London. Law and order were enforced throughout the empire, from whose highest courts appeals were submitted for final decision to the Judicial Committee of the Privy Council in London.

The five colonies with large populations of European ancestry, Canada, Newfoundland, Australia, New Zealand and South Africa, though subject to the imperial Parliament at Westminster, were virtually self-governing in their domestic affairs. Known since 1907 as the Dominions, they appointed their own High Commissioners to represent them in London. Foreign affairs and defence, however, were directed from a Dominions Department within the Colonial Office, and the king's declaration of war in 1914 was formally proclaimed in his name by his personal representative in each dominion, the Governor or Governor-General.

Australia

The population of Australia in 1914 was overwhelmingly derived from British stock (about a third were of Irish origin). Though three-quarters were native-born, Australians still referred to Britain as 'Home'.[7] A 'White Australia' was the keystone policy in a country hostile to Asian immigration and alarmed at the rise of Japan and Britain's strategic alliance with it which had been concluded in 1902, and renewed in 1905 and 1911. Having lost overall naval superiority and facing the challenge of Germany's growing fleet, the Royal Navy no longer felt able simultaneously to control events in the Pacific and defend the British Isles. At Britain's instigation, Australia introduced conscription in 1909, seven years before it became obligatory in a Britain under pressure of war, and in 1913 was the first dominion to establish its own navy.

Australia had been a federation – the Commonwealth of Australia – since 1901. The Liberal Prime Minister since 1913, Sir Joseph Cook, had a majority of only one in the lower house, and an election campaign was in full swing when war was declared. The winner, the Scottish-born Labour leader Andrew Fisher, whose party had favoured an independent defence force, played to pro-British sentiment. 'Our duty is clear', he declared, 'to gird up our loins and remember we are Britons'. He pledged 'our last man and last shilling'[8] to the cause. From a population of less than five million, Australia enlisted 417,000 men, 13 per cent of its manpower, of whom 332,000 were to serve overseas.

New Zealand

New Zealand, geographically furthest from Britain, was perhaps the dominion most openly attached to the 'Old

Country'. Economic ties were close, for four-fifths of New Zealand's exports went to Britain and three-fifths of its imports came from there; and, like Australia, New Zealand looked to the Royal Navy for protection. Like Australia, New Zealand introduced compulsory military service in 1909. This, together with a contribution towards the cost of a dreadnought for the Royal Navy, was New Zealand's response to Britain's request for assistance in bearing the burden of imperial defence. Ulster-born William Massey had been Prime Minister since 1912. On the declaration of war, both Massey and opposition Liberal Party leader Sir Joseph Ward pledged their support, Massey placing 'all we are and all we have' at Britain's disposal.[9] From a population of just over a million, including 40,000 Maoris, New Zealand enlisted 127,000, 19 per cent of its manpower, of whom 112,000 went to serve overseas. The proportion of volunteers was high: 14,000 joined up in the first week alone; volunteer Maori contingents totalled 2,000.

Canada

Canadian attitudes were shaped by the proximity of the United States. Its strong British attachment served to protect Canada from undue American influence and to mark Canadians as a distinct people on the North American continent. French Canadians had shown themselves averse to entanglement in imperial quarrels such as the Boer War, in which Canada, Australia and New Zealand had participated on Britain's side. US–Canadian relations became a dividing issue in the federal election of 1911. The Liberal Government of Sir Wilfred Laurier favoured a free trade agreement with the USA. The Conservatives under Robert Borden exploited latent suspicions of America and won the election.

Three years later and three days before Britain declared war, Borden promised Britain full support. Laurier declared a party truce, and this was endorsed, initially at least, by Henri Bourassa, the stalwart of French-Canadian nationalism in Quebec. Québécois did not respond to the call to arms with the same enthusiasm as Canadians of British stock. Their ties with France were remote. Newfoundland, Britain's oldest overseas possession (nominally an independent dominion until 1949), and with a population of 250,000, sent 6,000 men overseas, of whom a quarter would die.

The first Canadian contingent of 32,000, two-thirds British-born and 1,000 Québécois, left for England in October 1914. From a population of 7½ million, Canada called up 13.5 per cent of its manpower, 630,000 men, of whom 460,000 were to serve overseas. Canada's minuscule fleet of four ships was amalgamated in the Royal Navy.

South Africa

The Union of South Africa, incorporating in a single state the former Boer republics of the Orange Free State and Transvaal together with the British Cape Colony and Natal, had been established only in 1910. War in 1914 re-opened the bitter divisions of the Boer War (1899–1902). South Africans of British stock and many Afrikaners supported Prime Minister Louis Botha and his right-hand man, Jan Smuts, Minister of Defence. Smuts declared: 'Botha and I are not the men to desert Britain in this dark hour'.[10]

Other Afrikaners, however, were still smarting from the defeat of 1901, and a general election in 1915 would show half of all Afrikaner voters to be opposed to the war. Rebellion broke out in September 1914 among some unreconciled Afrikaners, who crossed into German South West Africa (present-day Namibia). Botha and Smuts subdued it by December and went on to conquer this German colony. The white population of South Africa was a little above 1¼ million. Of these, 136,000, or 11 per cent of its manpower, were enlisted, of whom 76,000 served in overseas campaigns, while a further 10,000 volunteers sailed for England and enlisted there. The South African Native National Congress (forerunner of the African National Congress), representing the black but unenfranchised majority, also voiced support for the war.

India

India was a not a country of white settlement like the dominions but a multi-racial subcontinent divided by language, religion and caste. Most of India was administered as a Crown colony by a tiny echelon of British officials, the Indian Civil Service, a mere 1,000 men. One third of India – 'British India' – was ruled by 600 native princes under British supervision. At the top of the pyramid was British officialdom, directed by the India Office in London, and on the spot through a Viceroy and his advisory councils in Delhi. Behind them stood an Indian army of 150,000 and a British garrison of 75,000 men, one-third of the entire British Army. British rule was avowedly paternalistic, though the Morley-Minto reforms of 1909 conceded increasing participation by native Indians in the administration. But neither Lord Morley, Secretary of State for India, nor Lord Minto, the viceroy, thought India ready for self-government on the model of the Dominions.

Nevertheless the public demonstration of submission to George V as King-Emperor at his coronation *durbar* at Delhi in 1911 symbolised a genuine allegiance, and opinion across India in 1914 was overwhelmingly pro-British. Aid was offered on a scale that the British Government itself would scarcely have dared to request. Even Gandhi, then in London, pledged India's 'desire to share the responsibilities of Empire'.[11] It was true that Indian members of the Congress Party[12] hoped that participation in the war would prove India's right to increasing self-government. It was also true that few Indians wanted to exchange British rule for German, a possibility that loomed when the Ottoman Empire joined the Central Powers in October 1914. But the prevailing sentiment among the most highly placed Indians was pride. Indian princes with long martial traditions of regimental honour freely offered their services. Britain was able to withdraw all but 15,000 British troops from India to meet the emergency and India provided a million men, of whom half served overseas and 390,000 in labour units.

⁂

Excluding India, the full complement of Dominion soldiers was 1,328,000, of whom 943,000 would be put in the field against the Central Powers. Enlistment from the colonies included black and coloured volunteers from the West Indies (15,600), from British East Africa (34,000) and British West Africa (25,000). In practice African 'volunteers' were often commandeered by tribal chieftains through whom the British ruled. In Nigeria, for instance, the Alafin of Oyo promised the local British resident to raise 30,000 men; after the war he was made a KCMG.[13] Many served in indispensable auxiliary roles as labourers and porters.

August 1914: 'a united Empire'[14]
The British Empire in August 1914 was united by ties of racial kinship in the Dominions and generally by common ideals

and loyalties, revived every four years by conferences of Dominion leaders with the British Prime Minister and Colonial Secretary in London. The 1911 conference was planned to coincide with George V's coronation and to 'raise the temperature of imperial patriotism'.[15] Empire patriotism in 1914 was also a spur to local nationalism, the 'young lions' in the imperial pride keen to prove their worth. Deference to Britain was often accompanied by demands from the Dominions for a greater say within the Empire as equal states by 'new nations bursting the colonial chrysalis'.[16] The term 'Commonwealth' rather than 'Empire' came to be used more and more.

Even so, 'Dominion over palm and pine'[17] remained vested in the Colonial Office and ultimately in the imperial Parliament, and imperial policy-making continued to be directed from Downing Street in war as in peace. 'Be on your guard against possible attack',[18] the Colonial Office somewhat portentously warned the Deputy Governor of Nigeria on 3 August. For a dozen years Britain's immediate priority had been Europe, not the empire – Germany's challenge to the balance of power, to Britain's naval supremacy and to the British Isles. Defence had long been considered by a Committee of Imperial Defence, consisting of Cabinet ministers and service chiefs.

When the crisis erupted in 1914, the loyal subordination of the 'colonials' was somewhat patronisingly (but as it turned out justifiably) taken for granted. On 5 August, the day after war was declared, a 'War Council' met at Downing Street to consider Britain's strategy and issue instructions across the empire as to how each part should contribute. Even as the British Expeditionary Force crossed the Channel, a rash of strikes on German Empire territories overseas erupted across the globe at Britain's behest from neighbouring British territories: on Togoland and in the Cameroons in West Africa; in German South West Africa and East Africa (present-day Tanzania); in German New Guinea and Samoa. Britain's purpose was strategic: to secure the German coaling stations and silence the wireless stations in Africa and the Pacific that served the German fleet, and so to forestall German naval operations and secure Britain's sea-lanes. As Kipling, long a prophet of war with Germany, had warned Britain in 'Big Steamers': 'If any one hinders our coming, you'll starve!'

The war would kindle anti-imperial tendencies in Quebec, India, the former Afrikaner republics, among Australians and Canadians of Irish Catholic descent and above all in Ireland itself. A minority of Muslims in Egypt, India and Nigeria murmured against fighting their co-religionists when Turkey entered the war. But these were noises off in 1914, albeit the storm over Ireland, stilled for the moment, would rumble on and break out again in 1916. Mismanaged campaigns under British commanders would diminish unquestioning deference towards Britain and deepen self-confidence and a sense of the Dominions' own nationhoods. But that lay in the future. Once war was declared, across the empire differences with the 'Mother Country' were drowned out by fervent expressions of loyalty.

Yet references to the empire in the British press in August 1914 were surprisingly few. Eyes in Britain remained anxiously fixed on the continent, where rapid German advances to west and east made it seem that all Europe might soon fall beneath the jackboot. In a poem published in *The Times* on 2 September, Kipling sounded a stark call to arms:

For all we have and are,
For all our children's fate,

Stand up and take the war.
The Hun is at the gate! ...

To a later generation such sentiments might sound over-blown. But at the time they struck the authentic note of kinship and shared values. Proof that allegiance to the 'Old Country' was more than an article of the constitution lies in the spontaneous response to the call to arms and in the Commonwealth war cemeteries in Flanders, Gallipoli and many another foreign field.

10

23 August 1914: Japan declares war on Germany

The Chance of a Millennium

Jonathan Clements

Since being driven to the brink of bankruptcy by the Russo-Japanese war of 1904–5, Japan had pursued a policy of expansion, particularly in mainland Asia, under the cover of international actions. Prime Minister Ōkuma Shigenobu hence regarded the outbreak of war as 'the chance of a millennium', and swiftly declared war on Germany on 23 August 1914.[1]

The precise terms of the 1902 Anglo-Japanese Alliance did not require Japan to enter the First World War on the British side, but Ōkuma decided to do so anyway, as a means of seizing German possessions in the Pacific and of consolidating Japan's position in China.

In his ultimatum to Germany, Ōkuma made a point of citing Japan's obligations under the Anglo-Japanese Alliance. In supposed deference to Japan's deal with Britain, Ōkuma proposed to '... take measures to remove the causes of all disturbance of peace in the Far East, and to safeguard general interests ... to secure firm and enduring peace in Eastern Asia

...'. Ironically, such a claim was made against the faint protests of the British Foreign Secretary, Sir Edward Grey, who
cautioned against any acts by the Japanese that might lead
to 'unfounded misapprehension' about Japan's intentions in
Asia.[2]

The problem, as the British realised, was that Japan would
be seen to be embarking upon a land-grab under the cover
of assisting its European ally – despite Grey's wording, such
a fear was anything but unfounded. However, the Japanese
Foreign Minister Makino Nobuaki parsed it very differently.
He noted that Japan had poured vast amounts of investment
into certain Chinese regions. The money might be 'industrial'
rather than 'political', but Makino argued that for industrial
investments to be secure, China required a secure government. In a policy redolent of Britain's Doctrine of Lapse on
the Indian subcontinent, for China to have secure government, the Japanese might be expected to interfere in Chinese
matters, be it through shoring up unstable regimes or offering
support to particular politicians or political parties.

Makino's rhetoric reflected a common conception among
Tokyo politicians in 1914, that Japan and China required
teikei (literally 'accord') on a vast range of policies. The two
countries, it was believed, needed to establish trade deals,
commercial liaisons, railway projects and even political
agreements with each other, in order to present a united front
towards, and perhaps even against, the white races.

To some extent, Chinese policymakers agreed with the
theory behind the Japanese plan, although not its colonial
implications. In August 1914, the Chinese President Yuan
Shikai had reportedly said, 'China, like Japan is of the yellow
race, and should not all make friends of the Europeans and
Americans who are of the white race?' But he had added that

once the First World War was over China and Japan might expect 'more powerful white adversaries', against whom they might need to cooperate.[3]

Such talk is one of the earliest incidences of a policy that would come to dominate Japanese militarism in the first half of the 20th century – the idea that Japan should become the hegemon of a Great East Asian Co-Prosperity Sphere, forming a bloc of nations that could stand up to the European powers. It was naturally assumed that China would be too weak to lead itself.

But though Yuan Shikai had offered vague assent towards general Japanese statements of intent, he does not seem to have wanted them to put such theories into practice. Despite his protestations, the Japanese launched an attack on German possessions in the Pacific, capturing a number of small islands and invading Chinese territory in order to oust the Germans from Shandong.

Japanese forces attacked the German naval base on the Shandong Peninsula in September 1914, shortly after war was officially declared. The 23,000 Japanese men were accompanied by a small force of 1,500 British soldiers. The port town of Qingdao (Tsingtao) held out for two months, but eventually surrendered – neutralising an important German military site, but also leaving a piece of Chinese territory in Japanese hands. Out in the Pacific, the Japanese navy took the initiative, seizing the Marianas, the Carolines and the Marshall Islands without significant resistance.

However, Japan's declaration of war against Germany cloaked a far more decisive and dangerous *undeclared* action against China, at the time a self-proclaimed neutral country. The seizure of Shandong was followed with a diplomatic assault in January 1915, with the presentation to China of the

Twenty-One Demands, which might be broadly summarised in five groups as:

1. The Japanese acquisition of Shandong was confirmed (that is, left to Japan, the de facto occupier, and Germany, the soon-to-be-vanquished former occupier, to determine).
2. Japan was to gain further rights of settlement and occupation along the South Manchuria railway, effectively extending Japanese influence into north-east China (Manchuria).
3. Several Chinese mines and refineries with Japanese shareholders were to be handed over to full Japanese control.
4. China was to offer no further territorial concessions to foreign powers, except Japan.
5. A cluster of further deals would establish Japanese control of the Chinese police force, the Chinese arms trade, Chinese government offices and the vague yet intimidating right of Japanese missionaries to 'preach' in China.

The Twenty-One Demands were a cunning continuation of Japan's soft expansion policy. Internal memos within the Japanese government acknowledged that a full-blown military attack on China would prove impossible to maintain, owing to resistance among the general population. But a China in hock to Japanese banks and beholden to its institutions and corporations would be easier to manage.

Although the Chinese unwillingly agreed to the first four groups of Demands, the nature of these negotiations would become an important issue at the Paris Peace Conference that followed the war. China would eventually enter the war as an Ally – in other words, on the 'same side' as Japan – at least in part as a response to the threat presented by the Japanese land-grab. Chinese diplomats would later argue that this made Japanese pressure an unseemly and invalid act against a fellow enemy of Germany.

Japan's role in the First World War was initially restricted to the Pacific sphere. In February 1915, Japanese marines formed part of a police action against a mutiny in Singapore by Indian soldiers. In late 1916, four Japanese battleships were sent on a long journey to the Mediterranean after a British request for naval aid in the European theatre. Based in Malta, the ships sailed on several hundred escort missions in the Mediterranean, and also took part in the rescue of over 7,000 seamen. In return, it was quietly agreed that Britain would support Japan's desire to hold on to Shandong after the war was over.

America did not share Britain's willingness to turn a blind eye to China's interests in Shandong, and the position of America and Japan as new allies was placed under threat by increasing tensions over Japan's actions in the Pacific. In an attempt to calm things down, the US Secretary of State Robert Lansing and the Japanese envoy Ishii Kikujirō concluded the Lansing-Ishii Agreement in 1917. This shaky compromise restated an old open-door policy, in which both America and Japan agreed to uphold Chinese territorial integrity. The US, however, also acknowledged that Japan had 'special interests' in China.

Both China and Japan would arrive at the Paris Peace Conference in 1919 determined to settle the question of Shandong, each unaware that the other had secured contradictory guarantees from the Great Powers in return for their cooperation during the war itself.

11

1 November 1914: Russia declares war on Turkey
The Ottomans' Last War – and After
Andrew Mango

The Ottoman Empire entered the First World War on the side of the Central Powers (Germany and Austria-Hungary) in November 1914. The sequence of events which led to this fatal decision and, four years later, to the dissolution of the Ottoman state is clear. On 2 August 1914, Sultan Mehmet V signed a secret treaty of alliance with Germany, negotiated by Enver Pasha, the most powerful and the most pro-German member of the Young Turks triumvirate which had seized power the previous year. On 10 August, the German cruisers *Goeben* and *Breslau*, with the Royal Navy in hot pursuit, were allowed to enter the Turkish Straits. They were theoretically turned over to the Ottoman navy and renamed *Yavuz* and *Midilli*. But they were still manned by their German crews commanded by Admiral Souchon, who was also given the command of the Ottoman navy. On 22 October, Souchon received a secret order from Enver, now Commander-in-Chief as well as War Minister, to sail into the Black Sea and attack the Russian navy without a prior declaration of war. The Russian navy and its shore bases suffered heavy damage. Russia responded by declaring war on the Ottoman Empire on 2 November. Britain and France followed suit on 5 November. The Ottoman Empire issued its own declaration of war on 11 November. Two days later, it reinforced it by proclaiming a *jihad* – holy war for Islam – on which the Kaiser set great store, believing that it would lead to a rebellion of the Muslim subjects of Russia, Britain and France. In fact it had little effect.[1]

But while this sequence of events is not in dispute, the underlying reason for them has been the object of passionate polemics. According to one school of thought, dominant in Turkey, but espoused also by some historians in the West, the Young Turks had been left no choice by the Entente. This is disputed by many historians who argue that the Young Turks rushed rashly into an adventure which spelled their doom.[2]

Defenders of the Young Turks argue that a change of British policy had led to their decision to throw in their lot with the Germans. Britain had traditionally supported the Ottoman Empire as a barrier against Russian expansion. But at the beginning of the 20th century British policy was gradually redirected. What became known as the Triple Entente of Britain, France and Russia gradually took shape and Germany came to be seen as Britain's main adversary. Monarchs helped change public opinion. In 1908 Britain's Francophile King Edward VII met the Russian Tsar Nicolas II in Reval (now Tallinn, the capital of Estonia, but at the time a Russian naval base in the Gulf of Finland). France and Russia had an alliance dating back to 1894. In 1904 Britain had signed the Entente Cordiale with France (which was still smarting at its defeat in the 1870–1 war with Prussia and the loss of Alsace-Lorraine), and in 1907 a similar Convention with Russia in order to reconcile their imperial interests. The Reval meeting precipitated the coup by the Young Turks who hoped in vain to prevent the loss of traditional British support. Britain's cool response to their overtures led them back to the policy of Sultan Abdülhamid II, who had seen Britain as the main threat and had turned to Germany for support. The Young Turks' revolution or, more correctly, military coup against the sultan was staged a month after the Reval meeting in order to pre-empt the appointment of a Christian governor of Ottoman Macedonia, agreed at Reval.

However, irrespective of the Reval agreement, Britain retained considerable interests and influence in the Ottoman Empire. While a German military mission trained the Ottoman army, a British mission worked alongside the Ottoman navy. True, the British attitude towards the Young Turks was at best suspicious, at worst unfriendly, fed by the ridiculous notion that the Young Turks were agents of a Masonic Jewish conspiracy against the monarchical order. But there were saner views in the Foreign Office, and as the threat of the Ottoman Empire tying its fortunes to Germany became imminent, the British Embassy in Istanbul made frantic efforts to ensure Ottoman neutrality in the coming conflict. But failure was anticipated, and on 2 August, the day the Ottoman-German secret alliance was signed, the First Lord of the Admiralty, Winston Churchill, took the prudent decision to sequestrate two Ottoman warships, *Sultan Osman* and *Reshadiye*, built in British yards and ready for delivery to the Ottomans.[3] To blame Churchill's decision for the Ottomans' entry into the War is disingenuous.

Defenders of the Young Turks argue also that one of the triumvirs, the Navy Minister, Jemal Pasha (Governor of Syria during the First World War, loathed by Arab nationalists for

The Ottoman Empire 1914

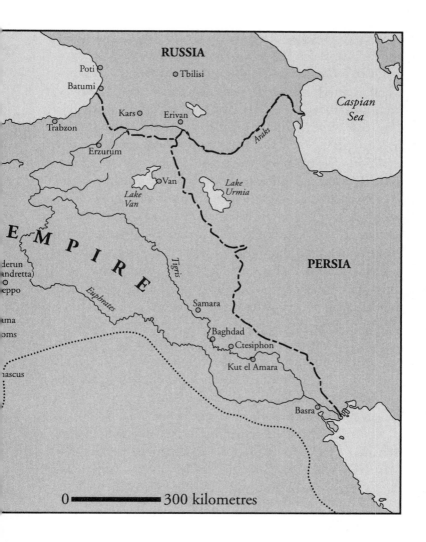

hanging Arabs who were intriguing with the Allies) had made overtures to the Allies when he was invited to attend French manoeuvres in June 1914, and had been rebuffed. However, Jemal's terms for Ottoman neutrality were stiff. He demanded from the Allies a guarantee of the territorial integrity of the Ottoman Empire, the return of the Aegean islands lost to Greece in the 1912 Balkan war, and Allied agreement to the abolition of extra-territorial privileges enjoyed by foreigners in the Ottoman Empire under the system of 'capitulations'. (The German and Austro-Hungarian Ambassadors in Istanbul were also unhappy that their nationals would lose the protection of the 'capitulations'. In addition, they feared that the Ottoman Empire would be a burden, rather than an asset, to their countries in the war.) The 'capitulations' and the concomitant restriction on the right of the Ottomans to impose import tariffs were particularly valued by France, which was the largest foreign investor in the Ottoman Empire. The French resistance to the ending of the 'capitulations' was to lead to the adjournment of the Lausanne Peace Conference in February 1923. But the resistance was overcome, and when the Treaty of Lausanne was finally signed on 24 July 1923, Turkey regained full economic independence.

As for Jemal's other demands, neither side in the looming war was prepared to force Greece to return the Aegean islands to Turkey. What Germany did was to offer the Young Turks the opportunity to compensate for their losses in the Balkans at the expense of the Russian Empire in the east. Enver swallowed the bait. He gambled on a quick victory in the east and lost.[4]

After the Entente powers had forced the Ottoman Empire to surrender in November 1918, they used their assumption of the Ottomans' wilful entry into the war to justify their designs to partition the remaining Ottoman territory in Asia Minor. This is why Turkish nationalists repudiated the imputation of war guilt. The leader of the Turkish armed resistance to the Entente, Mustafa Kemal (later Atatürk), defended publicly the view that the Ottomans had been left no choice other than entering the war on the German side. In fact, Mustafa Kemal had argued against Enver's decision to enter the war in 1914, as he doubted a German victory. In any case, he believed that the Ottoman Empire would be made to serve German ends, and that it should concentrate on defending its own core interests.

To this day, most Turkish historians argue that the Ottomans were left no choice by the Entente. They use this argument to rebut the accusation that the Young Turks (and their successors in the government of the Republic of Turkey) committed the crime of genocide when they deported close on a million Armenians from Asia Minor, with great loss of life. (The number of deportees and of Armenians killed during the deportation is subject to a fierce debate between rival nationalist historians.) The Armenians, most Turkish historians argue, were the authors of their own disaster, as their nationalist leaders gambled on a Russian victory, and urged their kinsmen to act as a Russian fifth column.

Thus the argument between proponents of choice and those of necessity in the decision of the rulers of the Ottoman Empire to enter the war in 1914 continues unabated to this day. But at a time when theories about the inevitable march of history (towards a future predictable by Marxists, among others) have been discredited by events, it is difficult to deny human agency in the outbreak of the First World War, in general, and the participation in it of the Ottoman Empire on the side of Germany and Austria-Hungary, in particular.

12

23 May 1915: Italy declares war on Austria-Hungary

Neutrality or Intervention? Italy's Long Road to War

Spencer Di Scala

The assassination of the heir to the Austrian throne Franz Ferdinand on 28 June 1914 touched off the final crisis that produced the First World War. During the previous 15 years several serious crises had occurred that might have set off a major conflict among the powers. In this delicately balanced diplomatic environment, Italy was in a good position – despite its weakness – to exploit its membership of the Triple Alliance in order to increase its influence. For example, in the 1891 renewal of the alliance, Austria-Hungary formally agreed to compensate Italy if it altered the status quo in the Balkans (Article 7). Nevertheless, with the passage of time and because of the re-orientation of Italian domestic politics in an increasingly democratic direction, shifts in the diplomatic balance, continued friction with its traditional Austrian enemy despite the alliance and the increasingly bellicose behaviour of its allies, the Italians became estranged from the alliance.

The Triple Alliance and 'Italian democracy in the making'

The origins of Italy's participation in the First World War and the crisis that followed at the Paris Peace Conference may be seen in the Triple Alliance, first signed between Italy and the Central Powers (Germany and Austria-Hungary) on 20 May 1882. Anxious to acquire colonies and Great Power status after unification in 1870, the Italians hoped to make Tunisia, where they constituted the largest European population, into a colony, but lost out to the French, long established in neighbouring Algeria.

The Italians attributed their failure to the lack of strong allies and resolved to end their diplomatic isolation. A German alliance would give them prestige, protection and economic advantages, but the Germans exacted a price: a rapprochement between Italy and its traditional enemy (but German ally), Austria-Hungary. Austria, against whom the unification struggle had taken place, had dominated the Italian peninsula for 150 years and still held territories inhabited by Italians, whom they treated as second-class citizens.

It was a bitter pill to swallow, but an alliance had advantages. Besides recognition of Italy as a Great Power, it would bolster the conservative Savoy dynasty in Italy and the conservative bloc in Europe. These benefits came at a low cost because the Triple Alliance was defensive, providing for mutual support if a member suffered an *unprovoked* attack by other powers. Preoccupied by the possibility of an eventual clash with Britain, with which it had cultural ties and whose fleet dominated the Mediterranean, Italy declared on 22 May 1882 that the alliance could not 'in any case' be regarded as directed against England, and the Austrians and Germans did likewise.[1] Since Russia was also linked to this bloc at least until 1890 with the lapse of the Reinsurance Treaty, and

France remained diplomatically isolated, the risk of Italy becoming embroiled in a European conflict was negligible.

In addition, the Triple Alliance bolstered crucial international support for the conservative Savoy dynasty during a turbulent time when revolts in the south, anarchist revolutionary conspiracies, assassination attempts and Liberal/Socialist efforts to democratise the country threatened its stability. Socialist leader Arturo Labriola, for example, argued that during Italy's *fin de siècle* crisis that threatened the Italian Parliament's viability between 1898 and 1901, consultation between the Italian and German rulers occurred in advance of all efforts to block the country's liberal evolution.[2]

In the years following the signing of the alliance in 1882 and 1914, Italian domestic conditions changed markedly as the country became more liberal. These years witnessed the defeat of the reaction of 1898 – an attempt at a conservative revision of the constitution that took place after the disorders of that year owing to the rising price of food – the foundation and growth in influence of the Italian Socialist Party and the extreme left, the arrival of quasi-universal manhood suffrage in 1912, and the Liberal Giolittian Era between 1901 and 1914. This 'Italian Democracy in the making'[3] clashed with the idea of Italian adherence to a conservative European bloc headed by the Germans and the Austrians. Leftists objected to ties with Austria, widely identified since the Risorgimento with supporting conservative policies, and to Germany, which they argued was not even a parliamentary regime because its government depended on the consent of the Emperor.[4] They sympathized instead with France, with its revolutionary traditions, its liberalism that had heavily influenced Risorgimento patriots, its role in aiding Italian unification and with its liberal Third Republic. From time to time, colonial issues caused problems between the two countries, but a common tradition, increasing commercial and financial ties and skilful French diplomacy knitted them together. The same openness marked relations with liberal Great Britain, which had influenced Count Cavour – who had guided the movement for Italian independence and had admired Britain's economic policies and its political moderation – favoured unification and served as home to many exile patriots.

Popular enmity focused, instead, on Austria because of the open sore of the Italian-speaking territories it still ruled, the *Irredenta* (the unredeemed lands) that included the city of Trent, the Trentino and Trieste. The Austrians mistreated the Italian minority, vetoing the foundation of an Italian university, allowing mobs to attack students, implementing other anti-Italian policies and rebuffing the attempts of Italian officials to resolve these issues. As a result, numerous anti-Austrian demonstrations took place in Italy. The unresolved problem of the *Irredenta* caused bad blood between the two countries and carried an emotional charge that was if anything stronger than that of the Alsace-Lorraine problem between France and Germany. In addition, the Austrians championed the Pope, who refused to accept the loss of Rome in September 1870 and frustrated Italian attempts to get the alliance to recognize the city as Italian territory. The tension between the two allies prompted the Austrian Chief of Staff Franz Conrad von Hötzendorff to insist several times on launching a surprise attack on Italy, most famously in 1908–9 when a severe earthquake destroyed the city of Messina and claimed 100,000 victims: 'The sooner the better to strike out against Italy.' Incensed at this attitude, Italian leftists vented their hatred of Austria.[5]

In sum, Italian popular opinion increasingly opposed the

alliance and would never have condoned fighting a war on the side of the Austrians. If in 1882 the Italians had declared that the Triple Alliance could never be regarded as directed against England, in 1896 they informed the Austrians and Germans that Italy 'could not participate in a war in which England and France should figure as the joint adversaries of the states included in the Triple Alliance.'[6] This was a warning to their allies that they would not participate in an offensive war because of their membership in the Triple Alliance; other warnings would follow up to the beginning of the First World War.

Given the tensions between the Italians and the Central Powers occasioned by open questions with Austria and the liberal evolution of the country, the chances for a rapprochement with France increased. The astute French Ambassador Camille Barrière closely followed the liberal evolution of the Italian political system and informed Foreign Minister Théophile Delcassé that a war against France would be the 'signal for revolution' in Italy. He undertook a series of long talks with Giulio Prinetti, a businessman and Foreign Minister in the liberal Giuseppe Zanardelli's government, which was most influenced by the even more liberal Giovanni Giolitti, the person who would dominate Italian politics until 1915.

In 1901 and 1902, Italian capital needs, a closer financial relationship fostered by Barrière, the new Liberal government and a French willingness to make concessions on Italy's imperial requests in Libya together provided the French Ambassador with an opportunity to bring about a formal understanding with Italy by recognizing its amity with France while remaining in the Triple Alliance. Barrière aimed to preclude any 'offensive obligations against France'. As already seen, the Italians had always presupposed that the Triple

Alliance did not oblige them to enter a war to aid their allies if they launched an unprovoked attack on another country. Asked to clarify what the French meant by 'offensive', he explained:

> that in speaking of the suppression in the Germanic treaty of all offensive clauses, [is meant] that which obliges Italy to bring her military support to Germany if we were to declare war, even though Italy is not attacked ... Such a disposition is offensive to the highest degree for it permits Germany, as in 1870, to provoke war without having declared it.[7]

Following diplomatic discussions and several friendly moves on the part of both countries, on 28 June 1902, the two men agreed on the final wording of the Franco-Italian agreement:

> In the case where France [or Italy] would be the object of direct or indirect aggression on the part of one or several Powers, Italy [or France] will maintain strict neutrality.
>
> The same will happen if France [or Italy], in consequence of a direct provocation, should find herself compelled in defence of her honour and her security to take the initiative in a declaration of war. In this event, the Government of the Republic [The Royal Government] shall have the duty to give previous information of its intention to H.M. Government [the Government of the Republic], thus permitting the latter to take cognizance that it is a case of direct provocation.[8]

Sometimes cited as an example of Italian duplicity, this

agreement hardly qualifies. Prinetti publicly announced the new friendship with France in Parliament, spoke to his allies and tried to get wording inserted into the text of a renewed Triple Alliance on the defensive nature of the treaty; German officials answered that since they had already stated that publicly, it would be superfluous to add it to the treaty, but that they were well aware of the rapprochement with France.[9] The Franco-Italian agreement signalled that the balance of power was shifting from the German-Austrian camp to a possible Anglo-French combination. England and France had come close to war over colonial difficulties at Fashoda in 1898, but had signed a convention in 1899 that practically eliminated the problem issues.[10] As the weakest of the Great Powers, Italy could not ignore indications of a possible Anglo-French realignment and the talks it held with France were in the context that Italy had established as early as 1882 and confirmed in 1896: the Triple Alliance as a defensive instrument; no support for a conflict provoked by its allies; no hostility against Britain or France. Moreover, the Prinetti-Barrière accord was in the same vein as much pre-First World War diplomacy, as shown by its similarity to Bismarck's 1887 secret Reinsurance Treaty with Russia. In that agreement, notwithstanding Germany's alliances with Austria-Hungary, Bismarck concurred with Russia that if Austria provoked a war against Russia, Germany would not come to its aid:

ARTICLE 1. In case one of the High Contracting Parties should find itself at war with a third Great Power, the other would maintain a benevolent neutrality towards it, and would devote its efforts to the localization of the conflict. This provision would not apply to a war against Austria or France in case this war should result from an attack

directed against one of these two latter Powers by one of
the High Contracting Parties.[11]

Bismarck had a similar fear to the Italians: that Germany
might be drawn into a war with Russia that it did not want,
to protect Austria's interests, not Germany's. Thus, Germany
did not agree to aid Austria in all circumstances, in particular
a war provoked by Austria for its own interests; the same was
true of the Italians, also with regard to Austria. Sorting out
all the complex alliances when a war breaks out is difficult,
but, regardless of treaties, countries do not agree to join their
allies under any and all circumstances, including a conflict
that one or more countries may start without consulting the
other alliance parties. By 1914 the Germans wanted to eliminate Russia as a rival and Austria wanted to do the same to
Serbia.[12] Their interests coincided rather than clashed; there
was collusion, not conflict, between the two, and they kept
Italy uninformed of their planned actions. Under those circumstances, the Italians could not be bound by an alliance
whose other participants excluded them from full participation while planning a provocation calculated to start a major
war in violation of their treaty obligations, and when they
repeatedly warned the Austrians and Germans that the *casus
foederis* would not come into being if they provoked such a
conflict.

Nevertheless, the Italians leveraged the Triple Alliance
in order to further their imperial designs in Libya and the
Balkans, just as other powers exploited changing diplomatic
situations elsewhere. Even so, Italy would not join its partners
when the First World War broke out. The reasons for Italy's
neutrality in August 1914 included the transformation of the
Triple Alliance into an offensive pact against its clearly stated

objections; its increasing democratization, bringing it closer to Britain and France; continued tensions with Austria; and its military weakness owing to its economic backwardness, which meant that of all the Great Powers, it could afford to spend the least on its army while needing to devote a greater proportion of its resources to it.[13]

The road to intervention

These considerations help explain why the Italians remained in the Triple Alliance, but not part of it. Italy's desire to take over Libya in 1911 and German anxiety for an early renewal of the Triple Alliance produced a deal by which Germany gave its assent to the Italian move and Italy agreed to renew the alliance in 1912.[14] Even if it was weak and unwilling to go along with the foreign policy of its allies, which it feared might lead to war, Italy was useful to the Germanic allies because, in case of a war with Russia and France, Austria's southern border would be secure if the Italians entered on the Germans' side. This would allow the Austrians to fight Serbia and to send a larger contingent to help the Germans against the Russians. Advantages for Germany included tying down French troops on the southern French border and the possible participation of Italian troops on their front with France.[15] At the very least, the alliance ensured that Italy would not ally with France and that Italy and Austria would not engage in a war against each other.

These calculations – at least on the Italian side – presumed that the alliance would remain defensive and that Germany and Austria would not precipitate a conflict. The Italians had informed both countries of this fundamental principle during the Balkan crises that preceded the First World War, most recently in August 1913 when Vienna requested Italian support in a military operation against Serbia during the second Balkan war. The Italians responded that the Triple Alliance did not come into play if one of the allies attacked another country.[16] The result: in October 1913 the Austrians sent an ultimatum to Serbia without informing the Italians, thus violating Article 1 of the alliance and ignoring a clear warning by Prime Minister Giolitti that Italy must be kept fully informed of all relevant diplomatic discussions.[17] After the assassination of Franz Ferdinand, the Austrians and Germans excluded the Italians from their discussions regarding the ultimatum sent to Serbia that provoked the First World War, violating the terms of the alliance because they believed (rightly) that the Italians would not join them.[18] The allies informed the Italians of the ultimatum at the same time as they did the other powers, leading Italy to state that the *casus foederis* had not come into effect and to declare its neutrality.[19]

For two weeks following the assassination of the archduke and his wife on 28 June, the Germanic powers kept Foreign Minster Antonino Di San Giuliano in the dark about their intentions, but the minister informed the German Ambassador in Rome that no Italian support for Austria would be forthcoming if the Austrians presented Serbia with demands 'incompatible' with Italy's liberal traditions, and motivated by 'tendencies, not yet dead either in Vienna or in Berlin, inspired by the Holy Alliance'. By 17 July, San Giuliano had got wind of Austro-German intentions to present Serbia with an ultimatum whose terms could not be fulfilled. He contacted the Russians and made proposals in a futile attempt to defuse the crisis and to avert the conflagration he expected. On the evening of 23 July Austria presented its ultimatum to Serbia, only informing its Italian ally the next day, along with the other European countries.[20]

When the Italian Prime Minister, Antonio Salandra, San Giuliano and the German Ambassador, Hans von Flotow, heard the terms of the ultimatum, all three blanched. San Giuliano told von Flotow that Austria did not have the right to take this step without the prior agreement of all its allies, that it had 'clearly demonstrated that it wishes to provoke a war' and that under the Triple Alliance Italy had 'no obligation whatsoever' to aid Austria if a war resulted from its 'provocative and aggressive act'. In addition, the Italians would claim compensation under Article 7 if Austria changed the status quo in the Balkans.[21]

The Italians were firmly convinced that Britain would be involved in any war that ensued and considered Germany's doubts on this point to be its greatest error. Given Italy's friendly relations with Britain, Italian assertions that the Triple Alliance could never be considered as directed against that country (agreed to by Germany and Austria), the vulnerability of the long Italian coastline and its major cities to British bombardment and Anglo-Italian agreements on the Mediterranean, the British connection was a fundamental consideration in the Italian decision, pointing to an eventual agreement with the Entente in the event of war.[22] Responding to a German request to join the Triple Alliance allies in the conflict, San Giuliano reiterated that the agreement did not oblige Italy to take part in an aggressive war. On 2 August Italy formally declared its neutrality and informed the Austrians that it would ask for compensation under Article 7 of the treaty.

Asked why he thought that the Central Powers followed such an aggressive policy in the final crisis Giovanni Giolitti said:

Frankly, I'll confess to you that I never would have believed
that there could have been two governments that were so
out of their minds as to undertake this monstrous war so
lightheartedly. I was aware of the intrigues and restless-
ness of the Austrian military faction; but I never would
have expected it from Germany, having had repeated occasions to ascertain that it exercised a moderating effect on
Vienna.[23]

It would have been folly for the Italians to join the Central
Powers in a war they had provoked in violation of the Triple
Alliance. Had they done so and contributed to victory, Salandra wrote, Italy would have been 'at most, the first of the
vassal states of the Empire'.[24]

Most importantly, the Italian people would never have sanctioned joining the war on the Austro-German side and were
strongly neutralist. Representing a majority of the population, both Socialist and Catholic Parties advocated remaining
neutral. The interventionists spoke only for small groups and
favoured war for very different reasons. After first supporting the party line, for example, revolutionary Socialist leader
Benito Mussolini proposed intervention on the Entente side,
arguing that the war was revolutionary. The party expelled
him and few Socialists followed him out of the organization.
Thirsty for war, the Nationalists first favoured intervention on
the German side, then, understanding the depth of popular
revulsion to this position, on the Entente side. Alarmed by the
prospect of authoritarianism taking over the continent, the
'democratic interventionists', led by former Socialist Leonida
Bissolati, viewed the war as a struggle to defend European
democracy and advocated immediate intervention to support
the Entente: a democratic Italy could not remain neutral in

such a struggle. The powerful Liberal establishment split. At first it favoured neutrality, but later one group leaning to the right and including Sonnino, promoted intervention on the Entente side because it saw the possibility of Italy strengthening its strategic position in the Mediterranean and feared increased Slav influence in the Balkans and Adriatic, vital to the country's security. Moreover, it feared a backlash from the Central Powers if they won the war. The left Liberals, led by Giolitti, opposed intervention because they believed that the country would be enormously damaged by a war and judged that Italy could receive the *Irredenta* and perhaps other gains from Austria by promising to maintain Italian neutrality.[25]

Eventually, interventionism won out. After San Giuliano's death, Sidney Sonnino replaced him. A convinced supporter of the Triple Alliance, he changed his mind as the Austrians stubbornly refused to relinquish the *Irredenta* in exchange for Italian neutrality. Instead, in response to the insistence of the Entente, he began the negotiations that would culminate on 26 April 1915 with the Pact of London, and finally intervention. The agreement committed Italy to intervene in the conflict within a month, ruled out a separate peace and spelled out Italian gains if the Entente won. Italy was to receive the *Irredenta* and a defensible frontier up to the Brenner Pass; about half the lands in Dalmatia it initially requested; and equitable compensation for any Allied gains in the colonies.

In light of the future dispute over the port city of Fiume at the Paris Peace Conference, it should be noted that the pact assigned Fiume to 'Croatia, Serbia, and Montenegro'. The city was majority Italian but surrounded by a Slav hinterland, and the Italian negotiators were willing to give it up because of its importance for a future Slav state. Guglielmo Imperiali, Italian Ambassador to London, who conducted the negotiations under the direction of his superiors, foresaw the grave problems that renouncing Fiume would cause, while requesting areas of Dalmatia not inhabited by Italians. In his diary for 6 March 1915, he wrote:

> There is perhaps too much Dalmatia [in the requests] while Fiume, incontestably Italian, is left out. This omission could cause us serious internal complications at the time of a victorious peace. I will recall for the record that in my talks in Rome with Salandra and Sonnino in November, I alluded to Fiume. The former rebuked me saying that you could not strangle a country depriving it of access to the sea. 'Live and let live!' However, I stick to my opinion.[26]

At the Peace Conference, the question of access to the sea for Yugoslavia was a powerful argument for the Americans in favour of assigning Fiume to that country despite the Italian majority in the core city.[27] However, the Italians considered domination of the Adriatic as absolutely necessary to their security, explaining their demands in Dalmatia.[28]

The territorial gains that Italy would realise in case of victory have been considered excessive, but while the British and French adopted this view after the war they were willing enough to negotiate at the time. It had been the Russians who objected to Italian demands, mostly because of their support for the Slavs. In fact, Sonnino received criticism from some quarters for not gaining enough territory, while sowing future problems by accepting territory inhabited by Austrians and Slavs.[29] However, by early 1915, the Salandra government had concluded that Italy stood to lose if it remained neutral, no matter who won the war, because the major problems of the day would be settled without its participation. Thus, the most important aspect of the Pact of London was that it gave Italy the security it had always sought in the Adriatic, if not control.[30] There was no notion that Austria-Hungary might disappear as a result of the conflict, nor did the Allies, including the Italians, desire it because of the problems that would ensue.[31] Moreover, the expectation that Russia would become a major Mediterranean power, and its close relationship with the Balkan Slavs, influenced Sonnino's obstinate demands for gains in the Adriatic in order to offset the supposed increase in Slavic authority and to protect Italy's post-war strategic position.[32]

There was, however, a major obstacle to be overcome before Italy could enter the conflict. The pact had to be ratified by Parliament – no easy task given its anti-war majority (Giolittians, Socialists and Catholics). Giolitti's supporters and their allies on this motion could have voted Salandra out of power, recalled Giolitti, and then voted against ratification. Since Parliament was closed, about 400 deputies (out of 508) left their calling cards at Giolitti's house as a sign of their support for his neutralism. Nevertheless, Giolitti, who was quoted as remarking that Italy could get 'plenty' [*parecchio*] in return for its neutrality, quickly discovered that Salandra had outmanoeuvered him.

Salandra resigned on 13 May, but pro-war demonstrations led by a small number of nationalists broke out and the police suppressed anti-war counter demonstrations.[33] Informed about the London agreement, Giolitti judged that Italy's honour demanded that it be fulfilled and withdrew from the political scene[34] – even though the Austrians had finally decided to make concessions, Parliament had manifested its support for his position and the military situation for the Entente had drastically deteriorated. Salandra returned as premier and on 20 May the Chamber of Deputies convened to ratify war and voted the government full powers to prepare for intervention. Just a few days later, Italy would declare war on Austria, citing the *Irredenta* as the cause. This dramatic switch to a war declaration by representatives opposed to it only a few days earlier gravely damaged parliamentary institutions, creating a precedent and leaving them subject to overthrow during the post-war period.[35]

In sum, the Pact of London promised Italy the Italian-speaking *Irredenta* and favourable adjustment of the Italian border with Austria-Hungary, primarily but not exclusively on defensive lines. These gains would have strengthened Italy's post-war position against either Austria-Hungary or a revived Germany that might have absorbed Austria. The new territories would have placed German-speaking and Slavic elements into Italy, but the country would still have had a much smaller minority population, 3 per cent, than other countries such as Czechoslovakia for which similar adjustments were made at the Paris Peace Conference.[36] These aims paled in comparison with French demands for control of the left bank of the Rhine after the German defeat and British and French colonial gains.[37] The Pact of London promised Italy 'just compensation' for any gains made by its allies in the colonies, but this compensation never arrived.[38]

On 23 May 1915 Italy declared war on Austria-Hungary, which, too late, offered to cede the *Irredenta* in return for Italian neutrality. A year later, on 28 August 1916, Italy declared war on Germany. It would pay a high price for its place at the peace table in 1919 and the deep divisions over its involvement in the war, together with disappointment about allied treatment of Italy's claims at the conference. The contention these controversies caused contributed significantly to the destruction of Italian democracy in the post-war years.

13

14 October 1915: Bulgaria declares war on Serbia

Bulgaria Choosing Sides
Alan Sharp

As Europe erupted into war in August 1914 the Bulgarian government declared 'strict and loyal neutrality'. It did so for two main reasons: first, Bulgaria had just fought two wars, the second of which it had lost badly and at great cost; secondly, it wanted to see how the conflict progressed and to ascertain what rewards it might gain either from remaining neutral or from joining one or other of the warring coalitions.

Bulgaria was an integral part of the ongoing Eastern question as the Ottomans struggled to maintain their hold on the Balkans, the emerging new states jostled for independence and territory and Austria-Hungary and Russia competed for influence and power. After the 1877–8 Russo-Turkish war, Bulgaria became an autonomous principality of the Ottoman Empire under the terms of the Treaty of Berlin, signed on 13 July 1878, though its territory was much smaller than the original Russian proposals in the earlier Treaty of San Stefano with the Ottomans, signed on 3 March. This was renegotiated at the behest of the Concert of Europe, orchestrated by

Bismarck, and left many Bulgarians outside the principality's boundaries. The problems posed by populations who found themselves as minorities in the 'wrong' country and the territorial disputes thus engendered, bedevilled – and continue to bedevil – relations between the Balkan states. In 1885 Bulgaria defeated Serbia, gaining Eastern Rumelia, and in 1887 Ferdinand of Saxe-Coburg-Gotha was elected prince, replacing the first incumbent, Alexander of Battenburg, who had withdrawn in 1886. Universally known as 'Foxy', Ferdinand timed his declaration of Bulgaria as an independent kingdom, and himself as King of the Bulgarians, to coincide with the Austro-Hungarian annexation of Bosnia-Herzegovina on 5 October 1908.[1]

In 1912, after the military weakness and diplomatic isolation of the Ottomans was exposed by the 1911 Italian attack on Libya, Bulgaria negotiated a pact with Serbia to partition Macedonia, the main remaining Ottoman territory in the Balkans. They were joined by Greece and Montenegro and, in October 1912, they attacked, driving the Turks from Thrace and Macedonia, and coming within 20 miles of Constantinople. The victors then fell out and, in June 1913 Bulgaria attacked Serbia and Greece, only to find itself helpless in the face of Romanian and Ottoman assaults. The resulting Treaty of Bucharest in July saw Bulgaria forfeit almost all the gains it had made in the first war, losing most of Macedonia to Serbia and Greece and all of southern Dobrudja to Romania. In the Treaty of Constantinople in September the Ottomans regained most of their lost territory in Thrace, though Bulgaria did retain the Adriatic port of Dedeagach (Alexandroupolis) and a narrow coastal strip.[2]

The outbreak of the First World War found Bulgaria battered, with both Ferdinand and his premier, Vasil Radoslavov,

Turkey, Greece and Bulgaria 1912–1923

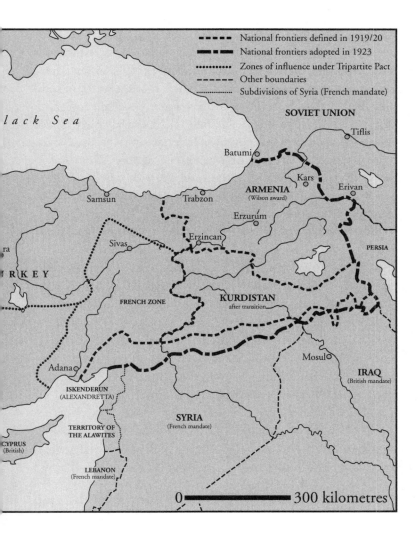

National frontiers defined in 1919/20
National frontiers adopted in 1923
Zones of influence under Tripartite Pact
Other boundaries
Subdivisions of Syria (French mandate)

Black Sea

SOVIET UNION

Tiflis

Batumi

Kars

ARMENIA
(Wilson award)

Erivan

Samsun

Trabzon

Erzurum

PERSIA

Sivas

Erzincan

TURKEY

FRENCH ZONE

KURDISTAN
after transition

Mosul

IRAQ
(British mandate)

Adana

ISKENDERUN
(ALEXANDRETTA)

SYRIA
(French mandate)

CYPRUS
(British)

TERRITORY OF
THE ALAWITES

LEBANON
(French mandate)

0 ▬▬▬▬▬ 300 kilometres

cautious, wanting to retrieve their losses but preferring to await events and suitors. Bulgaria had been supported, at different times, by both the Great Power rivals in the region but, more recently, Austria-Hungary had tended to see it as its natural ally, though Germany did not, Wilhelm II detested Ferdinand. Bulgaria's neutrality was valuable to the Central Powers, with money and armaments for the Ottomans passing across its territory but, as the tide of war turned against the Allies in 1915, with setbacks for Britain and France in Gallipoli and for Russia in the east, Ferdinand became more receptive to Austro-German inducements to join them.

The Central Powers were always at an advantage in any bidding war. The Entente had already made promises to Italy in the April 1915 Treaty of London, thus limiting their options. Both Serbia and Turkey possessed territory that Bulgaria wanted but whereas Austria and Germany prevailed upon their ally in September 1915 to cede land along the Maritsa River, giving Bulgaria control of a continuous railway connection to Dedeagach, the Entente could not persuade Serbia to give up parts of Macedonia. In February 1915 the Central Powers made Bulgaria a simple proposition – it could keep whatever it conquered. By contrast the Entente could offer only the possibility of Serbian land in Macedonia, provided Serbia gained compensation in Bosnia-Herzegovina, and assistance in negotiations with Greece over Kavalla and Romania over the Dobrudja.[3]

On 6 September 1915 Bulgaria agreed to fight Serbia in return for the Serbian portion of Macedonia and territory east of the Morava River. If either Greece or Romania or both joined the war on the Entente side, Bulgaria would also fight them, for the promise of Greek Thrace and part of the Dobrudja from Romania. After mobilising in September, on

14 October Bulgaria declared war on Serbia, joining the Austro-German offensive launched on 6 October which overran Serbia by January 1916. Ferdinand and Radaslavov had been very successful in extracting pledges concerning the territories that many Bulgarians thought should rightfully be theirs but Aleksandŭr Stamboliĭski, the leader of the opposition Bulgarian Agrarian National Union party, who would later head the Bulgarian delegation to the Paris Peace Conference, was both scathing and accurate. He warned Ferdinand, 'What your government is contemplating is frightful, terrible and catastrophic – and not just because of its content but also because there are not the necessary conditions to carry it through to a satisfactory outcome.' Bulgaria had embarked on a war it would not win.[4]

14

9 March 1916: Germany declares war on Portugal

Portuguese Intervention

Filipe Ribeiro de Meneses

On 9 March 1916, the German minister in Lisbon, Baron
Rosen, delivered his country's declaration of war against the
young Portuguese Republic, established in October 1910.
The imperial government in Berlin charged its Portuguese
counterpart with a long string of insults and breaches of
neutrality, which had culminated weeks earlier, on 23 February, with the forceful seizure by its armed forces, without
warning or prior negotiation, of some 80 German ships
which had sought refuge in Portuguese waters in 1914. The
document then refuted the Portuguese government's ration-
ale for the action by pointing out that the number of ships
seized far exceeded Portugal's actual economic needs, before
introducing a pointed insult: 'Through its procedure the
Portuguese government made it clear that it considers itself
England's vassal, since it subordinates all other considerations to English interests and desires'.[1] The declaration of
war concluded by noting that the actual seizure of the ships,
with the lowering of the German flag and its replacement by

the Portuguese pennant, and the 21-gun salute by a warship, was conceived as a deliberate provocation from which Germany could not back down.[2] The declaration of war ended a fortnight of intense diplomatic activity and speculation during which Portugal's minister in Berlin, Sidónio Pais, tried, without success, to mend fences between the two governments.

An agreement between Germany and Portugal was impossible to find at this late stage because the latter's government, headed by Afonso Costa, was determined to enter the conflict. The leader of the Democratic Party – the republic's most significant political formation – Costa placed great hopes in a Portuguese intervention in the European war. He was enjoying, for the first time since the regime's creation, an absolute majority in both houses of Parliament and a well-disposed President of the Republic, which meant that there would be no institutional obstruction of his designs. Portugal's intervention, through its resulting appeal to patriotism, would allow a strengthening of the bonds that kept together the Democratic Party's factions, which ranged from street-level agitators, crucial in times of crisis, to the staid *caciques* of rural Portugal, who guaranteed electoral victory. The war would breathe life into this coalition, enthusing its members and buying time for Costa's regenerative project before, inevitably, cracks began to appear. Military participation alongside the Western democracies would also improve the international standing of the radical republic, an oddity among Europe's monarchies. Not even the one-off balancing of the budget in 1913 by Costa had led to a general acceptance of the republic's legitimacy abroad. For Costa, it followed logically that an improved domestic standing would affect the regime's internal standing. A 'republican' war, built on equality of human and material sacrifice by members of all classes, would help to cement the regime in the eyes of the Portuguese people. Finally, the war, and participation in it alongside Britain, France and Belgium, would remove once and for all the threat than hung over the country's far-flung colonial possessions. These had been, as late as 1912, the object of negotiations between British and German diplomats. It was felt, thus, that one great sacrifice by Portugal's youth might secure the dream of a safe and prosperous Portugal, resting on a respected and respectable colonial empire. Interventionists such as Afonso Costa saw the increased prestige of the small nations who fought – Belgium and Serbia – and dreamed of foreign headlines of 'gallant little Portugal', fighting for Law, Civilisation and the Rights of Small Nations.

There was, however, no national consensus around the idea of intervention. As was the case in many other countries initially untouched by the conflict, a tremendous and often violent debate raged over whether or not to enter the war. Interventionists were thwarted by the strength of their opponents – a broad arc that stretched from revolutionary anarcho-syndicalists to reactionary monarchists – and by the material weakness of the Portuguese armed forces, unprepared for a clash with modern European forces (as was amply shown in Africa, where border clashes with German forces, notably in Angola, led to serious reverses). The result was that the Allies, while happy to exploit Lisbon's eagerness to help their cause, refrained from asking it to participate in the fighting, to the growing frustration of interventionists. The exception came in the autumn of 1914, when an Allied request for the delivery of French-made 75 mm guns owned by the Portuguese army was met with indignation by the

Minister of War, General Pereira d'Eça, who insisted that the guns be manned by Portuguese soldiers and that all branches of the army be included in the force to be sent to France. Mobilizing such a force proved, however, beyond the ability of the army, and the affair fizzled out. In order to prevent the occurrence of another such fiasco, Costa's Democratic Party, in power since a violent uprising in May 1915, prepared an army division for intervention in Europe, but was condemned to wait until the Allies changed their mind about the inclusion of Portugal in their ranks.

Such a change of mind would come only in 1916. Early in February of that year the Portuguese government was informed by London that Britain's weakened merchant marine would henceforth be used exclusively to supply Allied countries – which did not include Portugal.[3] With the imminent disappearance from Portuguese harbours of British merchant vessels – a circumstance which would spell the ruin of the country – it was understood, both in Lisbon and in London, that Portugal would have to make use of some (or all) of the large and modern German merchant ships lying at anchor in its harbours. Costa's Cabinet had many ways of bringing this about. It could, of course, negotiate with Germany for the use of enough vessels to meet the country's needs. This option, however, was never even contemplated in Lisbon, which suited London's desire for 'early and energetic action' on Lisbon's part.[4]

Costa saw in the British warning a golden opportunity to bring Portugal into the conflict. There was one obstacle, however: the fear of being at war with Germany without a British guarantee of protection of Portuguese interests (in other words, of a war against Germany running parallel to that being waged by the Allies). In order to ensure that

Portugal would be entitled to the full protection of the Allies, especially at sea and in its colonial possessions, the seizure of the German merchant vessels had to be carried out in accordance with an official request made under the terms of Portugal's ancient alliance with Britain, the pillar upon which rested Portugal's dealings with the rest of the world. This was what the Portuguese government now pointed out to the British, the Portuguese adding as a sweetener the possibility of sharing, at a commercial rate, the seized vessels with London. There was thus a trade-off: British use of the German ships, in return for allowing Portugal to join the Allies. Until this British request arrived there were days of very high tension in the Portuguese Cabinet. Minutes of its meetings reveal the extent of the panic which gripped ministers, many of whom gave full vent to Anglophobe sentiments. Some discerned a plot to deprive Portugal of its colonies, so that they might be used as a bargaining tool with Germany in any future peace negotiations. The desired request, however, eventually arrived, much to Costa's relief.[5]

None of this happened in secret. The government was leaking furiously, and sensitive information reached opposition parties and their newspapers. Agitation reigned in Portugal. People knew that a decisive moment had arrived, and that the most important question of the day was about to be resolved. Banking still on the long list of benefits to be derived from belligerence, Costa ordered, the very next day after the arrival of the British request, the military seizure of the German vessels. Announcing and explaining the measure to the country, Costa said Portugal needed the ships for economic reasons. Any surplus to requirement would be chartered at a commercial rate to the Allies. The reply to the resulting German ultimatum was taken, word-for-word, from a suggested British response,[6] and war quickly followed. Costa's great gamble, it seemed, had paid off: Portugal was finally at war. Little could he predict how painful the experience of war would be for Portugal, for the republic and for himself personally.

15

5 June 1916: Arab revolt against the Ottomans begins

The Hejaz: On the Road to the Arab Rebellion

Robert McNamara

The Ottoman Empire's entry into the First World War in November 1914 brought conflict to the Middle East. The Entente powers, Britain, France and Russia had little desire for war with Turkey, which distracted them from the key Western and Eastern Fronts. Moreover, the Sultan, utilising his position as Caliph (the spiritual leader of all the world's Muslims) had proclaimed jihad against the Entente powers. This was prompted by his German allies, who viewed the large Muslim populations in Russian Central Asia, British India, British-occupied Egypt and French North Africa as one of their enemies' weaknesses.[1] Within two months Jemal Pasha, a Turkish general and a leading member of the ruling triumvirate in Istanbul, had marched into the Sinai desert and attacked the British-controlled Suez canal. However, the Turkish offensive failed to spark off a revolt amongst the Muslim population of Egypt and was easily repulsed.

British efforts to knock Turkey out of the war were equally

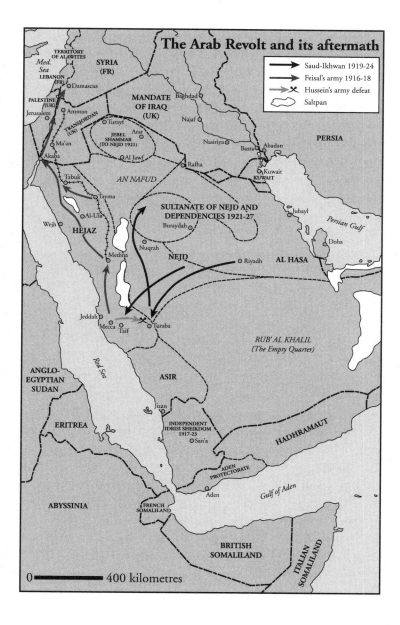

The Arab Revolt and its aftermath

→ Saud-Ikhwan 1919-24
→ Feisal's army 1916-18
→✗ Hussein's army defeat
Saltpan

Med. Sea
TERRITORY OF ALAWITES
SYRIA (FR)
LEBANON (FR)
Damascus
PALESTINE (UK)
Jerusalem
Amman
TRANSJORDAN (UK)
Ma'an
Akaba
Tabuk
Tayma
Al-Ula
Wejh
HEJAZ
Medina
Jeddah
Mecca
Taif
Turaba
MANDATE OF IRAQ (UK)
Baghdad
Najaf
JEBEL SHAMMAR (TO NEJD 1921)
Arar
Al Jawf
Rafha
Nasiriya
Basra
Abadan
Kuwait
KUWAIT
AN NAFUD
SULTANATE OF NEJD AND DEPENDENCIES 1921-27
Buraydah
Nuqrah
NEJD
Riyadh
AL HASA
Jubayl
Persian Gulf
Doha
PERSIA
Turayf
RUB' AL KHALIL (The Empty Quarter)
Red Sea
ANGLO-EGYPTIAN SUDAN
ASIR
ERITREA
Jizan
INDEPENDENT IDRISI SHEIKDOM 1917-23
San'a
HADHRAMAUT
ABYSSINIA
ADEN PROTECTORATE
Aden
Gulf of Aden
FRENCH SOMALILAND
BRITISH SOMALILAND
ITALIAN SOMALILAND

0 ——— 400 kilometres

187

unsuccessful. A bold attempt to seize the Dardanelles and open the Straits to Allied shipping, with the added benefit of almost certainly forcing Turkey to make peace, failed spectacularly. Neither the British Indian Army in Mesopotamia nor British forces in Egypt made much progress. By the summer of 1915, the Allied position in the Middle East had deteriorated substantially. This provided an opportunity for dissident Arabs opposed to Turkish rule to make a bold bid for the establishment of an independent Arab state in return for rebelling against their Ottoman overlords.

§

By the outbreak of the First World War, the Turks, who originated from the Central Asian steppes, had ruled the heartlands of the Arab world, encompassing the modern day states of Syria, Iraq, Jordan, Israel/Palestine, Saudi Arabia and Arab North Africa for over 1,000 years. Syria, Iraq, Jordan and Palestine were known as the Fertile Crescent due to the important rivers, the Jordan, Tigris and Euphrates that provided the water resources that made the areas conducive to human settlement. However, by 1914, the Arab lands of the Fertile Crescent and the Arabian peninsula, the cradle of one of the world's great civilisations and an all-conquering Islamic empire, were reduced to little more than barren, poverty-stricken, disease-ridden and ill-educated backwaters. The Ottomans, the last of the great Islamic Turkish tribes to forge a major empire, conquered the Arab lands in 1517 and ruled them, without serious opposition, for just over four centuries, mainly because Turkish rule relied heavily on local Arab collaborators and centralised rule from Constantinople was, as one observer noted, 'make believe'.[2] Outside the main urban centres – Damascus, Allepo, Mosul and Baghdad – Ottoman control was weak and the Arab-speaking communities largely ran themselves, with clan and tribal the main modes of control.[3] The Turkish-speaking governors, in theory, held supreme power in the Arab-speaking regions, though in practice linguistic barriers and a lack of military power meant they were dependent on local tribal leaders, the urban rich and religious leaders known as the 'notables' whose influence was the dominant fact of political life in the Ottoman Middle East in the 19th and early 20th centuries.[4] Only in the last decades of Ottoman rule, did proto-nationalist challenges begin to emerge in the Arab territories, partly driven by the penetration of Western ideas into sections of urban Arab opinion, particularly in Syria and the Lebanon. Meanwhile Ottoman Turkish rule in this period gradually became more heavy-handed and obtrusive as modern communications (the spread of railways and the telegraph) allowed more direct supervision of the Arab provinces to the discomfort of local notables, used to having considerable autonomy.[5]

Unsurprisingly, the first signs of a distinctively Arab nationalism begin to emerge in the urban areas of Ottoman Syria, where European and American cultural and educational influence grew in the late 19th century among Christian Arabs.[6] A handful of Syrian Christians educated in the American and French missionary schools in Lebanon established in the 19th century began to develop a quasi-secular Arab nationalism arguing that Turkish rule was a disaster for the Arabs.[7] George Antonius, in his 1938 book *The Arab Awakening*, perhaps the key text of modern Arab nationalism, saw in these very small cultural movements in late 19th-century Ottoman Syria the genesis of Arab nationalism. Antonius's views are not without their critics and he has been accused of over-emphasising these early movements' importance.[8] Some decades later, there were more concrete signs of a nascent Arab nationalism, spurred on by the 1908 Young Turks revolution in Constantinople. Arab reaction to the Young Turks was initially enthusiastic. The Committee of Union and Progress, in an early phase of liberalism, permitted political activity in the empire, including the formation of specifically Arab parties. Soon it became clear that this flirtation with liberalism and pluralism was merely a veneer behind which lurked a traditional Turkish nationalist agenda, reinforcing existing tendencies towards centralisation and Turkification of the empire.[9] After 1912, in a reaction to the end of this period of reform, parties with an Arab autonomy agenda began to emerge in Syria, though again their significance has been disputed.[10] Most Arabs, it has been considered by one authority, would have been content to 'remain within the frame of the Ottoman unity, as long as their proper place was recognised by the Turkish rulers'.[11]

※

The outbreak of the Arab Revolt in 1916 had its origins in the most underdeveloped of the Ottoman's Arab territories – the Hejaz – then a *vilayet* or province of the Ottoman Empire occupying the narrow strip of land that extends from just south of what is now the Jordanian port of Aquba to nearly as far as the northern border of the Yemen (now within the Kingdom of Saudi Arabia). The Hejaz's importance lay in the fact that it contained two of Islam's holiest sites: Mecca, the holiest city, and Medina, the first city to accept the word of the Prophet Muhammad. Its population probably totaled

500,000 Arabs in 1914. It depended on Ottoman subsidy and income from pilgrims making the haj.[12] It remained a pre-modern, highly traditional society with little nationalism evident.[13] It was rather ironic that the Arab Revolt began here.

From 1908 Sherif Hussein ibn Ali of the Hashemites occupied 'the most prestigious Arab-Islamic position within the Ottoman Empire', as Grand Sherif and Emir of Mecca.[14] The Hashemites' independence was circumscribed by the presence of a Turkish governor or *Vali* in Mecca, though the distance from Constantinople generally allowed the Emir of Mecca a reasonable degree of autonomy. The Emir of Mecca, Hussein ibn Ali,[15] was born in 1853 in Constantinople and together with his wife and four sons – Ali (1879–1935), Abdullah (1880–1951), Feisal (1883–1933), and Zeid (1898–1970) – lived much of his life there. Three of the four sons (Ali, Abdullah and Feisal) became kings of three of the successor states of the Ottoman Empire. The position of Grand Sherif of Mecca fell vacant in 1908 and that November Hussein was made sherif and returned to Hejaz. His son Abdullah testifies in his memoirs that Hussein was loyal to the Ottomans at this time though he opposed the secularising reforms of the Young Turks regime.[16] Hussein's priority was to consolidate his power base and increase his influence at the expense of the Turkish *Vali* though the British noted his toleration of brigandage.[17]

Hussein, however, needed to be circumspect in his challenges to Ottoman authority. His earliest achievements, with Ottoman consent, were to bring the increasingly fractious Bedouin tribes adjacent to the Hejaz under greater control.[18] His main ambition was to grow his own power, gain increased autonomy and make his office hereditary. But the tentacles of Ottoman control over the Hejaz were beginning to grow, not wither, as telegraph wires linked the Hejaz to Constantinople from the end of the 19th century and the Hejaz railway reached Medina in 1908. The Young Turks appear to have viewed its extension to Mecca as the cornerstone of the consolidation of more direct Ottoman rule in western Arabia. Conscious of this, Hussein assiduously resisted entreaties from the Young Turks to extend the line down to his power base at Mecca.[19] Hussein's autonomy, by 1914, was becoming increasingly restricted, leading his son Abdullah to complain to foreign diplomats about the tyranny of the Turks.[20] The installation of Vehib Bey as the *Vali* from April 1914, who vigorously clipped Hussein's wings, apparently led to initial Hashemite contacts with the British in 1914, prior to the outbreak of war.[21] British officials in Cairo had little interest in being drawn into the internal disputes of the Ottomans, though the meeting opened a channel of communication with the Hashemites that had later significance.[22] Given that there is little evidence of significant Arab nationalist pressures in the Hejaz, one can conclude that Hussein's Arab Revolt of June 1916 was rooted in a power struggle between the Hashemites, an elite whose privileges and autonomy were being threatened, and the Ottomans seeking to forge a modern centralised state. The First World War and the revolution in international politics it occasioned furnished Hussein with a unique opportunity to expand his power and become, in some respects, the father of Arab nationalism.

§

Throughout the 19th century, Britain was the Western country most committed to preserving the Ottoman Empire, seeing it as a vital barrier to Russian expansion. However, by 1914, the British had become rather indifferent to the fate of the empire. Their colonial disputes with Russia and France had been resolved, by 1907; and the Ottomans were increasingly unhappy that friendship with Britain had provided them with little protection against their enemies. Moreover, Britain repeatedly rebuffed Ottoman attempts to regain influence in Egypt (occupied by Britain from 1882). The decade before the First World War witnessed 'the almost complete abandonment by her of [Britain's] traditional Turcophil policy ...'.[23] The British remained intent that should the Ottoman Empire collapse, their interests in its southern flank, straddling the route to India, would be protected.[24]

In September 1914 Field Marshal Lord Kitchener, the British High Commissioner in Egypt, who was in London at the outbreak of hostilities, ordered Ronald Storrs, a British official in Cairo, to reactivate contacts with Hussein's son Abdullah as it became increasingly evident that Turkey was likely to enter the war on the side of the Central Powers. Storrs, who received a friendly reply, said that Britain would protect Hussein against aggression but also raised the tantalising possibility that a favourable outcome to the war might include the replacement of the Ottoman Sultan as Caliph by an Arab figure.[25] Hussein, on 8 December 1914, replied that he could not break with the Ottomans at present, but would do so should a suitable moment arrive.[26]

Storrs, according to the historian Elie Kedourie, continued to take local initiatives without recourse to London, which committed Britain almost completely to the general cause of Arab nationalism and an Arab Caliphate – the implication being that Hussein was a worthy candidate.[27] Hussein, apparently in return, did not endorse the Caliph's call for jihad;

instead maintaining a pointed silence. As Storrs was taking his Arab initiatives, the Entente powers were negotiating over the fate of the Ottoman Empire. The Russians were quickly promised control over the Straits and Constantinople.[28] France had its own shopping list: Cillicia, Syria and Palestine. An interdepartmental British government working group, the de Bunsen Committee,[29] established in April 1915, identified British territorial interests in a post-war settlement. Rather than an outright partition of Asiatic Turkey, it recommended that spheres of influence were preferable, though it remained open to the possibility of British annexations in the Middle East.

At much the same time, the British stepped up contacts with Hussein. Sir Henry McMahon, High Commissioner to Egypt from January 1915 (in succession to Kitchener, who had become Secretary of State for War), took tentative soundings on how to encourage the Arabs to split with the Ottomans as Hussein's alienation from them grew. Complaining about plots against him, Hussein sent his son Feisal to Damascus to meet Syrian nationalists whom Feisal reported were too weak to challenge the Ottomans.[30] He continued to Constantinople for negotiations with the Young Turk Junta, but these were fruitless as he refused to provide the assurances about autonomy and non-interference required, despite Feisal's best efforts. Feisal returned via Damascus, where he once more met with potential rebels in Syria and agreed the so-called 'Damascus Protocol' establishing the terms under which the Arabs would forge an alliance with Britain and take up arms against the Turks.[31] Feisal was sceptical that Britain would accept the Arabs' wide ranging and overly ambitious territorial demand for an independent Arab state. He also had little hope that a revolt would succeed. When he, his father and his brother Abdullah met for a council of war in June 1915, Feisal stated that he wished to see Turkey significantly weakened before the Arabs took to the field. Abdullah, however, was anxious to proceed with all possible haste and Hussein backed him.[32] The council of war offered the British an alliance if they accepted the Damascus Protocol. An unsigned letter of agreement from Hussein was sent to McMahon, with a covering letter from Abdullah to Storrs dated 14 July 1915.[33]

Hussein's opening gambit was certainly bold. He demanded recognition as king of an Arab state encompassing the whole of the Arabian peninsula (apart from Aden) as far north as Mersina and bounded by the Mediterranean, the Red Sea, the Persian Gulf and Persia (Iran). This would include all of modern-day Syria, Israel-Palestine, Jordan, Iraq, Saudi Arabia, the Gulf States and most of Yemen. Britain should also approve the proclamation of an Arabic Caliphate.[34] Unsurprisingly, British officials in Cairo thought Hussein's requests unrealistic, bordering 'upon the tragicomic'.[35] Nonetheless, the shattering of British confidence by the setback at Gallipoli is surely evidenced by McMahon's decision to engage in a lengthy correspondence of some ten letters with Hussein[36] concerning the boundaries of the Arab state and the amount of independence it would enjoy.[37] The British replies were 'at once deliberately vague and unwittingly obscure'.[38] McMahon believed his task was to tempt 'the Arab people onto the right path, detach them from the enemy and bring them on to our side'.[39] Early exchanges had failed to bring agreement when a new development occurred: the secret mission to Cairo of Muhammad Sherif al-Faruqi, an Arab staff officer in the Ottoman army and apparently a leading figure in the Arab nationalist group, *al Ahd*. In an interview in the autumn of 1915 with Brigadier Clayton, British Chief of Military Intelligence in Cairo, he revealed that Syrian Arab nationalist societies would take up arms if assured of explicit British support for an independent Arab state.[40] This appears to have convinced British officials and soldiers in Cairo that a deal acceptable to Sherif Hussein must be put on the table as soon as possible.[41] McMahon, without consulting the relevant Whitehall departments, in particular the India Office, which was aghast when it learned what had been offered, dispatched a letter to Hussein on 24 October 1915 outlining the extent of an Arab state subject to some exclusions for British and French interests. The lack of a map appended to the letter left certain issues open to interpretation. Was Palestine included in the exceptions that the British had made? How much of Syria was excluded? McMahon, in any case, had excluded considerable areas that Hussein desired in return for an Arab rising and he again delayed its launch. Had he known about the Anglo-French Sykes-Picot Agreement he would have been even more dubious about his new allies.

§

Sir Mark Sykes,[42] a baronet and a Conservative MP, was a rich and remarkably well-travelled expert on the Ottoman Empire and the Middle East. The outbreak of war saw him become a roving British government troubleshooter in the Middle East, due to his knowledge of the area. Sykes was an enthusiastic advocate of an Arab revolt and took the lead in Britain's negotiations with Georges Picot of France[43] regarding the partition of the Ottoman Empire.[44] France sought to extend the territory that it would directly control in the

Middle East as much as possible and to ensure that it enjoyed considerable influence in any potential Arab kingdom.[45] By the end of January 1916, Sykes and Picot had hammered out an agreement. Britain would annex the Tigris-Euphrates valley from the Arabian Gulf to Baghdad and enjoy indirect control (that is, priority in economic and political rights) in the area between the lines Akaba-Kuwait and Haifa-Tekrit, while France would have similar rights in the area delimited by the lines Haifa-Tekrit and the southern edge of Kurdistan. France would take direct control of modern-day Lebanon, coastal Syria and a considerable portion of central Anatolia. Britain seemed content to see the French act as a buffer between the British sphere and Russia, which it was assumed would be the dominant power in most of Asiatic Turkey. Palestine, apart from some strategic British bases, would be subject to international control, though this would later be changed to sole British control. Outside of Palestine and the areas of direct control, an Arab state or group of states would be allowed. However, this Arab state's independence would be circumscribed by being split into British and French spheres of influence. The British and French undoubtedly envisaged a system for the Middle East similar to those in Egypt and Morocco, where native governments existed but were dominated respectively by British and French officials. The agreement was signed on 31 January 1916, and after some modifications, endorsed by the British and French governments in February. However, it would only come into effect if Russia agreed and the Arabs rebelled. The first condition was fulfilled in May 1916 and the Arab Revolt began a month later.[46] The apparent incompatibility between the Sykes-Picot Agreement and the McMahon-Hussein correspondence was to be a source of later bitter controversy.[47]

In the final analysis foreknowledge of Sykes-Picot would have made little difference to Hussein. His road to revolt was forced upon him by the Turks, who were undoubtedly aware that he was parleying with the British. His prevarications might have continued until the end of the war had he not felt that an Ottoman attempt to depose him was imminent. Jemal, the Turkish commander in Syria, forced the pace. He placed Hussein under increasing pressure to provide a military contingent from the Hejaz to fight the British. Jemal also ruthlessly cracked down on Arab nationalist circles in Syria and within the army. He executed Arabs associated with nationalist parties and broke up Arab formations in Syria, sending them to other fronts, thus eliminating the threat of a major revolt by Arabs in the Ottoman army. Hussein, in response, continued to play a double game. He accepted McMahon's offer while maintaining relations with the Ottoman government, pressuring it to give him assurances regarding autonomy for the Hejaz. Enver Pasha and Jemal perceived an imminent break with Hussein, and Turkish forces prepared for a revolt. Hussein decided that he had to take the initiative, ordering his sons, Feisal, Abdullah and Ali, to organize the Hejaz for revolt. This began on 10 June 1916 with Hussein making a proclamation in Mecca and a simultaneous series of attacks on Turkish forces and infrastructure across the Hejaz.[48] War had come to the Arab world, though the immediate impact of Hussein's revolt was limited to the coastal areas of Hejaz. Its military impact was not on the scale that the British had once believed it would be.

16

30 August 1916: Turkey declares war on Romania

Romania Enters the War

Keith Hitchins

Romania did not enter the First World War until 27 August 1916. The delay had little to do with indecision about the preferred ally; the sympathies of a majority of politicians and the weight of public opinion lay with the Entente, particularly France. The commitment to war hinged on the satisfaction of territorial ambitions, calculations about the outcome of the war and the need to be at the peace table.

The chief responsibility for deciding on peace or war in 1914 and again in 1916 fell to Ion I C Brătianu (1864–1927). He was the foremost politician in Romania of the time. As the head of the powerful National Liberal Party and as the Prime Minister, he was responsible for domestic policy and, after the king, was the leading voice in foreign affairs. A reformer who thought government should deal creatively with changing economic and social conditions, he urged agrarian reform and universal suffrage. In international relations he sought for Romania a secure place in the European state system and recognition as a regional power.

His long-term goal was to unite all Romanians in a national state, a Greater Romania.[1]

At the time of Archduke Franz Ferdinand's assassination, Romania was allied with the Central Powers through secret treaties with Austria-Hungary and Germany dating from 1883. The Triple Alliance was important for King Carol (Prince, 1866–1881; King, 1881–1914) and those politicians who knew about the treaty because they judged Germany's military and economic power the primary guarantee of Romania's security. But Romania's relations with Austria-Hungary were never warm: the two countries waged a bitter tariff war between 1886 and 1893; in Balkan crises Austria-Hungary supported Bulgaria, which had become Romania's chief rival for regional predominance; and the Hungarian government denied national rights to the Romanians of Transylvania.[2]

The outbreak of war in 1914 forced difficult decisions on Romanian leaders. At a meeting of the Crown Council on 3 August only the king and one other member favoured entry into the war alongside Austria-Hungary and Germany. Brătianu urged a vote for neutrality, citing public support for the Entente and for the national aspirations of the Romanians of Transylvania. He justified ignoring any treaty commitment to the Triple Alliance by pointing out that Austria-Hungary had, in effect, violated its treaty with Romania by failing to inform its ally beforehand of its intention to deliver an ultimatum to Serbia. Not mentioned, but understood by all present, was the union of all Romanians in a national state, which could be achieved only by the annexation of Austro-Hungarian territories. The council voted for neutrality. The king, acknowledging himself as a constitutional monarch, acquiesced.[3] His death on 10 October left Brătianu in charge of foreign policy, as the new king, Carol's nephew Ferdinand, not as strong-willed as his uncle and confident of Brătianu's ability to lead, raised no objections to the course the Prime Minister was to follow.

During the next two years of neutrality Brătianu faced constant pressure from all sides to act. At home militant nationalists demanded intervention on the side of the Entente, and from outside both the Central Powers and the Entente offered threats and enticements. But Brătianu persevered. He watched closely the shifting fortunes on the battlefields and insisted that rewards for intervention justify the sacrifices of war. He could never free himself entirely from the anxiety that his country, militarily and economically, was ill-prepared for modern war.

Brătianu engaged in continuous negotiations with the Allies down to the spring of 1916, but he held back from joining them until they had guaranteed full support for Romania's war effort. He demanded regular deliveries of military supplies and equipment, an Allied offensive on the Eastern Front to coincide with the Romanian attack on Austria-Hungary, Allied military action against Bulgaria to spare Romania from having to fight a two-front war, and equal status for Romania with the principal Allies at the peace conference. He also insisted on a political treaty with the Allies that recognized Romania's territorial claims against Austria-Hungary, notably the cession of Transylvania, the Banat and Bukovina. He presented his conditions to the French Ambassador in Bucharest on 4 July 1916 and promised that if they were accepted the Romanian army would begin operations in early August.[4] He had finally been moved to act by what was in effect an ultimatum from France and Great Britain in June. They had informed him in plain terms that the time for decision had come, if he wished to achieve his ambitions. They wanted Romania to open a front against Austria-Hungary in order to support an imminent Russian offensive in Galicia. Brătianu himself had already come to a similar conclusion: that neutrality could no longer be sustained if he hoped to create a united Romanian state.[5]

The Allies thought Brătianu's pretensions exaggerated, and there was a consequent delay in negotiations. But the French offered a formula that finally brought agreement: if at the end of the war the Allies decided not to satisfy all Brătianu's demands, they would simply force him to do with less.[6] The way was thus clear for a formal agreement. On 17 August Brătianu and the representatives of France, Great Britain, Russia and Italy signed military and political conventions setting forth the conditions for Romania's entry into the war.

The final decision for war on the side of the Entente was made at a meeting of the Crown Council on 27 August. Brătianu, supported by the king, laid out the case for intervention and expressed confidence in the victory of the Entente and the country's 'national destiny'. A few members urged the continuation of neutrality, but, in the end, all but one approved Brătianu's motion for war.[7] That evening the Romanian minister in Vienna delivered his country's declaration of war to the Austro-Hungarian Foreign Ministry, and a few hours later Romanian troops crossed the frontier into Transylvania. Austria-Hungary and Germany responded with declarations of war on Romania on 28 August.

17

6 April 1917: United States Congress declares war on
Germany

America's Road to War

T G Fraser

On 23 October 1917, Battery C, 6th Field Artillery of the
American Expeditionary Forces in Europe bombarded
German lines, firing the first American shot of the First
World War. The order to open fire was given by Sergeant
Alexander L Arch of South Bend, Indiana, an immigrant
from Austria-Hungary, whose three fellow artillerymen
were of German-American origin.[2] Their adopted country
had not featured in the hectic round of diplomatic and military activity which engaged the European powers after the
Sarajevo assassination on 28 June 1914 that resulted in war.
The United States did not enter the war until 6 April 1917.
Separated by the North Atlantic Ocean from the European
continent, from where the vast majority of its population had
come, it had no obvious reason to involve itself in the competing interests of the European powers or in the nature of
their quarrels. Nor was America part of any alliance. It was
physically connected with only one of the belligerents, having

one of the longest, and most open, land borders in the world. This boundary stretched for some 3,000 miles demarcating it from the Dominion of Canada, an integral part of the British Empire.[3] That it was militarily undefended on either side says much about the relationship between the two. When Canada rallied to the imperial war effort in August 1914 it did so secure in the knowledge that no danger lay to the south. The American border with its southern neighbour, Mexico, was quite another matter, to which we will return.

Americans of European stock, or their forebears, had left their countries for a variety of reasons, whether to seek better economic opportunities, to escape famine or poverty or to flee from persecution and oppression, but leave Europe behind they had. Breaking their connection with the British Empire more than a century earlier, they had created a new nation which by the outbreak of war in 1914 had become one of the most vibrant economies in the world. Faced with the crisis that was engulfing Europe, it was hardly surprising that Americans' overwhelming sentiment was for neutrality. That view was clearly expressed by President Woodrow Wilson on 18 August 1914 when he enjoined strict neutrality on his countrymen.[4] No president, with the obvious exception of Abraham Lincoln, had ever been presented with the challenges that now faced Wilson.

Of Scottish and Ulster ancestral origins, Wilson was born in 1856 in Staunton, a small town in Virginia's Shenandoah Valley, the son of a Presbyterian clergyman who became a strong supporter of the Southern Confederacy. Some of his earliest memories were of the Civil War and its aftermath, and of seeing at first hand the defeated Confederate President Jefferson Davis and the Confederacy's legendary military commander, General Robert E Lee. His career had been in academia, becoming in 1902 President of Princeton University. A committed Democrat, in 1910 he was elected Governor of his adopted state of New Jersey. Two years later he was elected President, rather by default since the Republicans were divided between the rival camps of incumbent President William Howard Taft and former President Theodore Roosevelt, who between them substantially out-polled him in the popular vote.

A deeply devout Christian with a respected academic record, but in office on a minority vote, with no experience in foreign affairs, still less of military matters, Wilson's curriculum vitae in 1914 did not suggest that he was equipped to lead his country through such perilous times.[5] But, then, similar things might have been said of David Lloyd George, who was to become his British partner in war and peace, and whose pre-war record had been confined to high office in domestic politics (though his political compass was rather different). Wilson's inaugural address on 4 March 1913 said nothing about foreign affairs, but it did provide a clue as to how he and most Americans would come to view the war. The system of government that they had built up, he proclaimed, was a model which would endure against storm.[6] That storm, although he could never have guessed it, was not far off.

With a regular army numbering just 100,000, many of whom were serving in the Philippines and the recently created Panama Canal Zone, the country might have seemed a negligible military power, but that was only part of the story, and not the most important part. Those who cared to look back to the Civil War – and few Europeans did – would have appreciated its undoubted strength: the Union had mustered an army of 1 million from a population of some 22 million, a figure which does not, of course, include the armies of the

Confederacy. In 1865, its troops seasoned by four years of bitter conflict, the United States had claims to be considered the world's leading military power. Generals Grant and Sherman had directed operations on a truly continental scale. By 1914 America's military potential was there in plenty out of a population which by then numbered almost 100 million. With the exception of Russia, the American population dwarfed that of any of the European powers.[7]

Perhaps even more dramatic was the country's increasingly dominant position in the global economy. Its phenomenal agricultural and industrial surge after the Civil War was based upon an abundance of natural resources and raw materials, the ability to exploit these through new technologies, excellent internal communications, rampant capitalist enterprise, a sophisticated financial market and a seemingly limitless supply of young European immigrants. The development of the Great Plains in the last two decades of the 19th century had generated an agricultural surplus for which markets were sought in other parts of the world. In key areas of production, notably coal, iron and steel, the US was, by 1914, far outperforming Britain and Germany, its closest industrial competitors – and the same was true in new areas of economic activity such as the motor car.[8] It followed by simple mathematical logic that if these immense human and economic resources were mobilised on behalf of one of the First World War's combatants then that side would win, unless, that is, the deployment of American power in Europe could be pre-empted by a quick military or naval victory by the opposing side. This reality was understood, it seems, by the British Foreign Secretary, Sir Edward Grey.[9]

It was evident from the start of the war that Britain enjoyed certain advantages in appealing to American sentiment, not the least of which was a common language. People of British stock were still strongly represented in the American population, most obviously so in its higher social and political reaches. Although these Americans had twice fought a war against Great Britain, there was a joint heritage of constitutional government, democratic values and the English common law.[10] The late Victorian and Edwardian eras had seen a remarkable degree of inter-marriage between the American and British elites. In 1914 it was only a decade since Chicago's Mary Leiter had been Vicereine of India, the son of Jennie Jerome of New York was First Lord of the Admiralty, presiding over Britain's key weapon of war – and, of course, the first woman to take her seat in the British House of Commons would be the Virginian Nancy Astor, in 1918. Also prominent in Anglo-American circles, although by 1914 separated from her husband, was Consuelo, Duchess of Marlborough, whose Vanderbilt ancestor had settled in Long Island from Holland in the mid-17th century.[11] Leading Americans were familiar with Britain. Visiting the country during the summer of 1914 was the prominent Republican Senator from Massachusetts, and Wilson's ultimate nemesis, Henry Cabot Lodge. While supporting the policy of neutrality, he later recorded that he had strongly sympathized with the Allied cause.[12] For his part, Wilson had enjoyed holidays in the English Lake District.[13] Rather less tangibly, France could conjure up Lafayette and support for the American Revolution.

Sentiment, however, did not mean that public opinion favoured entering the war. These Allied advantages had to be set against three groups which were unsympathetic. After the anti-Jewish May Laws of 1882, over 2 million Russian Jews had come to the United States, most of them settling in New York City. They had no reason to favour the land of the pogrom. Their sentiments were heightened when it was learned that the Jews of the Pale of Settlement had welcomed the German advances in 1914, but had been badly treated once the Russian armies returned.[14] Nor did the large Irish-American population, seared as it was by the legacies of the Famine, harbour pro-British sentiments – quite the reverse. They were organised through the powerful Clan na Gael, led by Judge Daniel F Cohalan, Joseph McGarrity and John Devoy.[15] The German Americans, over 5 million of whom had migrated between 1820 and 1900, constituted one of the largest ethnic groups in the country by 1914. Their main area of settlement was the Midwest, especially in and around the cities of St Louis, Cincinnati, Milwaukee and Minneapolis-St Paul. As a group they were hard to categorise. Not only were they divided between Lutherans and Catholics, but before 1871 there had been no such political entity as Germany. What they shared was a pride in German culture, language and the accomplishments of the new German Empire. Branches of their cultural and athletic club, the Turnverein, studded the Midwest.[16]

The sympathies of those whose origins lay in the multi-national Austro-Hungarian Empire were much harder to pin down, with the Czechs, in particular, coming to favour the Allies.[17] From the very start of the conflict, Germany had disadvantages which counted against it in the battle for American opinion, and which were a gift to Allied and pro-Allied publicists. Most obviously, there was the violation of Belgian neutrality, which had been guaranteed by Britain, Austria, France, Russia and, crucially, Prussia in 1839. The German campaign, vigorously resisted by King Albert and his small army, was accompanied by atrocities against the civilian population, most notoriously the destruction of much of the historic university city of Louvain, including its unique library – an action which might have been wryly regarded by elderly Georgians who could recall the burning of Atlanta by Sherman's troops in November 1864, but which was regarded as an act of barbarism in the new century. These well-publicised atrocities reinforced the image of Germany as an aggressive and militaristic society. A scholar himself, Wilson keenly felt what the Germans had done to Louvain.[18]

Wilson's Secretary of State was William Jennings Bryan, a striking orator whose 'Cross of Gold' speech at the 1896 Democratic national convention had earned him an imperishable niche in American political history, but who was conspicuously unsuccessful when it came to the stump: he lost the presidential elections of 1896 and 1900 to William McKinley and then in 1908 to Taft. In 1913 he was a perfectly acceptable choice for the post; after August 1914 he was felt to be less successful.[19] Since Wilson preferred to keep the threads of foreign policy in his own hands, Bryan was increasingly marginalised in favour of Colonel Edward M House. House, whose honorary, and not military, title understandably perplexed the Germans, was an influential Democrat from Texas.[20] Once the war began he became a trusted, if unofficial, confidant and emissary of the President. House was well connected in Europe. In May 1914, a European tour saw him in Berlin, Paris and London. While in Berlin, he met Admiral Alfred von Tirpitz, the guiding hand behind the German naval expansion that had helped poison relations with Britain, the future Chief of the General Staff General Erich von Falkenhayn, and Arthur Zimmermann of the Foreign Office, whose fateful role in America's entry into the war would come three years later. He was also granted a private audience with Kaiser Wilhelm, who tried to impress upon him the merit of Germany, Britain and the United States standing together as the defenders of civilisation.[21] While in London House apparently found a sympathetic ear in Grey, also meeting the Prime Minister, Herbert Henry Asquith and his Chancellor of the Exchequer, David Lloyd George. Any chance that his mission would bring about a greater understanding among the Powers was brutally cut short on 28 June when the heir to the thrones of Austria-Hungary and his wife were murdered in Sarajevo. Within weeks, Britain, France, Russia, Belgium and Serbia were ranged against Germany and Austria-Hungary.[22]

The land war in Europe presented little challenge to American neutrality. The sea one, however, was a different matter. While Britain worked to expand its small regular force and associated territorial units into a mass army capable of sustaining a continental campaign, its principal weapon, the Royal Navy, was deployed to blockade Germany – a task for which the geographical position of the British Isles seemed providentially located. The legal basis for a blockade was a byword for obscurity, resting as it did on the Declaration of Paris of 1856 signed by Great Britain, Austria, France, Prussia, Russia, Sardinia and Turkey, and the Declaration of London of 1909, which had never been ratified by anyone. Probably as a result of this situation, Britain did not formally proclaim a blockade of Germany on the outbreak of war. The Federal blockade of the Confederacy during the Civil War was a handy precedent, however, and on 20 August 1914 the Declaration of London was unilaterally incorporated into the municipal law of the United Kingdom.[23] Britain's policy had to be finely judged. Germany and Austria-Hungary, with their great munitions factories in the Ruhr and Bohemia, could produce all the weapons that they needed, but they were vulnerable in other economic respects. While exerting the maximum pressure on the enemy, the British knew that they had to stop well short of alienating the United States.[24] Two points were at issue. The first was the complex concept of what constituted contraband of war. The Declaration of London had set out in some detail a list which comprised such obvious items as arms, explosives, military clothing and warships, and then added articles which might be designated conditional contraband. This latter list included foodstuffs, currency, and clothing and fabrics suitable for war use. A brave decision by Grey, approved by the Cabinet, was not to include cotton on the initial contraband list, despite the fact that it was used in the production of munitions. To do so would have associated Britain with a measure devastating to the economy of the southern states, leading to the enmity of their representatives in Congress. Even so, the disruption to trade caused by the war threatened to ruin the cotton farmers in the region – where Wilson's Democratic Party was dominant – although, fortunately, the effect proved to be short-lived. The second, and more crucial, matter was that of neutrality. This did not just affect the United States. Much of Germany's commerce passed through the great ports of Copenhagen and Rotterdam in neutral Denmark and the Netherlands, which were really extensions of Germany's economic system.[25] These issues had profound implications for the United States.

Despite these pressures, the crucial fact was that demand in Britain and France for American foodstuffs, raw materials and munitions proved to be almost insatiable, with far-reaching consequences for the country's economic prosperity and social structure. The war-time boom accelerated the movement of African Americans to the northern industrial cities, freeing them from the more overt institutionalised racism of the southern states. Since the administration rejected calls from German-American and pacifist groups for an arms embargo, the Royal Navy's command of the Atlantic and the North Sea ensured that the vast resources of the United States were the almost exclusive preserve of the Allies.[26] Grey later learned that had cotton been on the initial contraband list, the strength of feeling in the southern states might well have tipped the balance in favour of an arms embargo.[27] Given the impact of the war on the country's economy, it is perhaps hardly surprising that the administration's protests over the British blockade were muted, never really seriously threatening Anglo-American relations.

This stance stood in marked contrast to the US's response to Germany's naval campaign. The German surface fleet, notwithstanding the money and affection which had been lavished upon it, had no answer to the British blockade. Instead, the German leaders turned to a new, and as yet untried, naval vessel: the submarine or *Unterseeboot*, popularized in English as the U-boat. The U-boat campaign was instigated by Admiral Hugo von Pohl, who convinced his government to undertake attacks on merchant shipping in British and Irish waters – Tirpitz assuring the Kaiser that they would defeat Britain in six weeks. While it was true that Britain was heavily dependent upon imports, especially in food, such advice wildly overestimated the resources at Germany's disposal. When the blockade of Great Britain was announced on 4 February 1915, a mere 21 boats were available, of which a third could usually be at sea.[28]

The campaign brought into sudden and stark relief the rules of what had come to be termed 'cruiser warfare' under which a warship could only sink a merchant vessel if it resisted and even then the safety of those on board had to be ensured. While submarine commanders did try to observe this procedure, they could only do so by bringing their boat to the surface, a risky action since large British merchantmen were armed. In poor visibility or heavy seas it was difficult for a submarine commander to distinguish an Allied from a neutral vessel. There was the further complication of the possible fate of Americans sailing in Allied ships. In short, the submarine campaign of 1915 had no chance of success, while running the severe risk of alienating the United States should the established rules of warfare collapse, as they soon did in the most tragic manner.[29]

On 7 May 1915 *U-20*, commanded by Kapitänleutnant Walther Schwieger, was on patrol off the south coast of Ireland, near the Old Head of Kinsale. Schwieger fired a single torpedo at a large four-funnelled vessel, which sank in just 18 minutes. His victim was the Cunard liner *Lusitania,* en route to Liverpool from New York. Of its 1,924 passengers, 1,198 drowned, including 124 Americans. Although the Germans had issued a warning, what registered with American opinion was the loss of so many innocent civilian lives. In retrospect, the sinking of the *Lusitania* may be seen as marking a critical moment in America's road to war, but it did not seem so at the time. There was no overwhelming demand for the country to declare war on Germany, Wilson's somewhat sibylline response about being too proud to fight indicating that he still saw the United States as being above the conflict. The immediate consequences of the tragedy were an exchange of notes between Washington and Berlin, and a dramatic scaling back of Germany's submarine campaign. Bryan, who preferred a more even-handed policy towards Britain and Germany, resigned in June, being replaced by Robert Lansing.[30]

Although it did not precipitate a war with Germany, the sinking of the *Lusitania* contributed to a hardening of public opinion against it.[31] Ill-feeling against German intentions was further aroused by the actions of its agents. The Germans were naturally anxious to interrupt the flow of American munitions to Britain and France if they possibly could, but measures were taken which stretched the bounds of Germany's neutrality towards America. In January 1915, its Military Attaché, Franz von Papen, received authorization for a campaign of sabotage. Papen and his naval counterpart, Karl Boy-Ed, seem to have acted prudently, but in April they were joined from Germany by Franz von Rintelen, a naval reserve officer, who was less circumspect. The campaign which followed included attempts to sabotage munitions works, American ships and the Welland Canal in Canada. These activities did nothing to dent American supplies to the Allies, but they did create a sense, carefully fostered by Britain's intelligence chief Captain Guy Gaunt, of bungling interference in America's affairs. In August 1915 Rintelen was arrested by the British while trying to return to Germany, while in December Papen and Boy-Ed suffered the ignominy of expulsion from the United States as the result of their actions, although this measure was not extended to the Ambassador, Johann von Bernstorff.[32]

The year 1916, with the appalling carnage at the Somme and Verdun, saw no prospect of an immediate end to the war. At sea the rather inconclusive Battle of Jutland confirmed the Royal Navy's supremacy, but on the Eastern Front the Germans and Austrians increasingly held the upper hand. Britain's image in the United States suffered as a result of the execution of the leaders of the Easter Rising in Dublin, the only leading male commander to be spared being the

American-born Éamon de Valéra.[33] In addition to the war in Europe, Wilson had two other important preoccupations that year. The first involved the vexed relationship with Mexico, where he had already intervened with navy and marines in April 1914. In March 1916, the leader of one of the country's warring factions, Pancho Villa, raided the garrison town of Columbus, New Mexico, killing 15 Americans. The result was the deployment of a force under the command of Brigadier-General John J Pershing, soon to achieve fame in a wider arena.[34] Wilson's other challenge was domestic, since 1916 was election year. Riding on the back of the economic boom the country was enjoying, and buttressed by the refrain that he had kept the country out of war, Wilson narrowly defeated the well-respected Republican challenger, Charles Evans Hughes. If anything was confirmed by the result it was that public opinion remained set against war.[35]

Wilson was inaugurated for a second term on 5 March 1917, but by then Germany had embarked on a course that would transform the war and change the course of American history. Wilson sought to capitalise on his electoral victory through mediating in the conflict, despite strong reservations by Lansing and House. An appeal had been sent to the belligerents on 18 December 1916. Conscious of how dependent they had become on American resources, the British and French drafted an emollient response, but there was no echo from Berlin.[36] The dominant voices in Germany were no longer the Kaiser and his Chancellor, Theobald von Bethmann Hollweg, but its military leaders, Field-Marshal Paul von Hindenburg and General Erich Ludendorff. By the beginning of 1917 these two paladins had become convinced by the arguments of the naval commanders, Admirals Reinhard Scheer and Henning von Holtzendorff, as well as clamour from political circles, that Germany should unleash a campaign of unrestricted submarine warfare. This fateful course of action was agreed at a conference on 9 January, Hindenburg dismissing a reluctant Bethmann Hollweg's fears about the reaction in the United States. The submarine campaign was to begin on 1 February.[37] Once again, the German leadership had miscalculated, both the potential of its submarine fleet, and, much more seriously, the strength of the United States. On 31 January, the German Ambassador informed Wilson of the decision. On 3 February, Wilson announced to Congress the severance of relations with Germany.[38]

Even so, Wilson had yet to take the final decision for war. That task was facilitated by German Foreign Minister, Arthur Zimmermann. Zimmermann's brainwave was to create a diversion which, he believed, would frustrate any American moves to intervene effectively in the European conflict. In the event of war, Mexico, in alliance with Germany, was to attack the United States. In a further refinement, Japan was to be induced to join them. This latter dimension was fanciful at best. Although both Britain and the United States had come to harbour suspicions over Japanese intentions in the course of the war, Japan's leaders were not about to renege on the Anglo-Japanese Alliance which had served them well so far.[39] Mexico was a different matter since it had lost vast territories to its northern neighbour in the aftermath of the war of 1846–8. Mexico's reward for joining Germany was to be the re-conquest of its lost territories in Texas, New Mexico and Arizona. (New Mexico and Arizona, it may be recalled, had only become states of the Union as recently as 1912.) On 16 January 1917, Zimmermann sent a telegram outlining this to Bernstorff for forwarding to his counterpart in Mexico.[40]

What Zimmermann did not know, however, was that since

1916 British naval intelligence had been intercepting and deciphering both German and American diplomatic cable traffic. The Germans had come to an arrangement that they could send telegrams to their Ambassador in Washington from the American embassy in Berlin, but, of course, this simply meant that they fell into British hands, which was exactly what happened.[41] The British had to proceed with caution, since they could not reveal that they had been reading American traffic. Once they had decided how they could do so safely, they presented the American Ambassador to London, W H Page with the telegram, on 23 February. Wilson received it the following day, and decided it should be released to the press. Political and press reaction was electric. There remained the obvious question of the document's authenticity, but on 3 March Zimmermann confirmed it.[42]

Events then moved very quickly. The Americans made sure that their ships were clearly identified, but to no avail. Between 16 and 18 March three of their merchantmen were sunk, only one of which received a warning. The attackers made no effort to come to the aid of the crews. Exactly what Wilson was thinking in the light of these dramatic events remains elusive, but at a Cabinet meeting on 20 March it became clear that the opinion was for war. A meeting of Congress was called for 2 April. When it convened, castigating the German government for its submarine campaign, he asked for a declaration of war. War, he said, had been thrust upon them, but he made it clear that the quarrel was not with the German people. His message had a high moral content. The United States sought neither conquest nor dominion, pledging that the world had to be made safe for democracy. On 6 April, by 373 votes to 50, Congress endorsed Wilson's appeal. The same day, he signed the war resolution. The United States had joined the war.[43]

18

7 April 1917: Cuba and Panama declare war on Germany
Central America, the Caribbean and the First World War
Irene Fattacciu

By the time of the outbreak of the First World War in 1914, the United States had established itself as the main power in Central America and the Caribbean. The conflict was closely followed by politicians, businessmen and public opinion in the region but, given its dominant position, America's policy of neutrality made the direct involvement of the Central American states a very remote possibility.

In 1898 the United States had intervened decisively in the Hispano-Cuban war, subsequently occupying Cuba for four years and passing the Platt Amendment to the Cuban Constitution. The amendment gave Washington the right to intervene unilaterally in Cuban affairs to protect 'life, property, and individual liberty', and to establish military bases on the island.[1] This enabled it to safeguard its growing commercial interests, and the new Cuban-American relationship transformed both the US's foreign policy and its role in the region.

In 1904 President Theodore Roosevelt announced a cor-
ollary to the Monroe Doctrine that extended Monroe's
prohibition of European colonisation in the region to the
sanctioning of American intervention to prevent neighbouring countries falling under European control because of
political and financial instability. This became the foundation
of the policy pursued by Washington in the first quarter of
the 20th century.

This so-called 'dollar diplomacy' used diplomatic pressure,
commercial penetration and financial investment to uphold economic and political stability in the troubled countries of Central
America and the Caribbean in order to promote and secure
American interests. American companies such as the United
Fruit Company (founded in 1899) achieved control of much of
the productive land in Central America, and by investing in the
building of railways, shipping lines and other economic activities created deep and long-lasting ties with their host nations.[2]
The establishment of a direct connection between the Atlantic
and the Pacific Oceans was fundamental to American policy
and the Panama Canal opened in 1914, after Roosevelt had
engineered Panama's independence from Colombia in 1903. As
with Cuba this independence came at a high price, involving an
American presence at the heart of the country.

When war began in 1914, with the exception of Guatemala, where Germany's cultural influence was boosted by
propaganda and massive investments in the coffee plantations
and the country's electrical company, the region was broadly
sympathetic to the Allies.[3] Some volunteers from the large
communities of French and Italian migrants even returned
to defend their homelands. The war also affected American
policy towards the region. President Woodrow Wilson insti-
tuted a series of measures to counter local insurgencies and

the resurgence of European powers in the area. The United States on the one hand took charge of protecting private citizens of Britain, France or Germany, and on the other conducted a series of operations in the troubled countries of Central America to secure their loyalty and America's commercial interests. German commercial activities in the region were still strong and reports gathered by the US Office of Naval Intelligence through its network of military attachés scattered among Central America, Cuba and Haiti offered reasons for concern about German operations. During the years of neutrality US military interventions multiplied: Cuba (1906 and 1917); Nicaragua (1912); Haiti (1915); and the Dominican Republic (1916–24).[4]

The security of the strategic Panama Canal was vital to the United States. In 1912 America had claimed its intervention in Nicaragua was to stem political violence, but the real motive was to prevent the construction of a competing canal across the country, over which the Zelaya administration had opened negotiations with Germany in 1909. The occupation lasted until 1933. The Chamorro-Bryan Treaty (1916) transformed Nicaragua into a near protectorate and gave the United States the exclusive prerogative to build any inter-oceanic canal across the country.

By 1905 American companies owned 60 per cent of Cuba's sugar industry, which constituted another major American interest. In 1906 Washington had intervened, reluctantly, in an internal Cuban political struggle, but in 1917 2,000 marines were sent to the island with the sole task of protecting American sugar plantations.[5] In 1915 American troops went to Haiti ostensibly to restore order after an election, but the real reason lay in the refusal of the government to leave control of the country's finances with US banks. The military presence lasted until 1934 and the new government accepted a customs regime, which gave control to the United States over budgetary policy, customs and the army.[6] A debt crisis in 1916 in the Dominican Republic brought further American intervention, with the marines remaining for eight years. America negotiated a further extension of the Platt Amendment with both states, giving Washington full right of intervention to ensure stability and protect American economic interests.

On 6 April 1917 America declared war on Germany. Panama and Cuba immediately followed on 7 April, although Panamanian President Ramón Valdés had already assured the United States that Panama would defend the Panama Canal from any hostile attack. Militarily and economically Cuba was a precious ally for the United States. Its strategic position guarding the entrance to the Mexican Gulf prevented the penetration of German submarines and warships. Under the Espionage Act of July 1918 Cuba imposed a series of restrictions on German citizens on the island and confiscated their properties. Its vital contribution was sugar – as Hugh Thomas put it, 'in France the armies marched on stomachs filled from Havana'.[7] The sharp reduction of beet sugar from Germany and the huge demand for sugar in European countries such as Great Britain became a major boost for the Cuban industry, which doubled its revenue between 1914 and 1916.

American diplomatic pressure, combined with the economic damage caused by German submarine warfare, was an important factor in the subsequent actions of other regional states. Guatemala formally declared war on 23 April 1918, but its major focus remained on reconstruction following the devastation wrought by two huge earthquakes in December 1917 and January 1918. Nicaragua followed on 8 May 1918. Honduras had already broken diplomatic relations with

Germany in May 1917, but past frictions with the United States and a considerable German business presence delayed a formal declaration of war until 19 July 1918.

The Costa Rican declaration of war on 23 May 1918 was a curious case. President Federico Tinoco, who had seized power in 1917, hoped thereby to win favour in Washington, but Wilson stated in 1917 that the United States would not recognise any revolutionary government in the region. Hence America recognised neither the Costa Rican government, nor the arrival of an apparent new ally.[8]

The First World War marked an important stage in growing American dominance of an unstable political region. One of the major hopes of the states that had joined the war was that they would be able to exploit their presence at the Peace Conference to reduce their dependence on the United States. They would be disappointed, though Cuba, Guatemala, Haiti, Honduras and Nicaragua all became founder members of the League of Nations.[9]

19

13 April to 7 December 1917: South America and the First World War

In the Grasp of the United States
Edoardo Braschi

Although geographically part of the Americas, South America's development was profoundly influenced by Europe following Spain's colonisation of much of it in the mid-16th century, whilst Brazil (which is treated in another chapter), was a Portuguese colony. Bolivia, Ecuador, Peru and Uruguay – which would join Brazil as the South American representatives at the Paris Peace Conference in 1919 – all became independent republics between 1822 and 1830, beginning a process of modernisation often shaped by their relations with foreign powers.

On the eve of the First World War, all four countries were ruled by conservative Creole oligarchies operating policies of economic liberalism. French influences, both cultural and military, were dominant among the elite whilst Britain was the major market for their exports of food and raw materials and the main holder of South American debt. Germany was also a strong commercial and military influence.[1] The dominant regional economic and military power, however, was the United States and in 1914 it was a rapidly growing presence across the whole continent. Between 1900 and 1913 US exports to South America increased from $38 million to $146 million, whilst the beginnings of pan-American cooperation emerged in regional conferences held in 1889, 1902, 1905 and 1910. Various South American attempts to invoke a pan-American response to the war came to nothing, but US policy constituted a powerful factor in the decision-making of all four states.[2]

All four nations approached the war with prudence, each declaring a position of absolute neutrality. Uruguay did so on 4 August 1914, followed by Ecuador and Bolivia later that month. Peru made no formal declaration, but acted accordingly and soon released a statement confirming its neutral disposition. It had encountered major trade disruptions caused by a pre-war fall in sugar prices that may have affected the delay in its decision.[3] From the outset all governments applied strict regulations regarding the use of ports and facilities by belligerent forces, hoping to avoid any dangerous controversy.

For most South Americans the war seemed remote and meant little, but the region's strategic role in global trade was considered of great importance and relevance by all the warring powers.[4] Britain's attempts to curtail Germany's trade with neutrals – the Black List published in April 1916 – caused disruption to all the national economies, but Germany's unrestricted submarine warfare policy in early 1917 proved a much greater threat to vital commerce and occasioned diplomatic protests by all four states. British policies seemed unduly harsh, given the limited possibilities for trade with Germany, but Germany's action was considered unacceptable, endangering the economy of the entire region.

German influence was strongest in Bolivia, the only South American country in which it was the major commercial partner. A majority of Bolivians were sympathetic to Germany, and the military particularly so. The political leadership, however, especially after the election of General Ismael Montes as president, followed a strongly pro-American course. The Bolivian economy had been badly hit by the pre-war crisis and it could not afford to alienate American and European partnerships. On 17 March 1916, a German submarine sank the Dutch ship *Tubantia* carrying Sir. Luis Salinas, the Bolivian representative to Berlin. All on board were rescued but Bolivian resentment contributed to a growing rift with Germany.[5]

Peru was the closest of the South American countries to the United States. With strong cultural bonds with France and Britain, it shared American sympathy with the Allies, German propaganda having little effect outside clerical circles. On 4 June 1915, the Peruvian government interned a German liner after it violated Peruvian neutrality by staying too long in Callao, whilst the sinking of the Peruvian cargo vessel *Lorton* off the Spanish coast in January 1917 was a decisive factor in moving the country towards the Allies. During the lengthy diplomatic wrangle that followed, Peru could achieve no satisfaction from Germany.[6]

As a rather small and militarily weak country, Uruguay was particularly cautious, its policy strongly influenced by the United States but also by Argentina and Brazil. America's declaration of war on 6 April 1917, followed by Brazil's rupture of diplomatic relations with Germany encouraged a strong pro-Allied mood among Uruguayan public opinion, but President Viera reaffirmed neutrality. Uruguay had not suffered any diplomatic mistreatment or trade disruption by the German Empire. In June 1917 it issued a decree pledging sympathy and solidarity to all American nations but it continued to maintain its neutrality and good relations with Germany.[7]

Ecuador's situation was controversial. According to an official report, Germany's diplomatic representatives were considered unwelcome and the national elite was definitively pro-Allies.[8] However, of all four states, it was in Ecuador probably that the deepest German influence on society was felt, particularly in education, finance, industry and the Church. Relations with Britain and France were strained in September 1914 when the German cruiser *Leipzig* stayed in Ecuadorian waters longer than neutrality laws permitted. Britain and France accused Ecuador of not controlling its territorial waters effectively thus breaching its neutrality. Ecuador denied this but Britain and France requested US supervision to ensure compliance. The Ecuadorian government saw this as an outrage to national sovereignty but friendly relations were restored in early 1915. Ecuador's economy was struggling but the government saw, as yet, no reason to abandon neutrality.[9]

The United States declaration of war on 6 April 1917 was decisive in moving all four countries to sever relations with Germany. Bolivia was the first to do so, on 13 April, specifically mentioning the *Tubantia*, whose loss still rankled.[10] In October 1917, Peru and Uruguay followed suit. America's release of decoded dispatches from Count Karl von Luxburg, the German minister in Argentina, hinting at German intervention in Brazil, caused wide resentment, particularly in neighbouring Uruguay. On 5 October, frustrated by the lack of progress in its negotiations with Germany over the loss of the *Lorton* and hoping to gain the goodwill of the United

States in its disputes with Chile, Peru broke off diplomatic relations with Germany. On 7 October, encouraged by the imminent Brazilian declaration of war on Germany, President Viera, with parliamentary approval, also severed diplomatic links with Germany. Ecuador did the same on 7 December, influenced by the actions of its neighbours and the United States.[11]

Bolivia, Ecuador, Peru and Uruguay abandoned neutrality because of a mixture of economic necessity, United States influence and pan-Americanism sentiment.[12] Although each, particularly Bolivia, had commercial links to Germany, the strength of economic ties with the Allies and especially America proved predominant. The United States, with its commanding position, saw South America as its sphere of influence. Lacking the military, political or economic strength of Chile, Argentina or Brazil, the main objective of the wartime diplomacy of the four states was to gain the approval of the United States and its backing in regional South American disputes. Bolivia, for example, hoped that the United States would back a revision of its 1904 treaty with Chile under which it had lost all its coastline.[13] There was a strong desire for all four countries to retain the national feeling of being part of the same cultural and political entity that was Latin America. It was particularly vital for Ecuador, which 'merely joined the Allied side as testimony to the cause of American cooperation and her moral contribution to the ideals which the U.S and the Allies were striving to uphold'.[14]Finally each sought a seat at whatever peace conference would follow and hoped that this would enable advantages to be gained.

20

27 June 1917: Greece declares war on Austria-Hungary,
Bulgaria, Germany and Turkey

Greece and the First World War
Andrew Dalby

The route by which the Greek Prime Minister, Eleftherios
Venizelos, brought his country into the First World War could
hardly have been more tortuous. It began with a journey
from Salonica to London in December 1912 and ended with
a voyage from Salonica to Athens in June 1917.

Salonica, now the second city of Greece, was in early 1912
a European metropolis of the Ottoman Empire and the cradle
of the Young Turks movement. In that year Serbia, Bulgaria
and Greece made a joint attack on the empire's remaining
European possessions. All three had some claim to Salonica.
The Greek army reached the city on 8 November 1912, a few
hours ahead of the Bulgarians, and that was that. The peace
negotiations in London, the war that immediately followed
and the further negotiations in Bucharest made no difference
on this point: Salonica remained Greek territory.

Yet for almost a year during the First World War, while the
government in Athens remained neutral with a slant towards

Germany, Salonica was to be headquarters of a rival government, led by Venizelos, that had joined the Entente. Only after this traumatic episode had been brought to a traumatic end – only in July 1917 – would Greece as a nation declare war.

§

To return, then, to Venizelos's journey to London to attend peace talks in January 1913. As peace talks they were a waste of time, but to Venizelos personally, now aged 48 and in the third year of his premiership, this short stay in London was crucial. He forged good working relationships with Winston Churchill, First Lord of the Admiralty, and with David Lloyd George, then Chancellor of the Exchequer. At private meetings at 11 Downing Street the three of them delved into the common interests of Greece and Britain and the future of Cyprus, a British protectorate but a largely Greek-speaking territory that Greece very much wanted.[1] In London he also first met the woman who would be his second wife, Helena Schilizzi, a member of a wealthy Greek family firmly established in England.

These things surely helped to strengthen Venizelos's preference for Britain over other potential allies for Greece, but he was soon aware that he would face determined opposition whenever it might come to such a choice. Two months later Greece's King George, strolling in Salonica, was shot and killed by an anarchist. He had ruled for almost exactly 50 years; for three of these he and Venizelos had worked together with increasing mutual respect. The King's successor, his eldest son Constantine, was another matter. Proud of having personally led the army to its recent victories, convinced that he was 'responsible before God'[2] in matters of foreign policy, warmly conscious of his German military background (his brother-in-law, Kaiser Wilhelm II, was about to award him the rank of field-marshal in the German army), Constantine would be the last man to accept a prime minister's advice on the desirability of an alliance directed against Germany.

In June 1913, while the Balkan peace treaty was being uselessly signed in London, Venizelos was back in Salonica concluding a bilateral alliance with Serbia. One year later this alliance raised an unforeseen problem. If Austria invaded Serbia – as now seemed likely to happen – must the Greek army fight on Serbia's Austrian border? No, said Venizelos: since Serbia had provoked the conflict with Austria, Greece was not obliged to take part. Some thought this showed weakness, but Greece's army, defending threatened frontiers with Bulgaria and Turkey and about to send peacekeepers to Albania, was overstretched. There was another reason to hold back. King Constantine was being pressed by his wife's brother, Kaiser Wilhelm II, to bring Greece into an alliance with Germany.

Austro-Hungarian troops crossed the Serbian border on 12 August, by which time the Central Powers were at war with the Entente. In Greece the fact that the King's sympathies were with Germany, while the Prime Minister favoured the Entente, was at first academic: they agreed that Greece must remain neutral. Both knew this could not last, however. Wilhelm had told Constantine privately that Germany had a secret alliance with Turkey and was sending German warships to Constantinople; Venizelos knew this too.[3] On 29 October 1914, using German warships, the Turkish navy attacked Russian cities on the Black Sea coast, thus joining the war on the German side.

This opened a gap between the two men. Convinced that the Entente would win, Venizelos argued that since Turkey was at war, Greece, its historic enemy, could not remain neutral and must join Britain and France, naval powers, natural allies and probable victors. But Constantine foresaw a German victory. Under intense personal pressure to join Germany, he had softened his refusal with a promise to the Kaiser that Greece would stay neutral. To break this promise would be dishonest – and would open Greece to reprisals from Germany and a resurgent Ottoman Empire when they had won the war.

The gap between the King and the Prime Minister became unbridgeable a year later when Bulgaria declared for the Central Powers and attacked Serbia. Venizelos immediately assured Britain and France that Greece would fight in support of its ally. In hasty response to Venizelos's equally hasty invitation, French and British forces under General Maurice Sarrail disembarked at Salonica. The overt aim (though this was never practical) was to establish a base from which Serbia could be supported. Yet Constantine still stood firm for neutrality and would not commit Greece to war. Venizelos, with a fiery speech in Parliament denouncing the King's 'unconstitutional position', narrowly won a vote of confidence. Constantine dismissed him and his government on 7 October.

Thus the Salonica landing split Greece in two. Successive Athens governments clutched at neutrality; Salonica was de facto at war, and the Entente armies were recruiting Greek volunteers. Still, it was nearly a year before the split became a full-scale rebellion. Confident of British and French support, a triumvirate – Venizelos and two staunch allies, General Danglis and Admiral Koundouriotis, hero of the Balkan wars – left Athens secretly and proclaimed a

Provisional Government of National Defence. After a triumphal voyage around the Aegean they reached Salonica, where on 9 October General Sarrail, modestly and unofficially, joined the crowd that greeted them at the quayside. They set up their government in the villa that had been King Constantine's residence and declared war on Germany and Bulgaria. As Venizelos explained, 'Greece can never progress, or even exist, as a free and independent state except by continued maintenance of the closest contact with the Powers that rule the Mediterranean.'[4]

The Provisional Government established control of almost half of Greece. It had its own diplomacy (its base in the United Kingdom was Helena Schilizzi's London house at 51 Upper Brook Street)[5] and its own propaganda service. Entente forces and the British embassy's intelligence service steadily favoured Salonica, undermined King Constantine, destabilized Athens and blockaded southern Greece, causing famine during the winter of 1916/17.

The following summer London and Paris decided to finish the job. Their ultimatum to the Athens government demanded Constantine's abdication and the exile of a list of anti-Venizelists. Venizelos himself returned from Salonica on 21 June, and the young King Alexander, Constantine's second son, who had been allowed to succeed his father, had no choice but to invite him to form a government. The real balance of power was indicated by Venizelos's reported remark to the Russian Ambassador: 'If the new King turns out not to be a constitutionalist, we'll deal with him the way you did in Russia.'[6] Venizelos afterwards thought it a mistake that during these political manoeuvres he was on board the French navy's flagship La Justice: it could be said, and it was said, that his return to Athens was guaranteed by 'French bayonets'.

At any rate, on 2 July 1917 Greece declared war on Germany, Austria, Turkey and Bulgaria. On 26 August Venizelos spoke in Parliament for over four hours, justifying his policies, vilifying opponents and fence-sitters, explaining why he had 'decided to become a rebel' and concluding with bold promises concerning the future Peace Conference.

Greece knows that I have never failed to keep my word. By taking part in this world war alongside democracies impelled to unite in a truly holy alliance ... we shall regain the national territories we have lost; we shall reassert our national honour; we shall effectively defend our national interests at the Peace Congress and secure our national future. We will be a worthy member of the family of free nations that the Congress will organise, and hand on to our children the Greece that past generations could only dream of.[7]

21

22 July 1917: Siam declares war on Austria-Hungary and Germany

Why on Earth Was Siam a Participant in the First World War?

Andrew Dalby

In 1914, when war broke out in Europe it was not clear to King Vajiravudh whether it was in his country's interest to become involved. Germany was a rare interloper in South East Asia and Austria was an irrelevance: alliance with them offered nothing, and could bring annihilation, because two enemies of Germany – Britain and France – were daily and dominant presences. All the territories that bordered Siam were ruled by one or the other. The choice lay, therefore, between neutrality (the correct choice if Germany were to win) and alliance with Britain and France.

Siam had little love for France, whose protectorate over Cambodia in 1863, takeover of Laos in 1893 and annexation of the remaining Cambodian provinces of Battambang and Siemreap in 1907 had steadily deprived it of a vast swathe of its protective northern and eastern borderlands. The nightmare year 1893, when France had asserted its views on Laos with the help of gunboats threatening Bangkok, was not easily forgotten. Britain had played a similar imperial game. When in 1909 the small states in the middle Malay peninsula were given up to British protection, much was lost for very little advantage. Yet, when in the early 1890s Siam's north-western border was defined at the impulse of the British Burma government, very little was lost. That remained the case when in 1895 the northern frontier was sealed off at the point where newly enlarged British Burma met newly French Laos; there, with the sacrifice of two small tributary states, Britain and France were induced to let Siam remain independent.

Meanwhile there was increasing cultural and educational contact with Britain. British tutors and advisers were a familiar sight at Court; selected young Siamese, many of them from the vastly ramified royal family, attended British public schools and universities. The King's youngest full brother, Prajadhipok, who had just left Eton for officer training at Woolwich when war broke out in 1914, begged King George V in vain to allow him to go on active service. Siamese contacts with France were more limited, but here, too, Siamese students could be found, nearly all of them scholarship students rather than scions of the nobility, enjoying both the intellectual and worldly pleasures of Paris. King Vajiravudh personally favoured alliance with Britain, where he had studied, and he was anxious that Siam should play its part in the world as a modern nation state. Nationalism in his terms included readiness to fight for one's country and for the right side.

The choice became inescapably clear in 1917. On 6 April that year the United States joined the war. All three of the non-Asian countries with which Siam had long-standing relations and close economic ties were on the same side. Hesitating no longer, Siam declared war on Germany and Austria on 22 July. A military mission, accompanied by motor-ambulances and an air corps, led by the King's trusted brother, Chakrabongse, reached Marseille in August 1918, just in time to participate in the last weeks of the war against Germany.

The reward followed quickly: an invitation to the Peace Conference, with an allocation of two seats at plenary sessions, and, although Siam did nothing notable in Paris, it became a founder member of the League of Nations.[1]

22

14 August 1917: China declares war on Austria-Hungary and Germany

Labourers in Place of Soldiers
Jonathan Clements

The outbreak of the First World War split the Chinese government over the best means of action. Its first public act, on 6 August 1914, was to claim Chinese territory and Chinese waters to be off-limits to 'belligerent operations'– a statement borne out of the fear that sovereign Chinese terrain might become a battleground between foreign powers. However, a faction in the government had already realised the opportunity that the war presented for ousting Germany from its colonial possessions, notably the vast Shandong (Shantung) peninsula on China's north-east coast.

The diplomat Wellington Koo made a somewhat optimistic attempt to ask America to persuade Britain and Germany to mutually agree that Shandong could be handed back to China, and thereby avoid any hostilities there. But even as China proclaimed its neutrality, President Yuan Shikai was already offering the British 50,000 Chinese troops for a joint operation to take back Shandong's major city, Qingdao

(Tsingtao), and the nearby German naval base at Jiaozhou (Kiaochow) Bay.[1] However, John Jordan, the British Minister in China, rejected this offer, seemingly because he already trusted in Allied (read: Japanese) capabilities.

Yuan Shikai's government remained split between a 'reserved faction', hoping to preserve Chinese neutrality, and a 'realistic faction' that argued that China's best chance of not suffering from the war was to enter it on the winning side. Determined to stay neutral, Yuan sent Koo to bring up the Root-Takahira Agreement of 1908 with the Americans, particularly the clause in which Japan and the United States agreed to respect China's territorial integrity. Surely, Koo argued, this must mean that Japan was obliged to consult the US before landing troops in China? However, America was understandably reluctant to place itself on a war footing against two putative allies, merely to defend a territory that was not even under Chinese control, and Washington quickly found a loophole. The powers were only expected to consult each other 'in the case of internal disorders in China', and a Japanese invasion of Shandong was not 'internal'.

On 18 January 1915, having swiftly wrested Shandong from Germany, Japan presented China with its infamous Twenty-One Demands for further territory and concessions, printed, with a superfluous and rather ominous flourish, on paper that bore a watermark of dreadnoughts and machine guns.[2] The Demands were a blatant move to bully China into handing over territory ahead of the end of hostilities; many of the clauses only made sense if one assumed, as the Japanese did, that the war and subsequent Peace Conference would see the Western powers losing influence in Asia, and creating a new vacuum of influence and conquest that the Japanese hoped to fill.

The Twenty-One Demands also contained veiled threats that, if Yuan did not agree, Japan would instead find a group of Chinese revolutionaries that did, and would then offer sufficient support to them in order to topple Yuan's government. The document effectively urged China to act as if already defeated, in order to avert an actual physical invasion. It was also intensely secretive – Japan wanted the agreement to be made without the knowledge of the international community.

It was the minister Liang Shiyi who offered a wily strategy for outmanoeuvring the Japanese. If China were to enter the war on the Allied side, it would secure a place in the post-war negotiations that would surely follow a German defeat. China would then be a victor dividing the spoils, with the ideal opportunity to regain control of former German colonies. But China was politically unstable, still divided between rival north and south regimes, and hardly in a position to contribute troops. Brilliantly, Liang suggested *yigong dabing* – 'labourers in place of soldiers'. This would not only involve China intimately with the Allies, in the supply of the one commodity that China had in abundance, but might also be parsed as a means of retaining China's neutrality. It was a decidedly oriental obfuscation, but it was hoped to argue that these laundrymen, trench-diggers and road-makers who replaced able-bodied European men were operating in a non-military capacity, even though their presence would free thousands of Europeans to fight at the front.

Yuan caved in to the Twenty-One Demands on 25 May 1915. Koo drafted the Chinese response, deliberately couched in terms that he hoped would be renegotiable at a later stage. Since everyone expected that the war would be followed by a peace conference at which various treaties could be discussed, Koo was careful to note that China had been 'constrained to comply with the full terms of the Ultimatum'.[3] Before the Paris Peace Conference had even been scheduled, it had become China's last hope of extricating itself from the deals made in 1915, and one on which Koo was already banking.[4]

The first negotiations with the French, for private companies to hire Chinese labourers, began in June 1915. In order to keep the deal non-governmental on both sides, Liang arranged for the setting up of a Chinese labour supply company, Huimin, in May 1916, and the first labourers began arriving by ship in France, despite German diplomatic protests, in August 1916. Around the same time, the British overcame their misgivings about Chinese labour and began to ship some in for themselves.

The 57-year-old Yuan had died in June after an ill-fated and farcical attempt to proclaim himself emperor.[5] By October 1916, Beijing was under the control of a new warlord, Duan Qirui, who served as premier and kingmaker in the Republican government, supposedly under the command of the President but with substantially more temporal power. Encountering recruitment difficulties for their labourers in Shandong, the British offered concessions to the Chinese, including a 50-year stay on payments of China's punitive Boxer Indemnity, freedom of the Chinese to raise taxes and the promise of a seat at the putative post-war peace conference.[6]

Eventually, however, it was Germany itself that provoked China into entering the war, or at least provided a valid enough excuse. On 24 February 1917, the French vessel *Athos*, carrying 'coolies' for the war effort, was sunk by a German submarine – the Kaiser having authorised a return to unrestricted submarine warfare. The *Athos* sank with the loss of 543 Chinese lives and China severed diplomatic relations with Germany on 14 March.[7]

China officially declared war on Germany on 14 August 1917. However, this only created new problems elsewhere. In Canton, Sun Yatsen suddenly gained enough funding to set up a rival government, under the auspices of the Movement to Protect the Constitution. Although it had the rhetoric of pacifism and diplomacy, its seed money was believed to have been supplied by the German consulate in Shanghai, which was hoping to cut down China's war effort by destabilising the Beijing administration that had proclaimed it.[8]

'Little, if anything, can be expected of China in a military way', wrote Carroll K. Michener in *The American Review of Reviews*. 'She has no navy, and though there are in China upwards of half a million men under arms, they are neither trained nor equipped for warfare of the sort that is waged at the present day'. However, as Michener went on to concede, China's resources, including its manpower, 'will bulk largely in the scales that shall weigh the world's peace'.[9]

Eventually, some 140,000 labourers were transported from China to Europe by early 1918, when the recruitment drive stalled due to lack of available shipping.[10] The Chinese workers were a ubiquitous presence in the European theatre, although their story was swiftly occluded by nationalist narratives and memory. Their most telling erasure from history was in 1918 in Paris, when they were literally painted over in the cyclorama of the *Pantheon de la Guerre* monument, in order to make way for images of the Americans.[11] In all, 2,000 Chinese labourers were eventually buried in graves in France, including a large plot at Noyelles, overseen by an oriental portico, and surrounded by peonies and willows, planted in evocation of their distant origin.[12] But their participation in the war, intended to secure China the restoration of its lost territory, would soon be betrayed by the Great Powers in Paris.

23

26 October 1917: Brazil declares war on Germany
The Wavering Road
Edoardo Braschi

The First World War brought Brazil into contact with all the major world powers in a mix of contrasting connections, historic and economic. The only South American country colonised by the Portuguese Empire, it had a predominantly Afro-Luso ethnicity and a non-Spanish-speaking community. Since gaining independence from Portugal in 1822, Brazil's main relationships had been with Europe, though it retained some limited contact with its continental neighbours. Its main focus was on internal development. The abolition of slavery in 1888 and the end of monarchy in 1889 marked the end of the old system which was replaced by a federal republic,[1] dominated by the powerful coffee producers of Minas Gerais and São Paulo on whose exports the country depended. Unfortunately income from these was not sufficient and Brazil had had to raise large loans on the London market, thus creating strong economic and financial links with the United Kingdom. Its ruling class also had historical and cultural bonds with France, where many had studied.

Between 1902 and 1912 the Foreign Minister, Luis Branco, established a special relationship with the United States, giving it a privileged voice on Brazil's international relations. The US saw Brazil as an attractive Latin American market and quickly became a key commercial partner, providing 40 per cent of Brazilian imports by 1915,[2] whilst the outbreak of the war offered a 'propitious moment to increase their exports'.[3] Brazil's relationship with Germany was also blossoming because of its strategic commercial business, especially in terms of credit and shipping facilities. In 1913, Germany's economic importance was second only to Britain and later was only surpassed by the United States.[4] Brazil also modelled its military on the German example, and numerous officials were trained in Germany between 1906 and 1910.[5] Furthermore, there were many Brazilians with German origins in the southern states of Santa Clara and Rio Grande and in the city of São Paulo.[6] This tangled context is essential to understanding Brazilian ambiguity and indecision when faced with the outbreak of the First World War. The country, torn between competing loyalties,[7] struggled to balance its inclination towards neutrality with external pressures from the United States, Germany, France and Britain, with the added complication that Brazil's own economic interests and diplomatic decisions were in conflict.

The outbreak of the war in 1914 came as a shock for the Brazilian elite and President Hermes de Fonseca immediately declared a 'rigorous neutrality' and non-intervention.[8] Although the press and many upper-class Brazilians clearly sympathized with the Allies, others did not. The conflict was quickly perceived as a distant European affair[9] but also became a catalyst for raising Brazilian nationalism.[10] War had a huge economic impact, drastically reducing exports to

Europe and blocking foreign cash flow, which was especially vital to support coffee prices. Imports fell as never before.[11] Measures such as Britain's 1916 Trading with the Enemy Act prevented British and French citizens and businesses from any dealings with the enemy, which automatically affected German-Brazilian businesses. The British blockade of Germany also deprived Brazil of its second largest coffee market.[12] This caused widespread resentment among the Brazilian public and occasioned a formal diplomatic protest to Britain.[13] In addition, as the conflict developed, important commercial bonds with Germany (the withholding of £6 million of coffee sales by a German bank and the economic pre-eminence of Hamburg) became powerful arguments 'for adopting a circumspect and conciliatory attitude to Germany'.[14]

On the other hand, the sinking of Brazilian ships, beginning with the *Rio Branco* on 16 May 1916, strained relations, though Germany sought, successfully, to pacify the situation. Tensions increased in January 1917 when Germany announced a policy of unrestricted submarine warfare. The threat of the closure of all trade with Europe made Brazil's position even more difficult.[15] On 5 April 1917, another Brazilian steamer, the *Paraná*, was torpedoed off the French coast and Brazil reacted by breaking diplomatic relations with Germany on 11 April. Yet Brazil reaffirmed its neutrality after America declared war on Germany on 6 April 1917.[16] Foreign observers described Brazil's diplomacy as a waiting game.[17]

Internally, public opinion and senior figures perceived such a policy as ineffective and dangerous. Much of the blame fell on Lauro Müller, the Brazilian Foreign Minister, who was of German extraction. He was accused of pro-German bias and identified as the main reason for Brazil's passivity. Similarly, President Venceslao Brás faced growing pressure from the public for his lack of resolution and his administration's wavering. In May 1917 Müller was forced to resign.[18] His replacement, Nilo Peçanha, steered a more pro-American and anti-German course, but Brazilian neutrality in the war only ended on 1 June after the sinking of a third Brazilian vessel, *Tijuca*, on 23 May.

American warships could now use Brazilian ports but Brazil was not yet ready to declare war. Even when the Americans released decoded dispatches from the German minister in Argentina, Count Karl von Luxburg, hinting at German intervention in Brazil, Brás did not act. Although suspicions revived about earlier German projects to create a 'New Germany' in Brazil,[19] the Brazilian government did not make this a *casus belli* with Germany, but used the information for propaganda purposes only after war was declared.[20] The Brazilian elite had a lingering fear of American imperialism and were also re-evaluating their European links,[21] but economic considerations were paramount. Brazil now requisitioned 43 German ships held in its ports and leased 30 of them to France, which also agreed to buy a huge amount of Brazilian coffee.

Only after the sinking of a fourth Brazilian ship, the *Macau*, did Brás declare on 23 October 1917 that 'Germany had imposed a state of war upon Brazil' that required a 'belligerent retaliation in order to maintain the dignity of the nation'.[22] On 26 October the Senate unanimously approved a resolution recognising and proclaiming 'the state of the war initiated by the German government against Brazil',[23] becoming the only South American country to enter the war.[24] Brazil became a co-belligerent state rather than a formal ally of the United States and its European partners.[25] Formally it 'made no declaration of war against Germany but merely took official recognition of the state of belligerency forced upon her by hostile acts' – a statement that neatly represented the enigmatic Brazilian attitude to a conflict in which it was determined not to be dragged too deeply.[26]

Brazil's entry into the war had been driven principally by repeated German attacks, but also depended heavily upon the outbreak of hostilities between Germany and the United States.[27] Though there was strong sentiment in favour of the Allies and pressure from America, nonetheless Brazil exercised its national sovereignty in its path to war. As the American Ambassador in Rio, Edwin V Morgan declared on 26 October that Brazil 'did not follow because we led'.[28] By entering the war Brazil hoped to legitimate its presence among the Great Powers and to stand apart from the other South American countries during the peace process. Although its economic links with Germany led it to act cautiously in the early part of the war, as it progressed Brazil perceived greater economic advantages from joining the United States and the Allies, particularly in finding markets for its vital coffee crop. Brazil's diplomatic attitudes during the war can be very much explained in accordance with its own imperative economic necessity.[29] Unsurprisingly, the issues of the confiscated German ships and the consignments of Brazilian coffee trapped in German ports became top priorities for Brazil at the Paris Peace Conference in 1919.

24

12 January 1918: Liberia joins the war
Why Did Liberia Enter the First World War?
Mariella Hudson

The last thing Liberia wanted was to join the First World War. The foundling nation had only been an independent state for 67 years when war broke out, during which time its primary concern remained the struggle for its own survival. Liberia's sovereignty and economy remained fragile, largely from decades of aggressive land-grabbing by colonising nations such as Britain and France. Under the control of these powers, the west African lands surrounding Liberia were swept into war. The lone black republic 'already and quite unavoidably at war with bankruptcy, sickness, and extreme want', declared neutrality.[1] However, when the United States joined the Allies in 1917, Liberia could no longer afford to remain neutral and lose its most valuable supporter.

Liberia was created by the resettlement of freed American slaves in West Africa after 1820. An independent state from 26 July 1847, it lacked much of the inward investment offered to neighbouring lands colonised by the British and French.

While much of the rest of West Africa benefitted from extensive railroad systems and trade routes, Liberia had access to neither rail, nor harbours, nor riverside piers.[2] The economy also suffered from its reliance on agriculture over industry.[3]

The colonial powers encroached heavily on Liberian territory. Under treaties in 1885 and 1892 France and Britain acquired a total of 60,000 and 30,000 square miles of new land respectively, including some of the best agricultural land, coastal frontages, rivers, huge tracts of timber, fishing regions, arable valleys, native-growing crops[4] and mineral resources including gold and diamonds.[5] As a result, by 1910 Liberia was a quarter of the size it had been in 1866, having shrunk from 171,000 square miles to 43,000 square miles.[6] It had also lost possibly up to half its native population.[7] The United States, to which Liberia made frequent, but fruitless, appeals did nothing.

The nation did have a successful economic relationship with Germany, and in the three years from 1895 to 1898 German-Liberian trade multiplied five-fold, constituting just under a third of all Liberian exports, mainly leopard pelts and ivory, but the First World War was an economic disaster for Liberia.[8] The market for such goods collapsed and the loss of trade links with Germany created a British monopoly, bringing Liberia 'near the point of starvation'.[9] It had negotiated a loan from the United States in 1911 but a further request for finance in 1916 was refused in 1917, just as America entered the war.

Liberia had neither the money nor the resources to maintain an effective army but although its Secretary of State, Charles King, foresaw it being 'swept inevitably into a torrent of strife like a dot of wood carried on the surface of a rampaging river',[10] on 12 January 1918 Liberia declared war on

Germany. It did so because it needed American financial support and hence had to fulfil the role envisaged for it by American Secretary of State, Robert Lansing, as 'an ally in waiting'.[11] Its reward would be to become the only independent African nation to join the League of Nations as a founder member.

25

5 November 1918: Poland declares Independence

From Fighting in Three Armies to the Proclamation of an Independent Poland

Anita Prazmowska

Prior to the First World War a Polish state did not exist. It had finally been divided between Austria, Russia and Prussia in the third partition in 1795, though the endeavours of Poles to regain their independence kept the Polish question alive throughout the nineteenth century. When the war began none of the partitioning empires envisaged that Poland would once more become a political reality. But when Germany and Austria-Hungary initiated military action against the Russian Empire, the question of Polish independence once more became an issue in the military and political considerations of the three empires.[1] The explanation of the conundrum as to how a non-existent state could become an international issue lies in the military situation, as the Central Powers sought local support and the financial resources to underpin the war effort – from Poland, as well as elsewhere. Polish nationals who hoped for independence were, at the same time, encouraged by pronouncements made by the military leaders on both sides. At the end of the war an independent Poland emerged mainly because of the military collapse of the three empires that had controlled Polish territories before the war, but also because Polish national consciousness and organisational structures were sufficiently developed to enable Polish leaders to create a Polish government to supersede the German and Austro-Hungarian administrations.

Military action on Polish land

When war broke out, it was the Poles' misfortune that the fighting in the east took place mainly on ethnically Polish territories. Initially, Germany presumed that a swift victory in the west would require only minimal deployment of troops in the east. But when stalemate ensured on the Western Front, the Entente Powers imposed an economic blockade on the Central Powers. This caused Germany's military leaders to focus on what resources they could secure in the east. Thus the war on the Eastern Front had two objectives, to defeat Russia and to obtain the much needed resources that would enable Germany and Austria to continue the war. German and Austrian military leaders in the occupied Polish areas clashed both over which power would determine the Poles' fate and who had the right to exploit their lands.[2]

In the opening days of the war German troops entered the Russian-occupied Polish Kingdom areas without meeting any opposition. The Russian army had initially targeted military action against Austria-Hungary. On 15 September 1914, after a French request to relieve the pressure on Paris, the Russians changed their tactics and moved against the Germans in East Prussia. On 29–30 September General Hindenburg scored a major victory against the Russians at Tannenburg, followed by a German victory in the Battle of the Masurian Lakes.[3]

There was no consistent pattern to the military confrontations between the Russian and the Austro-Hungarian armies on Polish territories, with wins and losses on both sides. The initial Austro-Hungarian thrust into the Polish Kingdom in August was successful, resulting in the occupation of Chełm, Lublin, Kielce and Radom. In eastern Galicia the Russians were victorious, claiming the previously Austrian-held towns of Lwów, Przemyśl and Rzeszów. During the second half of September the Russians forced the Austrians out of the Lublin region that they had taken only weeks before,[4] and then, at the beginning of October, a joint German and Austrian action ousted the Russians from the Austrian territories and German forces stood poised to occupy Warsaw. However, the Russians regrouped and, once more on the offensive, retook Kraków, Łódź and Piotrków. This brought the military situation to a stalemate.

The offensive restarted in the spring of 1915 when, on 4 May, the Germans and Austrians breached the Russian front at Gorlice. Austrian troops reclaimed Przemyśl and Lwów. During the summer Austrian troops again took Lublin, while German troops advanced further into the Polish Kingdom, taking Warsaw (5 August), Modlin (20 August) and in the north Grodno (2 September) and Wilno (Vilnius) (18 September).[5] By October 1915, when the offensive stopped, the whole of the Polish Kingdom territories were under the administration of the Central Powers The German front stretched from the south to the north, running from Tarnopol, along the towns of Pińsk and Baranowicze to west of Riga on the Baltic coast, though the Germans did not capture Riga itself. The Russians had halted the German and Austrian advances but neither side could claim victory. The military situation on the Eastern Front was at an impasse.

The Polish Question

From the outset, neither Germany nor Austria-Hungary intended Poland to become an independent state. Their main priority was to exploit to the full the occupied territories. When the Austrian army had first entered the Polish Kingdom in August 1914 they established a skeleton Austrian administration (from which Poles were excluded) in order to raise revenue; but Russia's rapid recapture of these lands prevented this.[6] Germany did not initially plan to take territories in the east, and only started discussing occupation of a German-dominated state in the east after the early victories over the Russians in East Prussia. While it was generally agreed that the Polish Question would have to be addressed, within German military circles there was little clarity on it, so for the time being they decided to leave the matter to the Austrians.[7]

The two Central Powers quarrelled nevertheless over exploitation of the Polish coal mines. In September 1915 when the German and Austrian armies entered the Dąbrowa Basin area, after it had been abandoned by the Russians, the German military authorities immediately seized all the functioning mines. The Austrians protested and debates at the highest level determined how the exploitation of Polish resources would be jointly administered.[8] Further military successes highlighted the need for a clear policy on the division of Polish areas. In December 1915, it was agreed that Austria would establish its administration in the town of Kielce (later moved to Lublin). The Germans had control of the left bank of the Wisła River, with Warsaw the seat of their administration. Although they agreed to cooperate, as Austrian attention shifted to the Adriatic and the military confrontation with Italy, Germany came to dominate decision-making regarding the future of the occupied Polish territories.

Poles were not consulted during these first years of war. In all three empires they simply had to comply with mobilisation orders. They responded to the outbreak of the war in different ways, depending on where they lived and their wartime experiences. Poles within the Russian Empire cheered troops marching through Warsaw, giving voice to their approval of the war against Germany. This might have been just a sign of Poles succumbing to the general euphoria about the war, but it perhaps also indicates their deep dislike of Germany. It has been suggested that had the war been between the Russian and Austrian Empires, the Poles would have supported Austria, the least oppressive of the three partition Powers. Unlike the German and Russian governments, the Austrians never pursued a policy of eradicating Polish culture and language.[9] When they allied with Germany, however, this fed Polish antipathy towards Austria. Moreover, Russian victories might lead to the consolidation of Polish territories under Russian rule, which would be preferable to German domination of the region.

In Galicia, which at the outbreak of the war was part of the Austro-Hungarian Empire, popular opinion favoured the Austrian war effort against the hated Russian Empire, with local committees formed to offer support. On 28 July 1914, representatives of the Central National Committee encouraged the Austrian government to believe that its war against Russia would be supported by a national uprising in the Polish Kingdom areas. The Austrians, for their part, gave the

Poles vague assurances that after the war the Polish Question would be resolved. In German-held Poznań and Pomerania, civilian response to the outbreak of the war was unanimously hostile, but the efficiency of German mobilisation forced Polish men to comply with the call-up.[10]

All three partitioning powers employed censorship and wartime propaganda to reduce desertions and dissent. In their appeals to the Polish communities to rally against the enemy, each drew attention to the anti-Polish policies of its opponents. When the three empires finally issued separate statements about the future of Poland, this was a carefully calculated move designed to create problems for their opponents or to realise some particular immediate advantage. Current military rather than long-term political considerations influenced responses to the Polish Question: none of the three empires supported the Poles' wish for independence.

On 14 August 1914 Grand Duke Nicholas of Russia issued a Proclamation to his Polish subjects. For all its references to the resurrection of Poland, he made no real commitment to its restoration as an independent political state. On the contrary, the appeal for the Poles' support merely referred to the reunification of the Polish nation 'under the sceptre of the Russian Czar. Poland will be revitalized, free in her own faith, in her language, in self-government.'[11] As vague as this promise was, it was what some Polish leaders had hoped to hear. Roman Dmowski, a Polish representative to the Russian Duma and the leader of the National Democratic movement, had earlier advocated that the Poles should collaborate with the Russian Empire in order to combat Germany, which he saw as the greatest enemy of the Polish nation. The Grand Duke's declaration now emboldened some Poles who had already started planning some form of Polish voluntary units to fight in the war. When these proposals were put to the Russian army command, however, it quickly became apparent that the Poles hoped that these units would eventually become part of a larger Polish army. Since the Tsarist regime did not want to commit to this, the Polish plan was rejected as premature.[12]

In October 1914 the Russians agreed that the Poles could form the Puławski Legion, a separate partisan unit rather than part of the Tsarist army. As the Russian governor of the Polish Kingdom and Russian military command did not want to encourage patriotism among the Polish volunteers who joined it, the legion's role was somewhat restricted and was subject to contradictory instructions that tended to change frequently.[13] In May it was used to fight German units in the battle of Pakosław. Its military contribution can only have been minor, but for the Poles the existence of distinctly Polish units, with Polish commanders who used the Polish language in their communication with the soldiers was of enormous propaganda importance.

German long-term policies towards Poland and the Polish Question were determined initially by the hope that a peace treaty could be signed with Russia. Thus they did not wish to make any promises to the Poles. But in October 1914 the Prussian Minister of the Interior explained that it was not in Germany's interest to see the reconstruction of Poland, weak or strong, as in either case it would most likely ally itself with Russia. He was equally dismissive of any suggestion that the ethnically Polish territories might be united within the Austro-Hungarian Empire. As he explained, if Austria were dominated by Slav interests it would drift away from collaboration with Germany.[14] In the spring of 1916, when hopes of a separate peace with Russia receded, German political and military leaders once more deliberated the long-term future of the Polish territories. By then the idea of a Polish entity within the Austro-Hungarian Empire had been abandoned because the German High Command intended to incorporate the recently captured Baltic areas into Prussia. Instead, they now considered forming a Polish state which would be subordinate to Germany.[15] Such plans were, of course, dependent on military considerations, and when Germany occupied Warsaw ministers opened a dialogue with the Polish political elites, thus indicating that the door was open to other proposals.

Some Poles still hoped the Austrians would allow the creation of a Polish Kingdom within their empire with an arrangement akin to the Austro-Hungarian compromise of 1867, their aspirations encouraged by Austria's tolerance of Polish culture and Vienna's willingness to allow the Poles to raise their own military units. In 1910, the Austrian government had legislated to allow national groups to form riflemen's associations. The plan had been that these paramilitary organisations would play some, as yet unclear, role in the event of war with Russia.

In 1908 Józef Piłsudski, a leader of the Polish Socialists, had moved from the Russian to the Austrian-controlled Polish territories because he thought the Russians were unlikely to allow Polish independence. With Austrian approval, he established a Polish riflemen's association. On 12 August 1914, with Austrian tacit approval, Piłsudki led a group of approximately 150 riflemen into the Russian territories, hoping to spark a national uprising against the Russians. This would allow him to expand his military unit, now named the Polish Legion, into a regular army which would march onto Warsaw. In fact the passage of armed men in uniforms bearing Polish emblems caused only panic. The Austrians recalled Piłsudski and told him that the Polish Legion would be incorporated into the regular army under direct Austrian command. During the following months Piłudski struggled to retain control over the Polish units, refusing to cooperate in the recruitment of more Poles without receiving an assurance that they would remain under his command.

Polish lands under occupation

The war had a devastating effect on the Polish territories, not least because all three powers did their utmost to use whatever resources were available for their own war efforts, despite the clear consequences for the local civilian populations. When the Russians withdrew, they dismantled industrial plant and machinery and transported it to the interior. The workers were evacuated alongside the factories in which they had worked (in due course this would create a refugee problem). Where evacuation was not possible, industries and mines were destroyed, causing widespread unemployment in previously prosperous towns[16]

In the villages, the people were traumatised by military activities which paid little regard to their needs and safety. As a result most peasants did not care who won the war: it made little difference to them which armies marched through their fields and villages, all were equally destructive. The situation became more stable once the Polish territories were occupied by the Central Powers, but those who hoped for greater sympathy with Polish aspirations were quickly disabused. Far from being their liberator from Russian domination, the Germans and Austrians soon came to be seen as simply another occupying force, and just as determined to exploit Polish lands in aid of the war.

The two Central Powers' need of manpower, more than any other consideration, finally forced them to make political commitments to the Poles. In September 1916 the Austrians agreed to transform the Polish Legion into a Polish Auxiliary Corps, but they refused to appoint Pilsudski as its commander. On 18 October German and Austrian military leaders agreed to the creation of an independent Polish state to encourage Polish recruitment. On 5 November the Act of Two Emperors proclaimed the reconstruction of an independent Polish state. This was followed by an announcement that recruitment to a Polish Army would begin immediately.[17] In order to bolster the claim that a truly independent Polish state was being formed, the German authorities appointed an Interim Council of State which was to rule on behalf of the Poles, hand-picking wealthy Polish industrialists and landowners to guide their country to genuine independence. Piłsudski, unsurprisingly, remained sceptical. His anxiety was that the Germans would cynically use Polish soldiers without making any real commitment to the Polish cause.

The Entente Powers and the Polish Question

Meanwhile, in the West, most obviously in Paris, there were attempts to encourage political debate on the Polish Question. For French leaders the matter had both political and military implications and they found themselves in a quandary. On the one hand, they did not want to irritate the Russians by insisting that they make a commitment to the creation of an independent Polish state; on the other, it was obvious that any promises made to the Poles could destabilise the Germans and Austrians in the battle on the Eastern Front. The front line changed dramatically over Poland during the first two years of the war. Russian opposition to the emergence in France of Polish interest groups also played a role in French reticence in taking up the Poles' case.

Prominent Poles made direct appeals for support for their cause to the British, French, and finally also the US government. Inevitably, their lobbying activities were accompanied by plans to form Polish units which would fight alongside the French. These would symbolise the Polish contribution to the Entente war effort but, offering the French assistance at a time of great shortage of manpower, was also a means of eliciting post-war promises. Unfortunately, this initiative was not as politically useful as had been hoped, as the two Polish units formed were incorporated into the French Foreign Legion.

Among the self-appointed emissaries representing the Polish cause was the Polish pianist Ignacy Paderewski, who was residing in Switzerland when the war broke out. He and a number of other well-known Poles formed a Polish Victim Relief Fund – in reality, from the outset also a lobbying group that aimed to get the French government to make the restoration of Poland one of its war aims.[18] In 1915 Paderewski visited London, then toured the USA, where he lectured on Poland's independence and tried to raise funds. While all these activities increased international awareness of the Polish cause, they did not sway the French and British governments, which still needed Russia as their ally. In December 1915, Dmowski who had earlier thought that Poland would be best served by close collaboration with Russia, also arrived in Paris. Despairing of Russian support, he now concentrated on obtaining French and British backing. His efforts were only partly successful because his extreme nationalist ideas and well-known anti-Semitic views repelled politicians in both democratic countries.[19]

1916-1918

On 5 November 1916, Germany and Austria declared that they intended to restore Poland to the European map. This, more than any other event, forced the other Powers to declare their hands. The result was that the Polish Question became an issue in all debates on war aims. As most of the Polish territories had been part of the Russian Empire and had since been lost to Germany and Austria, Russia was the first to respond to the German-Austrian announcement – though only after the British and French governments had pressed the Russians to make a reasoned riposte to it. Boris Stürmer, the Russian Prime Minister, said that after the war the Polish regions would be united and granted autonomy within the Russian Empire. On 25 December Tsar Nicholas reiterated this commitment, and the new authority that took control following the Russian Revolution in February 1917 also repeated it. On 28 March, Pavel Milyukov, the Minister for Foreign Affairs of the Provisional Government which took power after the Tsar was forced to abdicate, issued a call to the Poles to unite in fighting the Central Powers. Since the Provisional Government was loath to make commitments before the elections to a constituent assembly, it did not make any firm promises on the Polish issue, only very general commitments to the restoration of a free Polish state, without any indication of its borders.[20]

Poland's future was fast engaging the attention of Poles of all backgrounds. In the German- and Austrian-occupied Polish areas hopes rose that, indeed, an independent Polish state would be established at the end of the war. While the German and Austrian authorities had been careful not to hand decision-making to the Poles, they had abolished the stringent Russian censorship laws and allowed publication of newspapers and books in Polish. This meant that the future of Poland could be openly debated and political leaders and others discussed it extensively.

Piłsudski, rather than the Interim Council of State, was now seen as the true defender of Polish interests. He had started to have doubts about cooperation with the Germans, which whom he came into increasing conflict. Public attention focused on his efforts to build a Polish army and his clashes with the German High Command. In April 1917 control over the Polish Legion had been transferred from the Austrians to the Germans, and for the first time Polish officers in the uniforms of the Polish Legion were seen in Warsaw. Piłsudski's reputation grew, and with it his role in determining German policies on the Polish Question. He was seen as the de facto Polish Minister for War. This, however, caused the German authorities to have doubts about the wisdom of the extensive recruitment drives to Polish military units, and their earlier promises and concessions – some of which they now tried to claw back.. By April the conflict between Piłsudski and the Legion and the German authorities was clear. When the Germans decided to change the Legion's status to that of units of the *Wehrmacht*,[21] Piłsudski objected. In July 1917, the Germans responded by imprisoning him – which only enhanced his reputation as a patriot.[22]

By the beginning of 1917 the Entente Powers had moved from viewing the Polish issue as a Russian problem to realising that pronouncements made by the Central Powers required them to respond. The outbreak of the Russian Revolution and the decrease of military activities on the Eastern Front meant the Entente Powers no longer had to worry about upsetting their Russian ally. They were also more willing to undermine the German war effort by appealing to Poles under German control. On 15 August Polish exiles in Switzerland and France formed the Polish National Committee (Komitet Narodowy Polski – KNP) to coordinate the work of Polish organisations in the West but, more importantly, to represent Polish political interests. The KNP renewed its call to raise further Polish units in France to fight with the Entente Powers.[23] On 20 September the French government recognised the KNP as an organisation which represented Polish interests. Britain followed suit on 15 October. On 30 October the US and Italian governments did likewise.

The Polish cause benefited from additional developments. On 22 January 1917 American President Woodrow Wilsons declared to the Senate that an independent and free Poland should be restored to the map of Europe. This he reinforced in Point 13 of the famous Fourteen Points declaration made on 8 January 1918, which stated that world peace would depend on an independent Poland. The October Revolution in Russia and the Soviet government's decision to sign a peace treaty with Germany in March 1918 tipped the balance finally and decisively. In June 1918 France and Britain declared that the restoration of Poland with access to the sea was one of their war aims. But the KNP did not want Poland to be treated merely as an object of Great Power politics. This explains why they continued with the calls for the formation of Polish military units to fight Germany. The French government appreciated the chance of further manpower which is why it signed a military agreement with the KNP stipulating that a Polish Army in France was to fight in the West under the command of General Haller.

These early discussions of the Polish Question with the Entente Powers were dominated by Dmowski, the leading personality with the KNP, while Paderewski remained for the time being in the United States, where he continued to lobby on Poland's behalf and raise funds. They both confidently anticipated that the Entente Powers would win the war, and that as a result the KNP would become the first government of an independent Poland. Both men thought in terms of a diplomatic victory, one whereby the winning side would recognise the principle of the restoration of Poland and then facilitate the process of defining its borders. Least of all did they expect that a Polish leader who had allied himself first with the Austrians and then with the Germans, would have a final say in the emergence of the first administration in Poland and furthermore would lead the fight to define Poland's borders in the north-east, the east and in the south-east.

In 1917 the situation in the Polish territories was far from clear. The outbreak of the Revolution in Russia meant that the Germans knew that the Russian war effort had come to an end. With no one to contest them, they did not need to be sensitive to Polish wishes, and they quickly reduced their commitment to the establishment of an independent state. The Austrians too felt that there was no need for their further involvement and passed responsibility for dealing with the Polish Question to the Germans. The changing situation also impacted on the Poles who now more forcefully than before divided along a number of lines. The pro-Russian and anti-German groups lost out, but those who had believed that Germany could be trusted also had doubts because of Piłsudski's arrest and the conflicts over the Polish military units. Revolutionary sections of the Socialist parties and trade unions, inspired by the Revolution in Russia, became vocal. The German and Austrian authorities tried to reduce the influence of the left-wing movements and sought cooperation with those who likewise feared revolutionary upsurges among the troops and workers.

Poland stood poised on the brink of a political revolution but also a nationalist one. In the circumstances, the German authorities established a Regency Council to collaborate with the two occupying powers. Consisting once more of hand-picked Polish conservatives, it was given the task of preparing an outline of the structure of an independent Polish state.[24] It was opposed by other political groups – the Socialists, peasant parties and the National Democratic parties – and although these were not fully formed national parties, they nevertheless proceeded to discuss the political future of an independent Poland.

The final German offensive in the west started in March 1918 but petered out in July, by October when it ended in defeat the Poles were preparing to take over those areas which they considered should be incorporated into their independent state.

The emergence of a free state of Poland

On 10 November 1918 the German authorities freed Piłsudski. His arrival in Warsaw turned into a triumphal procession. Polish military units, first in Warsaw and then in the rest of the Polish areas, transferred their allegiance to him as commander. The Regency Council handed over to Piłsudski the responsibility of forming a government. German troops withdrew after being disarmed, but without putting up a fight.[25]

Piłsudski benefited from the fact that other parties, even the Socialist Party which had harboured some radical aspirations, were willing to accept his authority. The Legion, together with Poles from the Austrian and German armies, now joined the newly formed Polish Army under Piłsudski's command. The road ahead was to be a difficult one. On the diplomatic front, the leaders of the KNP accepted reluctantly that Piłsudski and not they would form a first government. They nevertheless agreed to act as Polish representatives to the Paris Peace Conference where the battle for formal recognition still had to be fought. The borders of the new state, in particular in the east, were far from fixed. Local conflicts between national groups flared up with bloody consequences. Where possible the Polish army was deployed in support of the Polish communities. At the end of the First World War the existence of an independent Polish state was a reality against which no one could argue. Its final form, territorially and politically, was something that would be fought over throughout the following years.

26

28 June 1919: The Treaty of Versailles – part I
The End of the War and Peacemaking 1919
Alan Sharp

The First World War ended almost as precipitously as it had begun. In March 1918 Germany launched a massive offensive on the western front which nearly drove a wedge between the British and French armies. Subsequent attacks continued to menace Paris until June, but, like the other huge gambles that Germany had taken in seeking rapid victory in 1914 and launching unlimited submarine warfare in 1917, this also failed. In July and August the tide turned as the Allied Commander-in-Chief, Marshal Ferdinand Foch, unleashed a wave of offensives that forced the German armies into a steady retreat. Meanwhile Germany's allies crumbled. Bulgaria was granted an armistice on 29 September, whilst the Ottomans and Austria-Hungary began negotiations leading to their respective armistices on 30 October and 3 November. Faced with these defections and the prospect of apparently limitless supplies of men and munitions flooding across the Atlantic, Germany, on 4 October, sought an armistice from the American President, Woodrow Wilson. After an exchange of correspondence and negotiations with his allies this was granted and, at 11 am on 11 November 1918, the guns on the western front fell silent.[1]

Some 8 to 10 million servicemen had died, many more were wounded, some incapacitated physically or mentally for life. Millions more would die in continuing inter- and intra-state wars after 1918 and others would remain unborn because of wartime separations. These figures would be dwarfed by the effects of a virulent worldwide influenza epidemic whose spread was assisted by the massive wartime movements of men and goods. The British Treasury estimated £24 billion (in 1914 gold values) as the cost of Allied victory. In northern France and Belgium an area equivalent to neighbouring Holland lay devastated, leaving a legacy of human sacrifice and lethal debris which is still being unearthed a century later. In eastern Europe and the Balkans the damage was less concentrated but equally destructive.

The peacemakers who gathered in Paris in early 1919 faced the gargantuan task of reassembling a world that had torn itself apart. Their problems were compounded by the vacuum of power in eastern and central Europe caused by the sequential collapse between February 1917 and November 1918, of the Russian, Austro-Hungarian and German empires and the total defeat of the Ottomans. Former subjects of these multi-national empires now vied with each other to establish new states, justifying themselves on the principle of national self-determination, an idea that was easier to express than to apply in areas where an ethnographic map resembled a complex mosaic rather than neat, consolidated blocks. As an added concern, the spectre of revolution was, like Banquo's ghost, an unwelcome guest at the conference table as Russian bolshevism offered an alternative to Wilson's liberal vision for great swathes of Europe bereft of authority.

For six months Paris became the home of the leaders of the world's most powerful states as they tried to identify and deal with the problems that had led to war and the additional damage and complications that it had created. The conference opened on Saturday 18 January 1919, deliberately and ominously chosen to mark the forty-eighth anniversary of the proclamation of the German Empire in the Hall of Mirrors at Versailles following Prussia's victory in the Franco-Prussian war. It was dominated by the great powers, first in the Council of Ten (the heads of government of America, Britain, France, Italy and their foreign ministers, together with two Japanese representatives), the principal decision-making body until March 1919, and then in the Council of Four (Georges Clemenceau, David Lloyd George, Vittorio Orlando – respectively the French, British and Italian premiers – and Wilson) which replaced it until June. Their foreign ministers – Stephen Pichon, Arthur Balfour, Sidney Sonnino and Robert Lansing, together with Baron Makino of Japan – became the Council of Five, which undertook much of the detailed work on the new frontiers of Europe and the treaty with Austria. The smaller states were limited to brief appearances before these bodies: a few places on commissions or a meaningless and formal role in the Plenary Conference, which met only nine times; Clemenceau was characteristically blunt, telling them 'I make no mystery of it – there is a conference of the Great Powers going on in the next room.'[2]

By the end of March, with very little decided, pressure mounted on the leaders to find solutions to intractable international problems but also to tackle the complexities of redirecting the policies of their own states to accommodate the necessary adjustment from total war to peace. In a hectic six weeks the Four broke the log-jam of issues that seemed poised to wreck the conference. They argued, fought, threatened, compromised, but, crucially, they decided – often in a piecemeal and uncoordinated manner, but they heeded Clemenceau's admonition that 'Il faut aboutir' ('We must reach conclusions'). On 7 May the draft treaty, a hastily assembled document that no-one had read in its entirety, was handed to the German delegation at the Trianon palace. There were no face-to-face negotiations, the Germans were permitted to send written observations, most of which the Allies rejected. On 16 June Germany was given the final text of the treaty and, on 23 June, an ultimatum: sign within twenty-four hours or the war would resume. It capitulated and the treaty was signed on 28 June. This was not the end of peacemaking: treaties followed with Austria on 10 September, Bulgaria on 27 November, Hungary on 4 June 1920 and the Ottomans on 10 August 1920. When Mustafa Kemal overthrew the Ottomans, creating the modern state of Turkey, this final settlement was renegotiated at Lausanne, where the treaty was signed on 24 July 1923. Peacemaking had taken longer than the war itself.[3]

THE UNITED STATES OF AMERICA, THE BRITISH EMPIRE, FRANCE, ITALY and JAPAN,

These Powers being described in the present Treaty as the Principal Allied and Associated Powers,

BELGIUM, BOLIVIA, BRAZIL, CHINA, CUBA, ECUADOR, GREECE, GUATEMALA, HAITI, THE HEDJAZ, HONDURAS, LIBERIA, NICA-RAGUA, PANAMA, PERU, POLAND, PORTUGAL, ROUMANIA THE SERB - CROAT - SLOVENE STATE, SIAM, CZECHO - SLOVAKIA and URUGUAY,

These Powers constituting with the Principal Powers mentioned above the Allied and Associated Powers,

of the one part ;

And GERMANY

of the other part ;

Bearing in mind that on the request of the Imperial German Government an armistice was granted on November 11, 1918, to Germany by the Principal Allied and Associated Powers in order that a Treaty of Peace might be concluded with her, and

The Allied and Associated Powers being equally desirous that the war in which they were successively involved directly or indirectly and which originated in the declaration of war by Austria-Hungary on July 28, 1914, against Serbia, the declaration of war by Germany against Russia

27

28 June 1919: The Treaty of Versailles – part II
The Signature of the Treaty of Versailles
Alan Sharp

On Saturday 28 June 1919 those fortunate enough in the British delegation to have been allocated tickets for the Hall of Mirrors in the palace of Versailles, where the treaty with Germany would be signed, drove by motor car to the ceremony. The ladies, who were consigned to the terrace outside, had a less comfortable ride, squeezed into three dirty lorries. Esme Howard, a British diplomat recorded: 'The avenue up to the chateau lined with cavalry especially lancers all in French grey blue & steel helmets of same colours with lances with red and white pennons made a fine show.' The hall was very full – perhaps 1,000 people, thought Howard – and photographs show others standing on chairs in the corridors craning to catch a glimpse of proceedings. James Headlam-Morley, another British representative, thought the surroundings magnificent but was unimpressed by the ceremony.[1]

At 3 pm Clemenceau ordered 'Faites entrer les Allemands'. Johannes Bell and Hermann Müller proceeded, in silence,

Europe 1923

to seats opposite the rose and sandalwood table previously owned by Louis XIV and specially chosen by Clemenceau. Howard noted: 'They walked like men in a dream.' After Clemenceau made a short speech and it had been translated, the Germans signed, using their own fountain pens to thwart a French attempt to provide them with a pen supplied by the Leagues to recover Alsace-Lorraine.[2]

Sir William Orpen's painting, *The Signing of the Peace in the Hall of Mirrors, Versailles,* portrays the occasion as a much more orderly and dignified business than it actually was. In contrast to the canvas his eyewitness account described a hubbub of noise and movement in the hall as the Allied leaders penned their signatures:

> These were written without any dignity. People talked and cracked jokes to each other across tables. Lloyd George found a friend on his way up to sign his name, and as he had a story to tell him, the whole show was held up for a bit, but after all, it may have been a good story. All the 'frocks' [politicians] did all their tricks to perfection, President Wilson showed his back teeth; Lloyd George waved his Asquithian mane; Clemenceau whirled his grey-gloved hands about like windmills; Lansing drew his pictures and Mr Balfour slept.[3]

Orpen proved more successful in creating order from chaos than the subjects of his painting but he had the enormous advantage of being able to portray and manipulate them to his will. He impishly included himself as the figure bent in silhouette in the arched window behind Lloyd George and Clemenceau, and, more symbolically, added Orlando, who was not there, and omitted Smuts, the South African delegate who had signed the treaty only with the greatest reluctance, who was. The peacemakers were less fortunate; their ability to control events diminished as their armies dispersed or was often non-existent in the more remote corners of Europe and the wider world where they had no means available to enforce their decisions.

By 3.40 pm the ceremony was over, a 101-gun salute boomed, and the newsreel cameras captured Wilson, Clemenceau and Lloyd George on the terrace. The British representatives returned to Paris where their government treated them to an extra course at dinner – and free champagne, which Harold Nicolson pronounced very bad. Afterwards Howard and his wife 'walked back after to Majestic at about 1 a.m. People dancing singing in the street dragging cannons, pushing cars backwards etc. a v. good humoured carnival.' Clemenceau declared it 'une belle journée' (a wonderful day), Nicolson demurred, and Headlam-Morley regretted that it had, 'in every detail complied with the utmost insult to Germany ... Just the necessary note of reconciliation, of hope, of a change of view, was entirely wanting'. The conference which had begun on 18 January, the anniversary of the proclamation of the German Empire in the Hall of Mirrors in 1871, now 'laid the German Empire in the dust in the very place where it had risen in its glory.'[4]

28

The Peace Settlement Reviewed
Alan Sharp

The conflict the 1914 decision-makers had risked was not as short and successful as they had hoped and its consequences were much deeper and longer-lasting than they had imagined or intended. It was the seminal event of the twentieth century, becoming a test not simply of military prowess but of the ability of governments to respond to the challenges of total war, with those that failed experiencing defeat and revolution in varying degrees of intensity. Even victory did not guarantee the survival of a state's existing political structures, as Italy would soon discover. The peace conference now faced the formidable task of rebuilding a shattered world with the added difficulty that, in their 5 November 1918 pre-Armistice agreement with Germany, they had committed themselves to producing a settlement based on Wilson's inspirational articulations of liberal values in his 1918 speeches.[1]

The League of Nations
For Wilson the conference's key task was the creation of the League of Nations, embodying a new international order to

prevent the recurrence of such a disaster. In under a month, working from a composite Anglo-American script and driven by himself and his deputy, the prominent British Conservative, Lord Robert Cecil, his Commission presented the draft League Covenant to the Plenary Conference on 14 February 1919. Lord Eustace Percy, a British diplomat, judged that, 'As a matter of cold historical fact [the League] happened because Cecil and Wilson wanted it – and for no other reason!'[2]

Wilson's first draft of the Covenant in January 1919, like earlier British and French proposals,[3] had proposed an automatic sanction: 'Should any Contracting Power break or disregard its covenant ... it shall thereby *ipso facto* [automatically] ... become at war with all the members of the League.' This represented the core of his alternative international organisation, collective security, the absolute guarantee by all the members of a universal alliance of the political independence and territorial integrity of each member faced by an attack launched before all the League's mechanisms had been exhausted. The concept posed a revolutionary challenge to national sovereignty because this commitment meant that the fundamental decision for war or peace would be taken for each member by another government which had broken its international pledges. Faced with constitutional protests from his advisers and concerns from his major allies, Wilson amended his proposal, which eventually became Article 16: 'Should any Contracting Power break or disregard its covenant ... it shall thereby *ipso facto* be deemed to have committed an act of war against all the members of the League'. Now each member could formulate its own response, thus depriving the system of the immediacy and certainty on which it depended for its credibility.[4] Clemenceau spoke for many when he declared, 'There is an old system of alliances called

Turkey and the Near East 1923

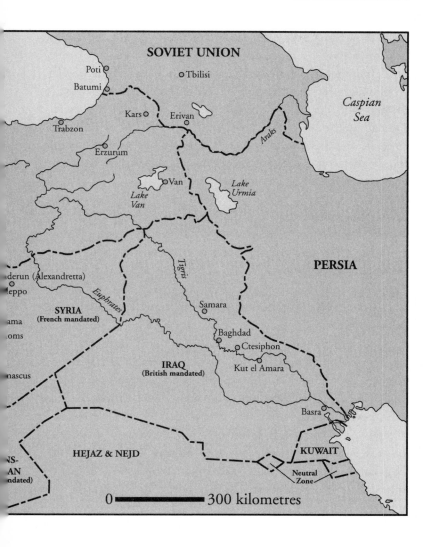

the Balance of Power – this system of alliances, which I do not renounce, will be my guiding thought at the Peace Conference.'[5] Nonetheless the conference found the League helpful in side-stepping the principle of self-determination to provide France with coal from the Saar and Poland with the use of Danzig as a port without awarding either state sovereignty over the respective inhabitants. It was also passed responsibility for minority protection for some national groups left on the wrong side of the new frontiers.[6]

The post-war world

A useful guide to measuring how stable international relations are likely to be at any given time asks whether an analysis of the attitudes of the principal actors suggests that they support or oppose the present state of affairs: are they *status quo* or revisionist in outlook, and what is the overall balance between them? There can be little doubt that many states in Europe and beyond in the 1920s and 1930s were revisionist, but whilst they might oppose the existing state of affairs they did not agree on what should replace it and very often their views on an alternative order were deeply opposed. The next key question is whether singly or collectively they had the power to translate aspirations into actualities. Throughout the 1920s and early 1930s they did not, but that balance began to alter radically as the 1930s progressed. It is also interesting to note that it is normally taken for granted that winners will favour the *status quo* and losers revision and, whilst this held true of the losers, this was not the case for many of the gainers from the post-war settlements.

To the east of Europe the Soviet Union gradually emerged from the wreckage of Tsarist Russia as the Bolsheviks triumphed in the complicated struggles following the fall of the

Romanovs. It posed a dual challenge to the settlement either as a centre of revolution or as a disgruntled state. In principle it was the ultimate revisionist, believing that the existing order of states was about to be overturned by the worldwide revolution which it was its function to promote and encourage. Normal diplomatic relations with other states were pointless since they would soon vanish. Yet, despite brief communist control of Munich and a slightly longer-lived regime in Hungary, by 1920 reality suggested that the world was not about to turn red. Foreign Minister Georgy Chicherin, called the Treaty of Tartu with Estonia signed on 2 February 1920, 'the first experiment in peaceful coexistence with bourgeois states' – a phrase more usually associated with the 1950s and 1960s.[7]

Even so, despite concluding border agreements with various neighbours, the Anglo-Russian trade treaty in 1921 or the more controversial Rapallo treaty with Germany in 1922, the Soviet Union's international stance was always ambiguous, preceding Fascist Italy and Nazi Germany in confronting other states with the problem of interpreting whether their actions and ultimate aims were driven by ideology or *realpolitik*. Although it was gradually able to reassert control over briefly independent areas like Georgia, Ukraine, Armenia and Azerbaijan the USSR suffered major territorial losses as a result of the First World War, civil conflict and subsequent confrontations. Finland and the three Baltic states gained their independence and, after the dramatic events of the Russo-Polish war of 1920, its frontier with Poland ended much further to the east than that recommended by the Paris Peace Conference. Unsurprisingly it wished to reverse these losses, though its power to do so was, for the moment, limited.

Moving west, newly independent Latvia, Lithuania and Estonia together with Romania, Poland and Czechoslovakia each had unfulfilled ambitions which made relationships between them difficult. In some cases they owed their very existence to the unpredictable sequential collapse of Austria-Hungary and the German and Russian empires and, even if Austria-Hungary had disappeared, it seemed inevitable that Russian and German power would eventually revive. In those circumstances it was essential that they cooperate to preserve their mutual independence but they did not. Disputes about territory and resources, like that between Czechoslovakia and Poland over Teschen, bedevilled relations between what the Germans referred to as 'season states' – states with limited life-spans. When Hitler dismembered Czechoslovakia in 1938 and 1939 the actions of neighbours who swooped to satisfy old territorial scores was symbolic of this disunity, which the French, hopeful of creating some sort of menace on Germany's eastern borders to compensate for the loss of their pre-war Russian alliance, viewed with despair, convinced as they were that Germany would attack the settlement in the east before turning west.[8]

Under the Treaty of Trianon Hungary lost two-thirds of its pre-war territory and nearly sixty per cent of its people, consigning some one-third of its Magyar population to become minorities in neighbouring states. It was a bitter revisionist throughout the inter-war period, moving closer to Hitler's Germany and eventually joining the Axis powers in the Second World War. Unlike Germany, however, Hungary did not have the power to support its demands for the revision of a settlement that emerged in June 1920, partly from decisions already taken about other states, at a time when, as one Hungarian official perceptively remarked, the Allies 'were frightfully bored by the whole Paris Peace Conference.'⁹

The tiny German-speaking rump state of Austria did not seek independence in 1919, instead wanting to join Germany. Given the difficulty the Allies had experienced in defeating Germany, and despite the tenets of self-determination, they were never going to allow Germany to increase its population by 8 million Austrians or 3 million Sudetenlanders from Czechoslovakia or to gain strategic advantages ensuring domination of the Balkans. Despite this unhappy beginning, compounded by enormous financial and economic problems, the Austrian republic came to value its national sovereignty before Hitler's forced *Anschluss* in March 1938 and re-emerged as an independent state after the Second World War. It might be classed, therefore, as one of the unexpected successes of the settlement.¹⁰

Germany clearly did not regard the settlement as a success and, throughout the period of the Weimar republic, the electorate made it plain that they expected their leaders to seek revision of the treaty, preferably by peaceful means. Most, including Hitler in *Mein Kampf*, accepted the loss of Alsace-Lorraine and few resented the transfer of part of Schleswig to Denmark, after a plebiscite, promised by Bismarck in 1864 but long postponed. The territory ceded to Poland was a very different matter: Germans regarded Poland as a failed state whose people had proved incapable of self-government in the eighteenth century and saw the transfer of Germans to Polish rule as intolerable. They resented the disarmament imposed by the treaty and saw reparations as a harsh burden. Gustav Stresemann, often portrayed as the acceptable face of Germany in the inter-war period, made no secret of the initial changes he wished to implement in the wake of the

1924 Dawes Plan, under which American credits to Germany seemed to have provided an answer to the problem of reparations, and the 1925 Locarno agreements. He accepted Germany's western frontiers but sought the return of Upper Silesia, Eupen-Malmédy and Danzig, a renegotiation of the access rights of the Polish Corridor, the reinstatement of full German sovereignty over its own territory and policies, proper protection for German minorities abroad and the recognition of Germany as a major power, to be symbolised by a permanent seat on the League of Nations Council and the right to hold colonial mandates. Germany may have suffered much fewer losses proportionately than Hungary but its greater international weight meant that it was the most important revisionist state even before Hitler came to power.[11]

Fearing for the future of France, with its smaller and ageing population, Clemenceau was acutely aware of the disparity both in population and birth rates between Germany and France. He believed, notwithstanding the settlement's adjustments, that a restored Germany would be much more powerful than a France which owed its present victory to a coalition of powers secured by a combination of skill and luck. In an ideal world France too would be a revisionist power – seeking to make the treaty even tougher – and indeed Poincaré's occupation of the Ruhr basin in January 1923 may have had this amongst its aims.[12] For the most part, however, French leaders accepted that Clemenceau had negotiated the best deal he could get, given that he had (apparently) secured a guarantee of French security from Britain and the United States, a long-term occupation of the Rhineland with the right to remain if Germany did not execute the treaty, a share of reparations, various restrictions on Germany's military and economic capacity, diminutions of German resources, including the product of the Saar coalfields for France, and a reduction of Germany's population and territory. In these circumstances France was thus the main defender of the post-war settlement in Europe. Its hope that Britain would be its major partner in executing the treaty would be sadly disappointed.

There was dismay in the British delegation about the draft treaty communicated to the Germans on 7 May. Joint meetings of the delegation and the cabinet, summoned to Paris for the purpose on 1 June, empowered Lloyd George to return to his negotiating partners to seek amendments to the clauses on the fate of Upper Silesia, reparations, the length and cost of the Allied occupation and German membership of the League. On the whole he did not enjoy huge success, except in obtaining a plebiscite for Upper Silesia, but this did not deter those who believed that revision was required and it has been argued that the inter-war British policy of appeasement – seeking to redress wrongs perceived to have been done to Germany – began in Paris.[13]

Britain was generally open to revision, tending to believe German leaders when they asserted that certain aspects of the treaty could not be fulfilled, but it also pined for a previous golden age in which it had, apparently, been able to divest itself of European responsibilities and concentrate on its destiny as a worldwide empire. It was difficult to convince the British that recent events had demonstrated that, without security in Europe, there could be no imperial security and that they had an active role to play in preserving European stability. They also found it hard to forget a past in which the enemy was France. There was a tendency to believe that Germany was no longer a menace but that France, in building submarines and a bomber force whilst maintaining the largest continental army, was reverting to type. As Paul Cambon, the veteran French ambassador in London remarked wanly to his successor, 'the misfortune is that the English are not yet aware that Napoleon is dead.'[14] The failure of the two principal European powers to cooperate on a firm policy of either treaty execution or revision was a tragedy.[15]

Belgium was entitled to particular consideration given its wartime experiences and losses but found its main ambitions at the peace conference blocked by Britain and France. Territorially, it hoped to regain areas lost in 1839, notably Luxembourg and parts of Holland, with the Dutch gaining German territory in compensation. But Paris in 1919 was not Vienna in 1815, such arrangements were now out of fashion, and the peacemakers, like the Dutch, would have none of it. Thus it gained only small amounts of German territory in Europe and Africa.[16]

Amongst the victors Italy was perhaps the most intense of the revisionist powers, choosing to regard a settlement in which it had made substantial strategic gains, not all of which could be justified in terms of self-determination, as the reflection of a 'mutilated victory'. The award of South Tyrol gave Italy an Alpine frontier with the tiny state of Austria on the Brenner Pass, whilst its gains in Dalmatia and Istria offered opportunities for further penetration of the Danubian basin and the Balkans. Yugoslavia, even with its French patron, did not present the same challenge to Italian influence as the pre-war powers had done. Whilst Italy did not make all the imperial gains it sought, the issue which caused deep resentment at home and huge problems both in Paris and beyond, was Fiume. Wilson, in particular, was determined to make no concession to the Italian demand for the city, which was not part of the bargain agreed in the 1915 Treaty of London and which was deemed to be an essential outlet to the Adriatic for Yugoslavia. Orlando's failure to convince his colleagues of the Italian case led him to quit the conference in April 1919, only to return empty-handed in early May, and was one of the reasons behind the downfall of his government on 19 June. Resentment at Italy's treatment, anger that its sacrifices were not sufficiently recognised and disappointment with the settlement, together with the deep divisions that entry into the war had already created, were major factors in the crisis of Italian liberal parliamentarianism which brought Mussolini and fascism to power in October 1922. Throughout the 1920s, and with increasing boldness in the 1930s, Mussolini's Italy was, as far as it dared to be, a revisionist state, determined to show the greater efficacy of fascist government in attaining its rightful dues.[17]

In the Balkans Bulgaria was the most dissatisfied of several unhappy states. Like the Germans, but possibly with more realistic expectations, the Bulgarians had hopes that they might benefit from the application of the principle of self-determination. They did not, losing Western Thrace to Greece and with it access to the Aegean, and also some strategically important land to Yugoslavia. Bulgaria actually lost little of its pre-war territory or population, but its neighbours expanded. Greece had fifty per cent more territory and population after the war than before, Romania doubled its size and people and Yugoslavia had three times more territory and population than pre-war Serbia.

Even so none was completely satisfied and each continued to seek readjustments to the settlement. Greek ambitions in Asia Minor suffered bloody defeat by Mustafa Kemal's revived Turkey, including the massacre of the Greek population of Smyrna, leading to a painful forced exchange of populations. Only one of Yugoslavia's seven frontiers was undisputed, whilst its wider ambitions clashed with those of the Italians. Its claim to the Banat of Temesvar was fiercely challenged by Romania, creating one of the most complicated tangles for the conference to settle, with massaged statistics, carefully distorted maps, great power rivalry and threats of the use of force all having an influence on the eventual partition of the area. This left 75,000 Romanians and 65,000 Slavs on the wrong sides of the new frontier, emphasising the impossibility of any perfect ethnographical solution in a region of intermingled populations.[18]

The Turks had to wait until 10 August 1920 for the Treaty of Sèvres, the last of the original five Parisian settlements. By then, however, as Kemal's nationalist revolt in Anatolia gathered momentum, circumstances were so different the Sultan's signature had no value. Sèvres was never ratified and, by the autumn of 1922, following a near renewal of hostilities after a confrontation between British and Turkish forces at Chanak, the Allies found themselves engaged in formulating the only negotiated settlement after the First World War with the victorious Kemal's representatives. The Treaty of Lausanne, signed on 24 July 1923, recognised the new secular Turkish republic, restored much of the territory in Europe and Asia Minor ceded under Sèvres, removed all the financial and extra-territorial privileges previously enjoyed by the great powers and, with the exception of new rules for the passage of warships through the Straits and a small demilitarised zone there, Turkey was restored to full sovereignty. Lausanne, negotiated by parties who had experienced both victory and defeat, proved to be the most successful and longest lasting of all the post-war treaties.[19]

In the former Ottoman possessions in the Middle East serious and enduring local rivalries were compounded by the ambitions of outside powers, most notably Britain and France, which had made a number of conflicting wartime promises or implied commitments to a variety of potential clients and to each other. The Hashemite clan dreamt of an independent Arabia including much of the Levant (the area of the Eastern Mediterranean). Their ambitions, apparently endorsed by British undertakings in 1915 given in the hope of encouraging an Arab revolt against the Ottomans, foundered on the determination of the British and French to control the area, on family feuds and on their own inability to defeat other Arab leaders with similar aims to establish hegemony.

The British refused to recognise Hussein, the Sherif of Mecca and titular leader of the Arab Revolt, as the King of the Arabs, accepting him only as the King of the Hejaz. Increasingly estranged from his sons, Feisal and Abdullah, whose success in acquiring their own thrones he resented, Hussein made a fatal blunder in 1924 by declaring himself Caliph, provoking the formidable Ibn Saud to invade and conquer the territory, driving him into exile. Ibn Saud eventually combined the Hejaz and Nejd into the kingdom of Saudi Arabia in 1932, embittering still further his relations with the Hashemites. Hussein's third son, Feisal, the effective leader of the Arabs throughout the military campaign and peace negotiations, tried to establish a kingdom in Syria, but this collapsed under French military pressure in July 1920. His subsequent and unforeseen reappearance as the King of Mesopotamia (Iraq) in 1921 came about as part of a British attempt to retain control of the region but to limit the costs involved after a serious revolt the previous year. His brother Abdullah was recompensed for renouncing any claim on Iraq by becoming the Emir of Transjordan (Jordan) in 1923. Feisal and Abdullah both retained ambitions to wrest control of

Syria from the French, each harboured dreams of leading a unified Arab state, and neither was an especially easy client for the British to handle.[20]

The establishment of Transjordan meant that the British, by dividing historic Palestine along the line of the Jordan river, were partially reneging on the promise given to the Jews in the Balfour Declaration to make it their national home. The practicalities of managing Jewish immigration and land purchase without alienating the existing population or exceeding productive capacity were extremely problematic. The repercussions of events elsewhere in the Arab world further complicated matters, spilling over into Palestine. Communal disturbances, leading to deaths in Jerusalem in 1920 and Jaffa in 1921, seemed to confirm the pessimistic predictions of British ministers opposed to involvement in the area that they would be left holding the line between discontented Arabs and disappointed Jews, though they still accepted the League of Nations mandate for Palestine on 24 July 1922.[21] It proved to be an awesome task.[22]

The First World War left the British empire both more secure and yet more vulnerable, since it was so large and difficult to police. The major conventional outside threats from Germany or Russia had dissipated and its other potential rivals were, for the moment at least, its allies. The sea routes through the Mediterranean and the Suez canal, or round the Cape of Good Hope, were secure. South Africa now controlled South-West Africa (Namibia) and Australia New Guinea (Papua New Guinea), and together with New Zealand, various islands south of the equator in the Pacific, removing any pre-war German menaces. Yet for each of the Dominions their wartime experiences and sacrifices had increased their sense of a separate identity and an awareness of interests which did not necessarily coincide with those of the 'mother country'. Even though it was George V's right to ratify the Treaty of Versailles simply on the advice of his Westminster parliament, it was judged politic to allow each of the Dominions to consider and approve the settlement before he did so. The marked lack of response from the Dominions to Britain's appeal for aid against Turkey during the 1922 Chanak crisis was a further indication that the world of 1914 had gone forever. Additionally, in India in particular, but also elsewhere in Africa and Asia, less official voices calling for self-determination were growing in strength, with the war exposing the myth of European invincibility and Wilson's apparent endorsement reinforcing existing and emerging movements. Violent unrest in Egypt and Ireland, which some attributed to the power of Bolshevik propaganda and influence, stretched British resources and emphasised that the major threats were now internal and ideological. These twin themes of increasing Dominion independence at one level and colonial discontent at another suggested interesting times ahead.[23]

In Asia the major loser, despite being an Allied power, was China whose hopes of regaining control of Shandong (Shantung), leased to the Germans under pressure in 1898 and reassigned to Japan under agreements forced upon it by the Japanese in 1915, were disappointed at the conference. This unleashed a portentous student protest in Beijing on 4 May 1919 and left a legacy of great bitterness in a deeply divided and troubled land. The immediate effect was that China refused to sign the Treaty of Versailles; in the longer term it increased its suspicion of the West and encouraged more militant Chinese nationalism.[24]

The major winner in the Far East was Japan which

emerged as an important regional power, temporarily gaining Shandong, which it returned to China after American pressure in 1922, and the German islands north of the equator in the Pacific. Its proposal of a racial equality clause in the League Covenant embarrassed Wilson and Cecil who were both aware of the strong opposition on the American west coast and in Australia and New Zealand to any measure that might increase the possibility of Japanese immigration. Wilson used a dubious technicality to defeat the motion. The payback came when Wilson, already under pressure from the Italian withdrawal from the conference and fearing that Japan would do likewise, conceded that it rather than China should have Shandong. At the same time, Japan's demands upon, and treatment of, China and its expansion into the Pacific, taken together with the naval implications of its alliance with Britain, underlined growing uncertainty in the United States about the ambitions of this emerging regional power.[25]

In addition to their concerns in the Far East, many Americans were deeply worried about the League of Nations and its implications for the United States and there was, among Irish and German-Americans in particular, anti-British and French sentiment. Wilson also had many bitter political opponents. Even so, given some judicious and properly presented concessions, he might have fulfilled his assurance to Smuts that he could pass the treaty through the Senate. Instead, on 19 November 1919 and again on 19 March 1920, a combination of a stubborn unwillingness to compromise together with sheer political ineptitude, perhaps born of a querulous invalid's growing sense of betrayal, ensured that he failed. America, whose financial, economic and, finally, military intervention in the war had been decisive, and whose contribution to peacemaking had been profound, now sought to withdraw, politically and militarily at least, into its pre-war shell.

The implications were enormous and far-reaching. America withdrew from all aspects of treaty enforcement, whether in terms of the occupation of Germany or of the membership of various commissions. If Lloyd George's strategy really was to play for time and count upon the Americans to assist Britain to ameliorate Germany's reparations bill, it collapsed because, instead of an American chair in a commission of five powers (America, Belgium, Britain, France and Italy) there were now only four members, with the French chair having a casting vote in the unlikely event that the Italians would risk the unnecessary alienation of France by siding with Britain against the usual Franco-Belgian combination. Any hope of packaging reparations and inter-allied debts into an overall settlement was destroyed by America's determination to enforce the repayment of its wartime loans. Most important of all, Wilson's League, widely touted as the safety mechanism which would correct the inevitable mistakes made in the pressure cauldron of Paris, was orphaned, left in the reluctant care of Britain and France, which disagreed at Geneva as they did elsewhere.[26]

Conclusion

It is clear that in the wake of the peace conferences there were more powers dissatisfied with their lot than those that were satisfied. On the other hand, even with the lamentable absence of the United States from the ranks of those responsible for treaty execution, Britain and France, whether or not supported by Italy, held the main levers of power in the post-war world and would continue to do so throughout the 1920s. It is also indisputable that, in September 1939, a second major conflict did begin and the key indictments against Versailles must centre on those terms that allegedly made such an outcome inevitable – perhaps including reparations, some of the new frontiers (particularly the Polish-German border) and the general treatment of Germany. Yet, inevitability is a concept that sits very uneasily with most historians and it must be questionable whether it is reasonable to hold the peacemakers of 1919, the last of whom left office for ever in October 1922, accountable for the decisions taken by their successors, who might have followed many alternative turnings on the road that it is claimed led directly from 1919 to 1939.[27]

The peace treaties have not enjoyed a sparkling reputation. In the words of Jan Christian Smuts, the South African delegate, 'such a chance comes but once in a whole era of history – and we missed it.'[28] The disappointment of many of the British and American experts found an effective voice in one of the most influential (and tendentious) polemics of the twentieth century, *The Economic Consequences of the Peace* by John Maynard Keynes. Leaving his role in Paris as a British Treasury adviser in June, Keynes had, by December 1919, published a coruscating attack on the peacemakers and all their works, condemning their settlement as vindictive and unworkable and casting a long shadow over future assessments of the treaties.[29] The prevailing perception remains that this was a huge opportunity spurned, that the treaties at the end of the war to end war and to make the world safe for democracy delivered neither outcome and that they had a large responsibility for the establishment of the dictatorships of the inter-war period and the outbreak of a second conflagration in 1939. Yet politics is the art of the possible and the peacemakers in Paris were constrained by domestic expectations, the limits of their own power to implement decisions and the overwhelming nature of their task. What is surprising is less that their settlement was imperfect, but that there was any settlement at all.[30]

Germany's revenge for the 1918 armistice came in the same railway carriage in the same clearing at Compiègne in June 1940. Many of the armistice terms were simply those of 1918 reversed. Versailles was dead – and yet the European territorial settlement in 1945 retained a remarkable similarity to that of 1919 and the victors were swift to revive the idea of a new international organization to replace the League, despite its poor record in the 1930s. The Nuremberg and Tokyo trials of Nazi and Japanese leaders resurrected, with greater success, the post-1919 attempt to extend the concept of war crimes beyond the operational to those responsible for political and military decisions. The legacy of 1919 would continue beyond 1945.

Notes

1. Introduction

1. Zara Steiner, *The Foreign Office and Foreign Policy 1898–1914* (Cambridge University Press: 1969) p 153
2. The Chinese delegation refused to sign and did not attend.
3. J A S Grenville, *Lord Salisbury and Foreign Policy* (Athlone Press, London: 1970) pp 165–6.
4. The principle is attributed to Nathan Bedford Forrest, a Confederate general in the American Civil War. On war planning, see Hew Strachan, *The First World War. Volume I: To Arms* (Oxford University Press: 2001) pp 165–207.
5. Christopher Clark, *The Sleepwalkers: How Europe went to War in 1914* (Penguin, London: 2013) pp 251–8, 285–8.

2. Serbia, Sarajevo and the Start of Conflict

1. See Ivo J Lederer, *Yugoslavia at the Paris Peace Conference: A Study in Frontiermaking* (Yale University Press, New Haven, CN: 1963); Andrej Mitrović, *Jugoslavija na Konferenciji mira, 1919–1920* (Zavod za

izdavanje udžbenika, Belgrade: 1969); Dejan Djokić, *Pašić and Trumbić: The Kingdom of Serbs, Croats and Slovenes* (Haus Publishing, London: 2010). I would like to thank Professor Ljubinka Trgovčević of Belgrade University for her comments on an earlier draft of this chapter.

2. See Thomas A Emmert, *Serbian Golgotha: Kosovo, 1389* (East European Monographs, Boulder, CO: 1990); Thomas A Emmert and Wayne S Vucinich (eds), *Kosovo: Legacy of a Medieval Battle* (University of Minnesota Press: 1991); Dejan Djokić, 'Whose Myth? Which Nation? The Serbian Kosovo Myth Revisited' in Jànos M Bak et al. (eds), *Uses and Abuses of the Middle Ages: Nineteenth to Twenty First Century* (Wilhelm Fink, Munich: 2009) pp 215–33.

3. Aleksandar-Aca Pavlović, *1914: Ljudi i događaji, ideje i ideali* (Jelena-Lela Pavlović, Belgrade: 2002) p 7.

4. Ibid, p 9.

5. Jovan M Jovanović, *Borba za narodno ujedinjenje, 1914–1918* (Geca Kon, Belgrade: 1935) p 19. Jovanović was Serbia's minister in Vienna during the events of June–July 1914. He bore no relation to, nor is to be confused with, several other Jovanovićs referred to in this text.

6. Among them was Dragoljub Jovanović, future leader of the Left faction of the inter-war Agrarian Union party. See his *Političke uspomene* (12 volumes, Kultura, Belgrade: 1997), Vol 1, p 52.

7. Mark Cornwall, 'Serbia' in Keith Wilson (ed), *Decisions for War, 1914* (UCL Press, London: 1995) pp 55–96, p 56.

8. See Christopher Clark, *The Sleepwalkers: How Europe Went to War in 1914* (Penguin, London: 2013) pp 367–76.

9. Andrej Mitrović, *Srbija u Prvom svetskom ratu* (2nd, revised edition, Stubovi kulture, Belgrade: 2004) pp 10–11. (English edition: *Serbia's Great War, 1914–1918*, Hurst, London: 2007).

10. Vladimir Dedijer, *Sarajevo 1914* (2 volumes, Prosveta, Belgrade: 1978) Vol 1, p 226. An earlier version was published in English as *The Road to Sarajevo* (MacGibbon & Key, London: 1967).

11. Princip and Čabrinović met in Sarajevo in 1912 and were brought together by, among other shared interests, their admiration of William Morris's *News from Nowhere*. A copy of the book with their signatures has been preserved. Dedijer, *Road to Sarajevo*, p 201.

12. The Bosnian-born Yugoslav Nobel prize-winning writer Ivo Andrić belonged to the revolutionary milieu of the Young Bosnia, as did several other prominent Croat and Serb writers. See Predrag Palavestra, 'Young Bosnia: Literary Action, 1908–1914', *Balcanica*, No. 41 (2010) pp 155–84, and a Young Bosnia-themed issue of the literary magazine *Gradac*, No. 175–77 (2011), guest-edited by Muharem Bazdulj.

13. The figures are from Vladislav Škarić, Osman Nuri Hadžić and Nikola Stojanović, *Bosna i Hercegovina pod austrougarskom upravom* (Geca Kon, Belgrade: 1938), as quoted in Ivo Banac, *The National Question in Yugoslavia: Origins, History, Politics* (Cornell University Press, Ithaca, NY: 1984) p 367n. See also Dedijer, *Road to Sarajevo*, pp 347–8; Mitrović, *Srbija*, pp 18–32.

14. Milada Paulová, *Jugoslovenski odbor: Povijest jugoslovenske emigracije za svjetskog rata od 1914–1918* (Prosvjetna nakladna zadruga, Zagreb: 1924); Connie Robinson, 'Yugoslavism in the Early Twentieth Century:

The Politics of the Yugoslav Committee' in Dejan Djokić and James Ker-Lindsay (eds), *New Perspectives on Yugoslavia: Key Issues and Controversies* (Routledge, London: 2011) pp. 10–26.

15. Mitrović, *Srbija*, p 11.

16. Mitrović, *Srbija*, pp 7–9, 15; Fritz Fellner, 'Die "Mission Hoyos"' in Vasa Čubrilović (ed), *Velike sile i Srbija pred Prvi svetski rat* (SANU, Belgrade: 1976) pp 387–410, and an appendix to the chapter: Alexander Hoyos, 'Meine Mission Nach Berlin', pp 411–18.

17. Clark, *The Sleepwalkers*, pp 402–3, 412.

18. See Andrej Mitrović, *Prodor na Balkan: Srbija u planovima Austro-ugarske i Nemačke, 1908–1918* (Zavod za udžbenike, Belgrade: 2011; first published 1981). Vernon Bogdanor has recently argued that the main reason for the war between Belgrade and Vienna was a conflict between German and South Slav nationalisms. See his lecture 'Sir Edward Grey and the Crisis of July 1914', delivered at the Legatum Institute, London, on 26 September 2013; available at: http://www.li.com/docs/default-source/default-document-library/sir-edward-grey-and-the-crisis-of-july-1914---with-vernon-bogdanor-(transcript)---september-2013.pdf, last accessed 5 March 2014.

19. Noel Malcolm, *Bosnia: A Short History* (Macmillan, London: 1996) p 150. See also Clark, *The Sleepwalkers*, Chapter 2.

20. As well as a small, but important, Jewish community which in 1910 totalled 11,868 people (0.6 per cent): Mitja Velikonja, *Religious Separation and Political Intolerance in Bosnia-Herzegovina* (Texas A & M University Press, College Station, TX: 2003) p 126.

According to the 1879 census, Serbs made up 43 per cent of the population of Bosnia-Herzegovina, Muslims 38 per cent and Croats 18 per cent: Robin Okey, *Taming Balkan Nationalism* (Oxford University Press, 2007) p 8.

21. See Okey, *Taming Balkan Nationalism*.

22. An English translation of the poem, by Amila Čelebić, is available at the 'Spirit of Bosnia' website, http://www.spiritofbosnia.org/volume-1-no-4–2006-october/stay-here/, last accessed 5 March 2014.

23. Dimitrije Djordjević, *Carinski rat Austro-ugarske i Srbije, 1906–1911* (Istorijski institut, Belgrade: 1962); Stevan K Pavlowitch, *Serbia: The History Behind the Name* (Hurst, London: 2002) pp 81–2; Michael Boro Petrovich, *A History of Modern Serbia* (2 volumes, Harcourt Brace Jovanovich, New York: 1976) Vol 2, pp 548–54, 562–4.

24. Pavlowitch, *Serbia*, p. 82; Petrovich, *History of Modern Serbia*, Vol 2, pp 554–62; Olga Popović-Obradović, *Parlamentarizam u Srbiji od 1903. do 1914. godine* (Službeni list SRJ, Belgrade: 1998); Dubravka Stojanović, *Srbija i demokratija, 1903–1914* (UDI, Belgrade: 2003).

25. Meštrović's major, and never completed, project, was *The Vidovdan Temple,* inspired by Kosovo mythology. See Andrew B Wachtel, *Making a Nation, Breaking a Nation: Literature and Cultural Politics in Yugoslavia* (Stanford University Press, 1998) pp 55–9.

26. Djordje Stanković, *Nikola Pašić i jugoslovensko pitanje* (2 volumes, BIGZ, Belgrade: 1985) Vol 2, pp 11–12.

27. For a contemporary analysis of the Zagreb and Friedjung trials, see RW Seton-Watson, *The Southern Slav Question and Habsburg Monarchy* (Constable & Co., London: 1911) Chapters 9 and 10. For a version of

events more sympathetic to Austria-Hungary, see Clark, *The Sleepwalkers*, pp 87–90.

28. Dedijer, *Sarajevo 1914*, Vol 1, p 18.

29. [General] Panta M Draškić, *Moji memoari* (SKZ, Belgrade: 1990) pp 76–7.

30. Ljuba [Ljubomir] Jovanović, 'Posle Vidova Dana 1914. godine', in *Krv slovenstva, 1914–1924: Spomenica desetogodišnjice svetskog rata* (Štamparija Save Radenkovića i brata, Belgrade: 1924) pp 9–23, p 15; Mitrović, *Srbija*, pp 11–12.

31. Novica Rakočević, *Crna Gora u Prvom svjetskom ratu, 1914–1918* (ITP 'Unireks', Podgorica: 1997), pp 23–6; Mitrović, *Srbija*, pp 13–14.

32. J M Jovanović, *Borba*, p 22.

33. Petrovich, *History of Modern Serbia*, Vol 2, pp 612–18; Mitrović, *Srbija*, pp 58–67; Clark, *The Sleepwalkers*, pp 451–67.

34. J M Jovanović, *Borba*, p 25.

35. Clark, *The Sleepwalkers*, p 456; J M Jovanović, *Borba*, pp 25–7.

36. J M Jovanović, *Borba*, p 26.

37. Draškić, *Moji memoari*, p 83. In a gentlemanly act, the Austrians arranged for Putnik's safe passage to Serbia. He promptly assumed the command of the Serbian army and oversaw its successful defence and counter-attack in August–September.

38. J M Jovanović, *Borba*, pp 27–8; Petrovich, *History of Modern Serbia*, Vol 2, p 616.

39. Petrovich, *History of Modern Serbia*, Vol 2, p 617.

40. Clark, *The Sleepwalkers*, p 464. The Austrian official was Alexander Musulin von Gomirje, who was of Croat origin.

41. Mitrović, *Srbija*, pp 67–8.

42. Lj. Jovanović, 'Posle Vidova Dana', pp 9–23, p 9. The citations are taken from an English translation, 'The Murder of Sarajevo', *Journal of the British Institute of International Affairs*, Vol 4, No. 2 (March 1925) pp 57–69, p 57.

43. Edith M Durham, 'Fresh Light on the Serajevo [sic] Crime', *Contemporary Review* (January 1925), pp 39–49; Sidney Bradshaw Fay, 'The Black Hand Plot That Led to the World War', *Current History*, Vol 23, No. 2 (November 1925) pp 196–207.

44. RW Seton-Watson, *Sarajevo: A Study in the Origins of the War* (Hutchinson, London: nd [1926]) pp 157–8.

45. Branislav Gligorijević, *Parlament i političke stranke u Jugoslaviji, 1919–1929* (ISI/Narodna knjiga, Belgrade: 1979) pp 207–9.

46. Dedijer, *Sarajevo 1914*, Vol 2, pp 117–19, 121. See also Vladimir Dedijer and Života Anić (compilers), *Dokumenti o spoljnoj politici Kraljevine Srbije* (10 volumes, SANU, Belgrade: 1980) Vol VII, Part 2.

47. Cornwall, 'Serbia', pp 56–7.

48. Dedijer, *Sarajevo 1914*, Vol 2, p 137.

49. J M Jovanović to RW Seton-Watson, Belgrade, 12 August 1925, in Hugh Seton-Watson et al (eds), *R.W. Seton-Watson and the Yugoslavs: Correspondence, 1906–1941* (2 volumes, British Academy & University of Zagreb – Institute of Croatian History, London & Zagreb: 1976) Vol 2, pp 138–9.

50. Dedijer, *Sarajevo 1914*, Vol 2, pp 137, 341–2n. Clark (*The Sleepwalkers*, pp 60–1) gives a good summary of this episode, but his contention that, in retrospect,

Pašić instructed Jovanović to issue a vague warning as 'a covering manoeuvre' is unconvincing.

51. Dedijer, *Sarajevo 1914*, Vol 2, pp 137–40.
52. Mitrović, *Srbija*, pp 35–6.
53. Slobodan Jovanović, *Apis: Moji savremenici*, Vol 10 (Avala, Windsor, Canada: 1962); David MacKenzie, *Apis: The Congenial Conspirator: The Life of Colonel Dragutin T. Dimitrijević* (East European Monographs, Boulder, CO: 1989); David MacKenzie, *The 'Black Hand' on Trial: Salonika, 1917* (East European Monographs, Boulder, CO: 1995); Milan Živanović, *Pukovnik Apis: Solunski proces 1917* (Milan Živanović, Belgrade: 1955); Veselin Masleša, *Mlada Bosna* (IP 'Veselin Masleša', Sarajevo: 1964).
54. Mitrović, *Srbija*, pp 5, 68 (for eyewitness statements); Petrovich, *History of Modern Serbia*, Vol 2, p 618.
55. Mitrović (*Srbija*, p 509) estimates that nearly 370,000 Serbian soldiers and at least 600,000 civilians died. More conservative estimates exist, but it is generally accepted that due to a combination of fighting, starvation and disease, Serbia's population losses during the war were in relative terms higher than those of any other country.

3. The Dual Monarchy Stumbles into War

1. G Vermes, *István Tisza* (New York: Colombia University Press, 1985) pp 217, 219; Sean McMeekin, *July 1914: Countdown to War* (Icon Books, London: 2013) pp 27–8.
2. Vermes, *Tisza*, pp 80, 117, 224; Luigi Albertini, *The Origins of the War of 1914*, 3 volumes (originally published Milan, 1942; trans and ed Isabella M Massey, Oxford University Press: 1953) Vol II, p 126; Bryan

Cartledge, *The Will to Survive: A History of Hungary* (3rd edition, C Hurst and Co, London: 2011) pp 286–7; Margaret MacMillan, *The War That Ended Peace: How Europe Abandoned Peace for the First World War* (Profile Books, 2013) p 464; Christopher Clark, *The Sleepwalkers: How Europe Went to War in 1914* (Penguin, London: 2013), p 397; McMeekin, *July 1914*, p 32.

3. Albertini, *Origins of War*, Vol II, pp 127–8; Clark, *The Sleepwalkers*, p 398; McMeekin, *July 1914*, p 41.

4. The Archduke was referring to Austria's victory in the Hungarian War of Independence in 1849. Albertini, *Origins of War*, Vol II, p 12; Vermes, *Tisza*, pp 94–5, 133, 215; Clark, *The Sleepwalkers*, p 397.

5. Vermes, *Tisza*, p 214.

6. Albertini, *Origins of War*, Vol I, pp 533–4; Vol II, p 17; Vermes, *Tisza*, pp 214, 216.

7. Albertini, *Origins of War*, Vol I, pp 383–4; Vol II, pp 125–6; Clark, *The Sleepwalkers*, p 396; MacMillan, *The War That Ended Peace*, p 452; McMeekin, *July 1914*, p 27.

8. Albertini, *Origins of War*, Vol II, p 128; Cartledge, *Will to Survive*, pp 293–4; Clark, *The Sleepwalkers*, pp 397–8; MacMillan, *The War That Ended Peace*, p 521; McMeekin, *July 1914*, p 32; Vermes, *Tisza*, p 220.

9. Albertini, *Origins of War*, Vol II, p 127; Cartledge, *Will to Survive*, pp 292–3; Vermes, *Tisza*, p 230.

10. Albertini, *Origins of War*, Vol II, p 124; Clark, *The Sleepwalkers*, p 399; McMeekin, *July 1914*, p 33.

11. Albertini, *Origins of War*, Vol II, p 134; Clark, *The Sleepwalkers*, pp 401–2; MacMillan, *The War That Ended Peace*, p 522; McMeekin, *July 1914*, pp 42–3, 95–7.

12. Albertini, *Origins of War*, Vol II, p 139.

13. Ibid, pp 138–9; Clark, *The Sleepwalkers*, pp 412–5; MacMillan, *The War That Ended Peace*, pp 522–3; McMeekin, *July 1914*, pp 97–105.

14. Albertini, *Origins of War*, Vol II, pp 165–6; Clark, *The Sleepwalkers*, pp 424–5; McMeekin, *July 1914*, p 108; Vermes, *Tisza*, p 222.

15. Albertini, *Origins of War*, Vol II, pp 166–7; Clark, *The Sleepwalkers*, pp 424–5.; MacMillan, *The War That Ended Peace*, p 530; McMeekin, *July 1914*, pp 109–13; Vermes, *Tisza*, pp 222–3.

16. Albertini, *Origins of War*, Vol II, pp 167–8; Cartledge, *Will to Survive*, pp 293–4; Clark, *The Sleepwalkers*, pp 424–5.; MacMillan, *The War That Ended Peace*, pp 530–1.

17. Vermes, *Tisza*, p 223.

18. Albertini, *Origins of War*, Vol II, pp 169–70; McMeekin, *July 1914*, p 116; Vermes, *Tisza*, pp 223–4.

19. Cartledge, *Will to Survive*, p 292; Vermes, *Tisza*, p 228.

20. Albertini, *Origins of War*, Vol II, p 172.

21. Ibid, p 175.

22. Albertini, *Origins of War*, Vol II, p 175; Cartledge, *Will to Survive*, pp 294–5; MacMillan, *The War That Ended Peace*, p 531; McMeekin, *July 1914*, pp 122–3.

23. Albertini (*Origins of War*, Vol II, p 176) renders the Kaiser's scrawl as 'What a man he is!'.

24. Cartledge, *Will to Survive* pp 294–5.; Clark, *The Sleepwalkers*, p 426; MacMillan, *The War That Ended Peace*, p 531.; Vermes, *Tisza*, p 230.

25. Clark, *The Sleepwalkers*, pp 425–6; MacMillan, *The War That Ended Peace*, p 529; McMeekin, *July 1914*, p 115.

26. Albertini, *Origins of War*, Vol II, p 177; Clark, *The Sleepwalkers*, p 426; MacMillan, *The War That Ended Peace*, p 530; McMeekin, *July 1914*, p 121.

27. Albertini, *Origins of War*, Vol II, p 256; McMeekin, *July 1914*, p 137.

28. Count M Károlyi, *Faith Without Illusion* (Jonathan Cape, London: 1956) p 56.

29. Albertini, *Origins of War*, Vol II, pp 287–8; Clark, *The Sleepwalkers*, pp 454–6; MacMillan, *The War That Ended Peace*, p 536; McMeekin, *July 1914*, p 142.

30. Albertini, *Origins of War*, Vol II, pp 256–8; Clark, *The Sleepwalkers*, pp 451–2; MacMillan, *The War That Ended Peace*, p 535.

31. Albertini (*Origins of War*, Vol II, p 264) argues persuasively that Berchtold feared, on the contrary, that the Germans would try to make the terms of the ultimatum even stiffer; and that he consequently wished to present them with a *fait accompli*. I prefer the majority view, which is reinforced by Fritz Fellner ('Austria-Hungary' in Keith Wilson (ed), *Decisions for War, 1914* (University College London Press: 1995, pp 27–54) and McMeekin, *July 1914*, pp 141–3.

32. Albertini, *Origins of War*, Vol II, pp 185, 208; Clark, *The Sleepwalkers*, p 427; McMeekin, *July 1914*, pp 126–7.

33. Albertini, *Origins of War*, Vol II, pp 220–31; McMeekin, *July 1914*, p 143.

34. Albertini, *Origins of War*, Vol II, pp 352–3.

35. Albertini, *Origins of War*, Vol II, pp 363–71; Clark, *The Sleepwalkers*, pp 457–65; MacMillan, *The War That Ended Peace*, pp 536–9; McMeekin, *July 1914*, pp 172–5, 197–201.

36. Albertini, *Origins of War*, Vol II, pp 377–86, 426; Clark, *The Sleepwalkers*, p 468; Vermes, *Tisza*, p 234.

37. Albertini, *Origins of War*, Vol II, pp 387–9; MacMillan, *The War That Ended Peace*, p 562; McMeekin, *July 1914*, pp 244–5.

38. Albertini, *Origins of War*, Vol II, pp 466–9, 522–5; Clark, *The Sleepwalkers*, pp 522–3; M. Hastings, *Catastrophe: Europe Goes to War 1914* (William Collins, London: 2013), p 77.

39. Albertini, *Origins of War*, Vol II, p 665; MacMillan, *The War That Ended Peace*, pp 570–1; McMeekin (*July, 1914*, pp 281–2) reverses the order of Bethmann's two telegrams.

40. Albertini, *Origins of War*, Vol II, pp 658–61.

41. Albertini, *Origins of War*, Vol II, p 673.

42. Wilson, *Decisions for War*, p 22.

43. Albertini, *Origins of War*, Vol II, pp 658–9; Cartledge, *Will to Survive*, p 296; Hastings, *Catastrophe* pp 29–30.

44. Albertini, *Origins of War*, Vol II, p. 670; Hastings, *Catastrophe* p 73.

45. Hastings, *Catastrophe* pp 148–52.

4. The Problem of Germany

1. I am grateful, as always, to Professor Tom Fraser for his advice and support and particularly to Baroness Ruth Henig for her insightful suggestions and encouragement.

2. David Fromkin, *Europe's Last Summer* (Vintage, London: 2005) p 138.

3. Keith Wilson (ed), *Forging the Collective Memory: Government and International Historians through Two World Wars* (Berghahn, Oxford: 1996).

4. David Lloyd George, *War Memoirs* (2 volumes, Odhams Press, London: 1938) Vol I, p 32.

5. Fritz Fischer, *Griff Nach der Weltmacht* (Droste Verlag, Düsseldorf, 1961); translated as *Germany's Aims in the First World War* (Chatto and Windus, London: 1967); Ruth Henig, *The Origins of the First World War* (Routledge, London: 1989) pp 32–40; Annika Mombauer, *The Origins of the First World War: Controversies and Consensus* (Longman, London: 2002) pp 21–126.

6. Ibid, pp127–49. This was not the case in East Germany, where his views, even though he was not a Marxist, matched the existing orthodoxy.

7. Fritz Fischer, *Krieg der Illusionen* (Droste Verlag, Düsseldorf: 1969); translated as *War of Illusions* (Chatto and Windus, London: 1975); Mombauer, *Origins*, pp 149–53.

8. Henig, *Origins of the First World War*, p 43; John Röhl, 'Germany' in Keith Wilson (ed), *Decisions for War, 1914* (UCL Press, London: 1995) pp 27–54. Notable critics of such an interpretation include Niall Ferguson, *The Pity of War* (Allen Lane, London: 1998), Sean McMeekin, *The Russian Origins of the First World War* (Belknap of Harvard University Press, Cambridge, MA: 2013) and Christopher Clark, *The Sleepwalkers* (Penguin, London: 2013).

9. William Carr, *A History of Germany 1815–1985* (3rd edition, Edward Arnold, London: 1987) pp 167–8.

10. Volker Berghahn, *Germany and the Approach of War in 1914* (Macmillan, London: 1973) pp 186, 192.

11. Imanuel Geiss (ed) *July 1914, The Outbreak of the First World War: Selected Documents* (Batsford, London: 1967) p 122.

12. Fromkin, *Europe's Last Summer*, p 164.

13. Jonathan Steinberg, *Tirpitz and the Birth of the German Battle Fleet* (Macdonald, London: 1965); Berghahn, *Germany*, pp 43–64.

14. Wilhelm von Stumm, of the German Foreign Office, remarked in 1916, 'If we had not attacked then, Russia would have attacked us two years later, and then it would have been much better armed and would have had the railway lines in Poland – half of Prussia would have been devastated.' Röhl, 'Germany', p 33. McMeekin suggests that this assessment of Germany's strategic advantage was flawed (*July 1914: Countdown to War* (Icon Books, London: 2013) p 387.

15. Volker Berghahn was a strong supporter of such an idea, whilst historians from the University of Bielefeld, in particular Hans-Ulrich Wehler and Jürgen Kocka, believed German domestic problems were a key element in its foreign policy (Mombauer, *Origins*, pp 153–4. For alternative views, see Richard Evans (ed), *Society and Politics in Wilhelmine Germany* (Croom Helm, London: 1978) and David Blackbourn and Geoff Eley, *The Peculiarities of German History. Bourgeois Society and Politics in Nineteenth-Century Germany* (Oxford University Press: 1984).

16. Clark, *The Sleepwalkers*, p 178.

17. Fromkin *Europe's Last Summer*, p 149.

18. Clark, *The Sleepwalkers*, pp 412–13.

19. Not all were so optimistic; Arthur Zimmerman, of the German Foreign Office, told Hoyos on 5 July, that there

was a '90 per cent probability of a European war if you take action against Serbia' (Rőhl, 'Germany', p 37).

20. Ibid, p 35.

21. Clark, *The Sleepwalkers*, pp 423–30, 517–19; Fromkin, *Europe's Last Summer*, pp 162–9, Berghahn, *Germany*, pp 189–93.

22. Geiss, *July 1914*, pp 149–50, 123.

23. Fromkin, *Europe's Last Summer*, pp 190, 195; Clark, *The Sleepwalkers*, p 522.

24. Geiss, *July 1914*, pp 186–7.

25. Clark, *The Sleepwalkers*, p 495. In support of his argument Clark cites Sidney Fay, *The Origins of the First World War* (2 vols, Macmillan, New York: 1928), Vol II, pp 360–2.

26. See Vernon Bogdanor, 'Sir Edward Grey and the Crisis of July 1914', September 1913, http://www.li.com/docs/default-source/default-document-library/sir-edward-grey-and-the-crisis-of-july-1914---with-vernon-bogdanor-(transcript)---september-2013.pdf, last accessed 24 March 2014; Geiss, *July 1914*, p 237.

27. Ibid, pp 238, 256–7.

28. Ibid, p 236 (italics in original); Clark, *The Sleepwalkers*, pp 522–3; Röhl, 'Germany', p 39.

29. Geiss, *July 1914*, pp 259–60.

30. James Joll, *The Origins of the First World War* (Longman, London: 1984) p 18.

31. Clark, *The Sleepwalkers*, pp 525–7; Röhl, 'Germany', p 39.

32. Fritz Fellner, 'Austria-Hungary' in Wilson, *Decisions for War*, p 22.

33. Ibid, pp 21–2.

34. Carr, *History of Germany*, p 211; Clark, *The Sleepwalkers*, pp 530–3, 541–51.
35. Geiss, *July 1914*, pp 300–1, 315.

5. From Steamroller to Empty Chair

1. J W Headlam-Morley, *A Memoir of the Paris Peace Conference 1919* (Methuen, London: 1972) p. 6.
2. Herbert Hoover, *The Hoover Memoirs*, 3 volumes (Hollis and Carter, London: 1952) Vol 1, p 411.
3. David Robin Watson, *Georges Clemenceau: A Political Biography* (Eyre Methuen, London: 1974) pp 315–316.
4. 'The Necessity for Intervention', *The Russian Outlook*, 1:3 (24 May 1919) p 66.
5. 'What Russia Has Done for The Common Cause', *Bulletin of the Russian Liberation Committee* (5 April 1919) p 1.
6. Published in English as Fritz Fischer, *Germany's Aims in the First World War* (Chatto and Windus, London: 1967).
7. Joshua Sanborn, 'Russian Historiography on the Origins of the First World War since the Fischer Controversy', *Journal of Contemporary History*, Vol 48 No. 2 (2013) pp 350–62.
8. Keith Neilson, 'Russia', in Keith Wilson (ed), *Decisions for War, 1914* (UCL Press, London: 1995) pp 97–120; D W Spring, 'Russia and the Coming of War' in R J W Evans and H Pogge von Strandmann, (eds), *The Coming of the First World War* (Oxford University Press: 1988) pp 57–86; and Dominic Lieven, *Russia and the Origins of the First World War* (Macmillan, London: 1983). Sean McMeekin's recent *The Russian Origins of the First World War* (Belknap of Harvard University Press,

Cambridge Mass.: 2011), a recent attempt to cast Russia as an aggressive imperialist power rather like Fischer's Germany, is rather conspiracy-oriented, and lacks the nuance of these earlier studies.

9. Robert K Massie, *Nicholas and Alexandra* (Victor Gollancz, London: 1967) pp 244–5

10. Vladimir Gurko, J E Wallace Sterling, Xenia Joukoff Eudin and H H Fisher (eds), *Features and Figures of the Past: government and opinion in the reign of Nicholas II*, trans. Laura Matveev (Stanford University Press, Palo Alto, CA: 1939) p 537.

11. Sergei Sazanov, *Fateful Years 1906–1916* (Jonathan Cape, London: 1928) pp 150–151.

12. Lieven, *Origins*, p 139.

13. Hans Rogger, *Russia in the Age of Modernisation and Revolution 1881–1917* (Longman, London: 1983) p 164–6.

14. Ronald Bobroff, 'Behind the Balkan Wars: Russian Policy toward Bulgaria and the Turkish Straits, 1912–13', *Russian Review*, 59:1 (2000) pp 76–95.

15. Rogger, *Russia*, p 173.

16. B Williams, 'Great Britain and Russia, 1905 to the 1907 Convention', and D W Sweet and R T B Langhorne, 'Great Britain and Russia, 1907–1914' in F H Hinsley, (ed), *British Foreign Policy under Sir Edward Grey* (Cambridge University Press: 1977) pp 133–47, pp 236–55.

17. On this see Peter Gatrell, *Government, Industry and Rearmament in Russia 1900–1914: the last argument of tsarism* (Cambridge University Press: 1994).

18. Lieven, *Origins*, pp 142–4.

19. Joshua Sanborn, 'The Mobilization of 1914 and the Question of the Russian Nation: A Reexamination', *Slavic Review*, 59:2 (2000) pp 267–89.

20. Gurko et al, *Features and Figures*, p 538.

21. Matthew Rendle, *Defenders of the Motherland: The Tsarist Elite in Revolutionary Russia* (Oxford University Press: 2010) p 18. Durnovo's memorandum is printed in Frank Golder (ed.), *Documents of Russian History 1914–1917* (The Century Company, New York: 1927) pp 3–23.

22. Robert Service, *Lenin: A Biography* (Macmillan, London: 2000) pp 226–7.

23. Alfred Senn, *Emergence of Modern Lithuania* (Colombia University Press, New York: 1959) pp 18–19.

24. W Harrison, 'Mackenzie Wallace's View of the Russian Revolution of 1905–1907', *Oxford Slavonic Papers*, New Series 4 (1971) pp 73–82; Michael Hughes, 'Bernard Pares, Russian Studies and the Promotion of Anglo-Russian Friendship 1907–1914', *Slavonic and East European Review*, 78:3 (July 2000) pp 510–35; Michael R Palmer, 'The British Nexus and the Russian Liberals 1905–1917', PhD thesis (University of Aberdeen:2000).

25. 'Russia's Advance', *Daily Mail*, 14 August 1914, p 2; *The Times*, 3 October 1914, p 9. On the 'steam-roller' motif, see Keith Neilson, 'Watching the "steamroller": British observers and the Russian army before 1914', *Journal of Strategic Studies*, 8:2 (1985) pp 199–217.

26. Percy Dearmer, 'The Soul of Russia', *Nineteenth Century*, 77 (January–June 1915) p 81. For examples, see James Simpson, *The Self-Discovery of Russia* (Constable, London: 1916), Charles Sarolea, *Europe's Debt to Russia* (Heinemann, London: 1915) and Donald

Mackenzie Wallace, *Our Russian Ally* (Macmillan, London: 1914). Hughes discusses efforts to promote an understanding of Russian culture in Britain, as a way of cementing the alliance, in 'Searching for the Soul of Russia: British Perceptions of Russia during the First World War', *Twentieth Century British History* 20:2 (2009) pp 198–226.

27. Morgan Phillips Price, *My Three Revolutions* (Allen and Unwin, London: 1969) p 23.

28. See Keith Neilson, '"Joyrides"? British Intelligence and propaganda in Russia 1914–1917', *Historical Journal*, 24 (1981) pp 885–906; and M L Sanders, 'British Film Propaganda during the First World War', *Historical Journal of Film, Radio and Television* , 3 (1983) pp 117–29.

29. Bryan Perrett and Anthony Lord, *The Czar's British Squadron* (William Kimber and Co, London: 1981).

30. Keith Neilson, *Strategy and Supply: The Anglo-Russian Alliance 1914–1917* (Allen & Unwin, London: 1984).

31. On the impact of war domestically, see Peter Gatrell, *Russia's First World War: A Social and Economic History* (Pearson Longman, Harlow: 2005). On the Eastern Front, see Norman Stone, *The Eastern Front 1914–1917* (Hodder and Stoughton, London: 1975).

32. Stone, *Eastern Front*, pp 225–6. See also Marvin Lyons (ed), *Vladimir Mikhailovich Bezobrazov: Diary of the Commander of the Russian Imperial Guard 1914–1917* (Dramco Publishers, Boynton Beach, Florida: 1994).

33. See Peter Gatrell, *A Whole Empire Walking: Refugees in Russia during World War One* (Indiana University Press, Bloomington: 2005).

34. On the war industries committees, see Lewis Siegelbaum, *The Politics of Industrial Mobilization in Russia, 1915–1917: A Study of the War Industries Committees* (Palgrave Macmillan, London: 1984).

35. Michael C Hickey (ed), *Competing Voices from the Russian Revolution* (Greenwood, Oxford: 2007) pp 33–4.

36. Miliukov's speech is reproduced in Frank Golder (ed), *Documents of Russian History, 1914–1917* (The Century Company, New York: 1927) pp 154–166.

37. For example, Sarah Badcock, *Politics and the People in Revolutionary Russia: a provincial history* (Cambridge University Press: 2007), and Aaron Retish, *Russia's Peasants in Revolution and Civil War: citizenship, identity and the creation of the Soviet State 1914–1922* (Cambridge University Press: 2008).

38. Russell E Snow, 'The Russian Revolution of 1917–18 in Transbaikalia', *Soviet Studies*, 23:2 (1971) pp 201–15.

39. David Mandel, 'October in the Ivanovo-Kineshma industrial region' in Edith Rogovin Frankel, Jonathan Frankel and Baruch Knei-Paz, (eds), *Revolution in Russia: Reassessments of 1917* (Cambridge University Press: 1991) pp 157–87.

40. On the Russian Civil War, see Evan Mawdsley, *The Russian Civil War* (Unwin Hyman, London: 1987); Geoff Swain, *The Origins of the Russian Civil War* (Longman, London: 1996); Jonathan D Smele, *Civil War in Siberia: the Anti-Bolshevik Government of Admiral Kolchak 1918–1920* (Cambridge University Press: 1996); and Peter Kenez, *Civil War in South Russia* (University of California Press, Berkeley, CA: 1971).

41. Zourab Avalishvili, *The Independence of Georgia in International Politics 1918–1921* (Headley Brothers, London: 1940) p 143.

42. See for example, Charlotte Alston, 'The Suggested Basis for a Russian Federal Republic: Britain, Anti-Bolshevik Russia and the Border States at the Paris Peace Conference, 1919', *History*, Vol. 91, No. 301 (January 2006) pp 24–44.

43. Aleksander Kerensky, former Prime Minister in the second Provisional Government, appeared in London in 1918 campaigning for intervention. General Bicharakhov arrived in the British capital in 1919 with plans for effective military support for the Whites; and Pavel Miliukov, former Foreign Minister in the Provisional Government, led a delegation which included both socialists and former members of the Council of State. Jonathan Smele, '"*Mania grandiosa*" and "The Turning Point in World History": Kerensky in London in 1918', *Revolutionary Russia*, 20:1 (June 2007) pp 1–34; 'General Bicharakhoff in London', *The Russian Outlook*, 1:2 (17 May 1919) p 43; Author?, 'A Russian Delegation to Europe', *The Russian Commonwealth*, 1:5–6 (20 January 1919) p 110.

44. Stephen Bonsal, *Suitors and Suppliants: The Little Nations at Versailles* (Prentice Hall, New York: 1946) p 20.

45. On Russia at the Paris Peace Conference, see John M Thompson, *Russia, Bolshevism and the Versailles Peace* (Princeton University Press: 1966) and Keith Neilson, 'That Elusive Entity British policy in Russia: the Impact of Russia on British Policy at the Paris Peace Conference' in Michael Dockrill and John Fisher

(eds) *The Paris Peace Conference, 1919: Peace Without Victory?* (Palgrave, Basingstoke: 2001). On the Baltic States at the Peace Conference, see Charlotte Alston, *Antonius Piip, Zigfrids Meierovics and Augustinas Voldermaras: The Baltic States* (Haus Publishing, London: 2010).

46. 'Copie de la note remise par la Conférence Russe à la Conférence de la Paix', National Archives, Kew, London, FO 608/184. Russian Political Conference Memorandum to Clemenceau, 24 May 1919; cited in Malbone W Graham, *Diplomatic Recognition of the Border States, Volume II: Estonia* (California University Press, Berkeley: 1939) pp 259–60.

47. William C Bullitt, *The Bullitt Mission to Russia: Testimony before the Committee on Foreign Relations United States Senate* (B W Huebsch, New York: 1919) gives a full account of the fate of Bullitt's proposals.

48. *Foreign Papers Relating to the Foreign Relations of the United States: 1919: The Paris Peace Conference*, 13 volumes (United States Government Printing Office, Washington, 1942–7) pp 300, 361, 369, http://digital.library.wisc.edu/1711.dl/FRUS.FRUS1919vRussia, accessed 14 March 2014; Paul Mantoux, *The Deliberations of the Council of Four (March 24–June 28 1919: notes of the official interpreter, Paul Mantoux), Volume II: From the Delivery of the Peace Terms to the Signing of the Treaty of Versailles* (Princeton University Press: 1992) p 194.

49. Esme Howard, *Theatre of Life* (Hodder and Stoughton, London: 1936) p 277.

6. How France Entered the First World War

1. J F V Keiger *Raymond Poincaré* (Cambridge University Press: 1997), p 164; J F V Keiger, *France and the Origins of the First World War* (Macmillan, Basingstoke: 1983) pp 145–6.

2. B F Martin, *The Hypocrisy of Justice in the Belle Epoque* (Louisiana State University Press, Baton Rouge, LA: 1984).

3. M B Hayne, *The French Foreign Office and the Origins of the First World War 1898–1914* (Clarendon Press, Oxford: 1993) pp 271–2.

4. Gerd Krumeich, *Armaments and Politics in France on the eve of the First World War: The Introduction of Three Year Conscription 1913–1914* (Berg, Leamington Spa: 1984).

5. Gustave Dupin, *M Poincaré et la Guerre de 1914,* (Librairie du Travail, Paris: 1935); Raymond Poincaré, *Les Responsibilités de la Guerre, Quatorze Questions par René Gerin, Quatorze Réponses par Raymond Poincaré* (Payot, Paris: 1930); Jacques Droz, *Les causes de la Première Guerre Mondiale, Essai d'Historiographie* (Editions du Seuil, Paris: 1973) pp 26–32.

6. Maurice Paléologue, *La Russe des Tsars pendant la Grande Guerre* (Librairie Plon, Paris: 1921) pp 22–47; Raymond Poincaré, *Au Service de la France: Neuf Années de Souvenirs,* 11 volumes (Librairie Plon, Paris: 1926–1974), *Volume IV: L'Union Sacrée 1914,* pp 221–431; Raymond Poincaré, *Les Origines de la Guerre: Conférences prononcées en 1921* (Librairie Plon, Paris: 1921); René Viviani *As We See It: France and the truth about the War* (Hodder and Stoughton, London: 1923); Poincaré's diary, in the manuscript

department of the Bibliothèque Nationale, Paris, has been utilized by Keiger in *Raymond Poincaré* and *France and the Origins of the First World War*. A completely different interpretation is given by Christopher Clark, *The Sleepwalkers: How Europe went to War in 1914* (Penguin, London: 2013) pp 442–50.

7. Luigi Albertini, *The Origins of the War of 1914*, 3 volumes (originally published Milano, 1942; trans and ed Isabella M Massey, Oxford University Press, 1953), Vol II, p 593.

8. Keiger, *Origins*, pp 153 and 193; Albertini, *Origins of the War of 1914*, Vol II, p 593; P M H Bell, *France and Britain 1900–1940 Entente and Estrangement* (Longman, Harlow: 1996) pp 55–9.

9. Recent studies which attribute blame to Russian and thus indirectly to French policy are Sean McMeekin, *The Russian Origins of the First World War* (Belknap Press of Harvard University Press, Cambridge Mass.: 2011) and *July 1914: Countdown to War* (Icon Books, London 2013), and Clark, *The Sleepwalkers*.

10. Keiger, *Origins*, pp 153–5 and *Poincaré* pp 165–70.

11. Laurent Villatte, *La République du Diplomates: Paul et Jules Cambon 1843–1935* (Science Infuse, Paris: 2002) pp 310–20.

12. Jean-Jacques Becker *Le Carnet B, Les Pouvoirs Publics et l'antimilitarisme avant la Guerre de 1914*, (Editions Klincksieck, Paris, 1973); Annie Kriegel and Jean-Jacques Becker *1914 La Guerre et le Mouvement Ouvrier Français* (Librairie Armand Colin Paris, 1964); Jean-Yves Le Naour *L'Affaire Malvy* (Hachette, Paris 2007).

13. James Joll, *The Second International 1889–1914* (Weidenfeld and Nicolson, 1955); Jean-Pierre Rioux *Jean Jaurès* (Perrin, Paris, 2005); Gilles Heuré *Gustave Hervé, Itinéraire d'un provocateur*, (Edition La Découverte, Paris, 1997).

14. Jean Stengers, 'Le dernier discours de Jaurès' in Ernest Labrousse (ed), *Actes du Colloque, Jaurès et la Nation* (Publications de la Faculté de Lettres et Sciences Humaines de Toulouse, Toulouse: 1965) p 104.

15. Jean-Jacques Becker and Gerd Krumeich, *La Grande Guerre, Une Histoire Franco-Allemande* (Editions Tallardier, Paris: 2008); Jean-Jacques Becker *L'Année 14* (Armand Colin, Paris, 2004).

7. Belgium: the Victim

1. For texts, see Great Britain, Foreign Office, *British and Foreign State Papers* (HMSO, London: 1856) Vol 27, pp 1001, 994.

2. Aside from judicial proceedings, the government remained entirely francophone, as did the officer corps, but not the troops.

3. The folder – with scribbles – is located in the Belgian Foreign Ministry archive in Classement Independance, Neutralité, Défense militaire de la Belgique, Garantie des Puissances, Vol 15.

4. Chef de cabinet. The term Prime Minister was not used until November 1918.

5. Margaret MacMillan, *The War that Ended Peace: The Road to 1914* (Random House, New York: 2013) p 539.

6. Lieutenant General Emile Galet, *Albert, King of the Belgians in the Great War*, trans Major-General Sir

Ernest Swinton (Houghton Mifflin, New York: 1931)
pp 22–3. War was in fact not declared in 1914.

7. Henri Haag, *Le comte Charles de Broqueville*, Vol 1
(Collêge Érasme, Louvain-la Neuve: 1990) p 190.

8. Until assured by Germany that it would not be violated,
the Netherlands proposed a joint Belgo-Dutch defense
of Dutch Limburg.

9. Albert's mother was Princess Marie of
Hohenzollern-Sigmaringen.

10. For text, see Belgian Grey Book, *Diplomatic
Correspondence Respecting the War (July 24–August
29)* in Great Britain, Foreign Office, *Collected
Diplomatic Documents relating to the Outbreak of
the European War* (HMSO, London: 1915) pp 309–11.
Hereafter *Documents: European War.*

11. Christopher Clark, *The Sleepwalkers: How Europe went
to War in 1914* (HarperCollins, New York: 2013) pp 549,
551.

12. Sean McMeekin, *July 1914: Countdown to War* (Basic
Books, New York: 2013) p 361.

13. For text, see Belgian Grey Book, pp 311–12. Texts of
ultimatum and response are more conveniently located
in Hugh Gibson, *A Journal from Our Legation in
Belgium* (Doubleday, Page, Garden City, NY: 1917)
pp 16–19. For a participant's account of the drafting
of the reply, see Albert de Bassompierre, *La Nuit du 2
au 3 août 1914 au Ministère des Affaires Étrangères de
Belgique* (Librairie academique, Paris: 1916) in *Seeds
of Conflict*, Series 5: *Germany and World Conflict*, Part
I (Kraus Reprint, Nendeln: 1976). A good summary
of the crisis from the Belgian viewpoint is Robert
Devleeshouwer, *Les Belges et le danger de guerre,*

1910–1914 (Éditions Nauwelaerts, Leuven: 1958)
pp 229–328.

14. Jean Stengers, 'Belgium' in Keith Wilson (ed), *Decisions for War, 1914* (St Martin's Press, New York: 1995)
pp 162–3.

15. Max Hastings, *Catastrophe, 1914: Europe Goes to War* (Alfred A Knopf, New York: 2013) p 90.

16. Great Britain, Foreign Office, *British Documents on the Origin of the War, 1898–1914*, G P Gooch and Harold Temperley (eds), Vol 11 (HMSO, London: 1916) p 351, hereafter *British Documents*; *The German White Book*, Appendix, p 438 in *Documents: European War*; Belgian Grey Book, p 317; *The British Diplomatic Correspondence*, p 111 in *Documents: European War*; Baron Eugène Beyens, *Deux Années à Berlin* (2 volumes, Librairie Plon, Paris: 1931) Vol II, p 270.

17. Brand Whitlock, *Belgium, a Personal Narrative* (D Appleton, New York: 1919) p 63.

18. Austria did not declare war on Belgium until 28 August, but was assumed to be acting in concert with Germany (which did not declare war on Belgium).

19. Daniel H Thomas, *The Guarantee of Belgian Independence and Neutrality in European Diplomacy, 1830s–1930s* (D H Thomas Publishing Co, Kingston, Rhode Island: 1983) p 502.

20. *British Documents*, p 351.

8. Britain and the Outbreak of War

1. Zara Steiner, *Britain and the Origins of the First World War* (Macmillan, London: 1977) p 215; Kenneth Morgan, *Lloyd George* (Book Club Associates, London: 1974) p 81.

2. John Grigg, *Lloyd George: From Peace to War 1912–1916* (HarperCollins, London: 1997) p 137.

3. Michael and Eleanor Brock (eds), *H. H. Asquith Letters to Venetia Stanley* (Oxford University Press: 1982) p 93. See pp 94–109 for the subsequent letters.

4. Steiner, *Britain and the Origins*, p 222; Keith Wilson, 'Britain' in K Wilson (ed), *Decisions for War, 1914* (UCL Press, London: 1995) pp 182–3; G M Trevelyan, *Grey of Falloden* (Longmans, London: 1937) pp 245–6.

5. British newspapers changed the pre-war spelling of Servia to Serbia to counter any connotations of servility. Brock, *Asquith Letters,* pp 122–3.

6. G W Monger, *The End of Isolation: British Foreign Policy 1900–1907* (Nelson, London: 1963) *passim*; Samuel R Williamson, *The Politics of Grand Strategy: Britain and France Prepare for War, 1904–1914* (Ashfield, London: 1990) p 90; Michael Howard, *The Continental Commitment: The Dilemma of British Defence Policy in the Era of Two World Wars* (Pelican, London: 1972) pp 31–51.

7. Monger, *End of Isolation*, pp 19–45; Jonathan Steinberg, *Yesterday's Deterrent: Tirpitz and the Birth of the German Battle Fleet* (Macdonald, London: 1965) pp 31–60.

8. Christopher Andrew, 'The Entente Cordiale from its Origins to 1914' in Neville Waites, (ed), *Troubled Neighbours: France-British Relations in the Twentieth Century* (Weidenfeld & Nicolson, London: 1971) pp 11–39; Monger, *End of Isolation*, pp 104–46, 281–95.

9. Keith M Wilson, *The Policy of the Entente: Essays on the Determinants of British Foreign Policy, 1904–1914* (Cambridge University Press: 1985) p 47.

10. William Mulligan, *The Origins of the First World War* (Cambridge University Press: 2010) p 5; Hew Strachan, *The First World War, Vol I: To Arms* (Oxford University Press: 2001) pp 51–5; David Lloyd George, *War Memoirs* (2 volumes, Odhams, 1938 edition) Vol I, p 58.

11. Those who knew were: the Prime Ministers, Henry Campbell-Bannerman, until 1908, then Asquith; the War Minister, Haldane; the First Lord of the Admiralty, Lord Tweedmouth until 1908, then Reginald McKenna until 1911, then Winston Churchill; and the Liberal leader in the House of Lords, first Lord Ripon, then Lord Crewe. John and Peter Coogan, 'The British Cabinet and the Anglo-French Staff Talks, 1905–1914: Who Knew What and When Did He Know It?', *Journal of British Studies*, 24 (January 1985) pp 110–31. On the details of the military talks, see Williamson, *Politics of Grand Strategy*, pp 59–114.

12. Grey of Falloden, *Twenty-Five Years* (2 volumes, Hodder and Stoughton, London: 1925) Vol I, pp 97–8; Brock, *Asquith Letters*, p 112.

13. Wilson, *Policy of the Entente*, p 51.

14. Wilson, *Decisions for War*, p 187.

15. Wilson, *Policy of the Entente*, p 78.

16. Brock, *Asquith Letters*, p 125.

17. Michael Ekstein and Steiner, 'The Sarajevo Crisis' in F H Hinsley (ed), *British Foreign Policy under Sir Edward Grey* (Cambridge University Press: 1977) pp 397–410, 401.

18. Wilson, *Decisions for War*, p 188; Trevelyan, *Grey of Falloden*, p 268; Ekstein and Steiner, 'Sarajevo Crisis', pp 403–5.

19. Wilson, *Decisions for War,* pp 189 –91; Ekstein and Steiner, 'Sarajevo Crisis', pp 403–5.
20. Wilson, *Policy of the Entente*, p 136; Wilson, *Decisions for War,* p 191.
21. Ibid, pp191–2
22. Brock, *Asquith Letters*, p 140.
23. Harold Nicolson, *Lord Carnock* (Constable, London: 1930) pp 419–20; Wilson, *Decisions for War,* pp 198–9.
24. Brock, *Asquith Letters*, p 146
25. Wilson, *Policy of the Entente*, pp 139–40.
26. K Morgan (ed), *Lloyd George Family Letters, 1885–1936* (Oxford University Press: 1973) p 167; Frances Lloyd George, *The Years That Are Past* (Hutchinson, London: 1967) pp 73–4.
27. Brock, *Asquith Letters*, p 150; Wilson, *Policy of the Entente*, p 142; Nicolson, *Lord Carnock*, pp 423–6.
28. Wilson *Decisions for War,* p 177; General Huguet, *Britain and the War: A French Indictment* (Cassell, London: 1928) p 26.
29. Max Hastings, *Catastrophe: Europe Goes to War 1914* (William Collins, London: 2013) pp 200–58, 286–355.

9. How the Empire Went to War

1. My thanks are due to Dr Peter Neville, Dr Philip Webb and Dr Peter Yearwood.
2. David Lloyd George, *War Memoirs* (2 volumes, Odhams, 1938) Vol 1, p 42.
3. Antony Lentin, *General Smuts: South Africa* (Haus Publishing, London: 2010) p 30.
4. 3 August 1914. Quoted in George Dangerfield, *The Damnable Question: A Study in Anglo-Irish Relations* (Quartet Books, London: 1979) pp 122–3.

5. Apart from the Dominions and India, Britain ruled Ceylon, Aden, Mauritius and the Seychelles in the Indian Ocean, Gibraltar, Malta and Cyprus in the Mediterranean. Britain's African territories included Nigeria, the Gold Coast (Ghana), the Gambia, Sierra Leone, the Anglo-Egyptian Sudan, British Somaliland, the East Africa Protectorate (Kenya), Uganda, Nyasaland and Rhodesia (Zimbabwe). In East and South East Asia, British possessions stretched from Hong Kong to Malaya, Burma (Myanmar), Singapore and parts of Borneo, and a string of Pacific islands. British colonies in the Caribbean included Jamaica, Trinidad, British Guyana (Guyana), British Honduras (Belize), the Bahamas and Bermuda; and in the South Atlantic, the Falkland Islands and South Georgia.

6. The title of a book by the explorer H M Stanley (1890).

7. W D McIntyre, 'Australia, New Zealand, and the Pacific Islands' in Judith M Brown and R Louis (eds), *The Oxford History of the British Empire* (5 volumes, Oxford University Press: 1998–9), *Vol IV: The Twentieth Century*, pp 667–92, 668.

8. Carl Bridge, *William Hughes: Australia* (Haus Publishing, London: 2011) p 29.

9. James Watson, *William Massey: New Zealand* (Haus Publishing, London: 2010) p 45.

10. Lentin, *Smuts*, p 30.

11. Hugh Purcell, *The Maharajah of Bikaner: India* (Haus Publishing, London: 2010) pp 27–8.

12. Originally an association intended to foster dialogue with the British authorities.

13. J K Matthew, 'Reluctant Allies: Nigerian responses to military recruitment 1914–1918' in M E Page

(ed), *Africa and the First World War* (Macmillan, Basingstoke: 1987) p 97.

14. *The Times* headline, 7 August 1914, echoing the king's message to the Dominions on 4 August and prefiguring the title of a speech by Asquith on 5 September.

15. Philip Kerr, quoted in M Beloff, *Britain's Liberal Empire: Imperial Sunset 1897–1921* (Methuen, London: 1969) p 136.

16. Richard Jebb, 1899, quoted in R Hyam, 'The British Empire in the Edwardian Era' in Brown and Louis, *Oxford History of the British Empire*, Vol IV, pp 47–63, 57.

17. Rudyard Kipling, 'Recessional' (1897).

18. Lugard, secret dispatch, 9 January 1915, National Archives, Kew, London, Co583/30/4984.

10. The Chance of a Millennium

1. Hata Ikuhiko, 'Continental Expansion 1905–1941' in Peter Duus (ed), *Cambridge History of Japan, Vol 6: The Twentieth Century* (Cambridge University Press: 1989) pp 271–314, p 279.

2. W G Beasley, *Japanese Imperialism* (Clarendon Press, Oxford: 1991) pp 109–10.

3. Ibid, p 112.

11. The Ottomans' Last War – and After

1. Andrew Mango, *Atatürk* (John Murray, London: 1999) pp 133–6.

2. Mango, *From the Sultan to Atatürk* (Haus Publishing, London: 2009), pp 7–8.

3. Mango, *Atatürk*, p 134.

4. Mango, *From the Sultan to Atatürk*, pp 7 et seq.

12. Neutrality or Intervention? Italy's Long Road to War

1. English translations of the texts of the declarations appended to the Triple Alliance are in Alfred F Pribram, *The Secret Treaties of Austria-Hungary, 1879–1914*, English edition Archibald Cary Coolidge (ed), trans Denys P Myers and J G D'Arcy Paul (Harvard University Press, Cambridge, MA: 1920) Vol 1, pp 69, 71, 72, 73.

2. He developed this argument in his *Storia di dieci anni* (Il Viandante, Milan: 1910).

3. The phrase is A William Salomone's, who introduced it in his fundamental work, *Italy in the Giolittian Era: Italian Democracy in the Making 1900–1914* (University of Pennsylvania Press, Philadelphia: 1945; 1960 edition).

4. See the book by Socialist leader Ivanoe Bonomi, originally published in 1906, *Le vie nuove del socialismo* (Sestante, Rome: 1944).

5. David G Herrmann, *The Arming of Europe and the Making of the First World War* (Princeton University Press: 1996) pp 108–9. For the reaction among leftists in Italy, see Spencer Di Scala, *Dilemmas of Italian Socialism: The Politics of Filippo Turati* (University of Massachusetts Press, Amherst, MA: 1980) pp 126–7.

6. Pribram, *Secret Treaties*, p 11.

7. The story is told in detail by J Fred MacDonald, *Camille Barrière: Ambassador Extraordinaire, on French Diplomacy 1898–1902 and the Coming of World War I* (2012), http://www.jfredmacdonald.com/camillebarrere/chapter5.htm, accessed 21 October, 5 and 10 November 2013, who provides the quote cited here.

8. Cited in René Albrecht-Carrié, *A Diplomatic History of Europe Since the Congress of Vienna* (Harper's, New

York: 1958) pp 234–5; see also his general account of this development beginning on p 232.

9. Both MacDonald, *Camille Barrière* and Albrecht-Carrié, *Diplomatic History of Europe* (p 234) agree on this point.

10. Albrecht-Carrié, *Diplomatic History of Europe* rightly insists on this point; see pp 232–3.

11. The text of the Reinsurance Treaty may be conveniently found in Pribram, *Secret Treaties of Austria-Hungary*, Vol I, pp 275, 277, 279.

12. David Fromkin, *Europe's Last Summer: Who Started the Great War in 1914?* (Vintage Books, New York: 2004) pp 272–5.

13. See the discussion in Di Scala, *Dilemmas*, p 128 and the statistics in Herrmann, *Arming of* Europe, p 237.

14. William C Askew, *Europe and Italy's Acquisition of Libya, 1911–1912* (Duke University Press, Durham, NC: 1942) remains the most detailed account of these negotiations.

15. Agreements within the alliance called for half the Italian army to be sent to the German front to help fight the French, but no one thought this was possible. However, this did not exclude the participation of some Italian contingents, just as the Italians sent troops to help the French fight the Germans during the First World War.

16. Giovanni Giolitti, *Memorie della mia vita* (Garzanti, Milan:1967), pp 311–12, 316–17.

17. The English text of the article requiring consultation is in Pribram, *Secret Treaties*, pp 65 and 67.

18. See Albrecht-Carrié, *Diplomatic History of Europe*, p 329.

19. Di Scala, *Vittorio Orlando: Italy* (Haus Publishing, London: 2010) pp 34–40.

20. Mark Thompson, *The White War: Life and Death on the Italian Front 1915–1918* (Basic Books, New York: 2008) p 20, describes how the Germanic powers hid their intentions.

21. Giorgio Candeloro, *Storia dell'Italia moderna* (Feltrinelli, Milan: 1989) Vol 8, pp 31–2.

22. San Giuliano's summary of the conversations, summarized here, upon learning of the terms of the Austrian ultimatum is in Antonio Salandra, *La neutralita' italiana 1914–1915* (Mondadori, Milan: 1928) pp 76–8.

23. Olindo Malagodi, *Conversazioni della Guerra 1914–1919* (Ricciardi, Milan-Naples: 1960) Vol I, pp 85–6.

24. Salandra, *La neutralita' italiana*, pp 83–93.

25. More details of this manoeuvering can be found in Di Scala, *Orlando*, pp 40–9.

26. Guglielmo Imperiali, *Diario (1915–1919)* (Rubbettino, Catanzaro: 2006) pp 131–2.

27. Ibid, p 143.

28. Ibid, pp 132–50.

29. Sidney Sonnino, *Carteggio 1914–1916* (Laterza, Rome: 1974) pp 318–21.

30. René Albrecht-Carrié, 'The Present Significance of the Treaty of London of 1915', *The Political Science Quarterly*, Vol. 54, No. 3 (September 1939), p 366.

31. Leo Valiani, 'Documenti francesi sull'Italia e il movimento Yugoslavo', *Rivista Storica Italiana*, 80, No. 2 (1968), pp 351–64. One of the possible problems, clearly identified by the Italians, was that the Germans

might take over Austria, bringing a much more dangerous power to the Italian borders.

32. H James Burgwyn, *The Legend of the Mutilated Victory: Italy, the Great War, and the Paris Peace Conference, 1915–1919* (Greenwood Press, Westport: 1993) p 23.

33. Istituto Giangiacomo Feltrinelli, *Dalle Carte di Giovanni Giolitti: Quarant'anni di politica italiana*, (3 volumes, Feltrinelli, Milan:1962) Vol III, Claudio Pavone (ed), *Dai podromi della grande guerra al fascismo 1910–1928*, pp 170–2.

34. Giolitti thought that the Pact of London was not legally binding, since it had not been accepted by Parliament, and that Italy's problems could be resolved by diplomatic means. See Malagodi, *Conversazioni della Guerra*, pp 83–5.

35. Di Scala, 'Parliamentary Socialists, the Statuto, and the Giolittian System', *The Australian Journal of Politics and History*, 25, No. 2 (August 1979) pp 155–68.

36. Di Scala, *Orlando*, pp 53–5, and Burgwyn, *Legend of the Mutilated Victory*, p 23.

37. For the enormity of the British and French gains in the Middle East, and the enormous impact of their policies, see David Fromkin, *A Peace to End All Peace* (Holt, New York: 1989).

38. See Di Scala, *Orlando*, pp 170–1, which cites relevant documents, and Burgwyn, *Legend of the Mutilated Victory*, pp 296–8. For a fuller discussion of colonial issues at the Paris Peace Conference, see René Albrecht-Carrié, 'Italian Colonial Problems in 1919' *Political Science Quarterly*, 58, No. 4 (December 1943) pp 562–80

and 'Italian Colonial Policy' *The Journal of Modern History*, 18, No. 2 (June 1946) pp. 123–47.

13. Bulgaria Choosing Sides

1. R J Crampton, *Aleksandŭr Stamboliĭski: Bulgaria* (Haus Publishing, London: 2009) pp 10–13.
2. Hew Strachan, *The First World War, Vol I: To Arms* (Oxford University Press, 2001) pp 49–51, 56–7; Christopher Clark, *The Sleepwalkers: How Europe went to War in 1914* (Penguin, London: 2013) pp 249–58; Crampton, *Stamboliĭski*, pp 44–52.
3. Z A B Zeman, *A Diplomatic History of the First World War* (Weidenfeld and Nicolson, London: 1971) pp 74–6.
4. Crampton, *Stamboliĭski*, pp 53–5.

14. Portuguese Intervention

1. *Portugal na Primeira Guerra Mundial (1914–1918)* Vol I, *As Negociações Diplomáticas até à Declaração de Guerra*, (Ministério dos Negócios Estrangeiros, Lisbon: 1997) Document 415, 'Declaration of War', pp 346–50, 348.
2. Ibid, Document 415, pp 346–50.
3. Ibid, Document 362, pp 308–9. See also A H de Oliveira Marques (ed), *O Segundo Governo de Afonso Costa, 1915–1916* (Publicações Europa-América, Lisbon: 1974), pp 111–20, for Afonso Costa's account to the rest of the Cabinet of his discussion on this subject with the British minister, Sir Lancelot Carnegie, and for the reaction of his government colleagues.
4. *Portugal na Primeira Guerra Mundial*, Vol I, Document 371, pp 313–14.
5. Ibid, Document 370, p 313.

6. Ibid, Documents 398, pp 333–4 and Document 400, pp 335–6. See also Filipe Ribeiro de Meneses, *Afonso Costa: Portugal* (Haus Publishing, London: 2010) pp 39–49.

15. The Hejaz: On the Road to the Arab Rebellion

1. Quoted in Hew Strachan, *The First World War, Vol I: To Arms* (Oxford University Press: 2001) p 696.

2. David Fromkin, *A Peace to End all Peace* (Phoenix, London: 1989) p 35.

3. Ira Lapidus, *A History of Islamic Societies* (Cambridge University Press, 2002) p 535.

4. As characterized in Albert Hourani, 'Ottoman Reform and the Politics of Notables' in William R Polk and Richard L Chambers (eds), *Beginnings of Modernization in the Middle East: Nineteenth Century* (University of Chicago Press, 1969) pp 41–68.

5. James L Gelvin, *Divided Loyalties: Nationalism and Mass politics in Syria at the close of Empire* (University of California Press, Berkeley: 1998) p 13.

6. M E Yapp, *The Making of the Modern Near East, 1792–1923* (Macmillan, London: 1987) pp 132–3.

7. See for instance, C Ernest Dawn, *From Ottomanism to Arabism: Essays on the Origins of Arab Nationalism* (University of Illinois Press, Urbana: 1973) pp 10–11.

8. Amongst critical looks at Antonius, are Sylvia G Haim, '"The Arab Awakening", A Source for the Historian?', *Die Welt des Islams*, 11 (1953); Elie Kedourie, *England and the Middle East: The Destruction of the Ottoman Empire, 1914–1921* (Boulder, London: 1987) pp 29–66 and 107–41; Elie Kedourie, *In the Anglo-Arab Labyrinth: The McMahon-Hussein Correspondence*

and Its Interpretations 1914–1939 (Cambridge University Press, 1976) pp 64–136 and 266–9; Albert Hourani, '"*The Arab Awakening*", Forty Years Later' in Derek Hopwood (ed), *Studies in Arab History: The Antonius Lectures, 1978–87* (Macmillan, London: 1990) pp. 21–40.

9. See C Ernest Dawn, 'The Origins of Arab Nationalism' in Rashid Khalidi et al. (eds), *The Origins of Arab Nationalism* (Oxford University Press, New York: 1991) pp 18–19.

10. Eliezer Tauber, *The Emergence of the Arab Movements* (Frank Cass, London & Portland: 1993) p 406. Dawn, *From Ottomanism to Arabism*, pp 152–3. puts the figure at only 144.

11. Majid Khadduri, *Political Trends in the Arab World: The Role of Ideas and Ideals in Politics* (The Johns Hopkins University Press, Baltimore, MA: 1970) p 19.

12. W Ochsenwald, *Religion, Society and the State in Arabia* (Columbia University Press: 1984) p 17.

13. W Ochsenwald, 'Ironic origins: Arab nationalism in the Hijaz' in Khalidi et al.,*Origins of Arab Nationalism*, p 190.

14. William Cleveland, *A History of the Middle East* (Westview, Boulder, CO: 2009) p 157.

15. What follows is substantially based on R Baker, *King Husain and the kingdom of Hejaz* (Oleander Press, New York: 1979); Kedourie, *In the Anglo-Arab Labyrinth*; A Susser and A Shmuelevitz, (eds), *The Hashemites in the Modern Arab World* (Frank Cass, London: 1995); J Morris, *The Hashemite Kings* (Faber & Faber, London: 1959); Joshua Titelbaum, *The Rise and Fall of the Hashemite Kingdom of Arabia* (Hurst,

London: 2001); Haifa Alangaria, *The Struggle for Power in Arabia: Ibn Saud, Hussein and Great Britain 1914–1924* (Ithaca Press, Reading: 1998).

16. J Nevo, 'Abdullah's memoirs as historical source material' in Susser and Shmuelevitz, *Hashemites in the Modern Arab World*, p 166.

17. Sir Louis Mallet to Sir Edward Grey, 18 March 1914, in G P Gooch and Harold Temperley, *British Documents on the Origins of the War 1898–1918*, Vol X, Part II (HMSO, London: 1938) p 827; hereafter *British Documents*.

18. Alangaria, *Struggle for Power in Arabia*, p 63.

19. James Nicholson, 'The Hejaz railway', *Asian Affairs*, Vol 37, No. 3 (2006), pp 320–36 for the story of the railway.

20. Titelbaum, *Rise and Fall of the Hashemite Kingdom*, p 69.

21. Ibid, pp 69–70.

22. Lord Kitchener to Sir Edward Grey, 6 February 1914, in *British Documents*, Vol X, Part II, p 827 See also, Kedourie, *In the Anglo-Arab Labyrinth*, p 5.

23. M S Anderson, *The Eastern Question, 1774–1923* (Macmillan, London: 1966) p 260.

24. See Marian Kent, 'Great Britain and the End of the Ottoman Empire, 1900–23' in Marian Kent (ed), *The Great Powers and the End of the Ottoman Empire* (G. Allen and Unwin, London: 1984) pp 173–85 for an account of British pre-war policy towards the Ottomans.

25. C Ernest Dawn, 'The Amir of Mecca Al-Husayn Ibn-'Ali and the Origin of the Arab Revolt', *Proceedings of the American Philosophical Society*, Vol 104, No. 1 (15

February 1960) pp 11–34, 22; Kedourie, *England and the Middle East*, pp 19, 52.

26. Teitelbaum, Joshua (1998) 'Sherif Hussein ibn Ali and the Hashemite vision of the post-Ottoman order: from chieftaincy to suzerainty', *Middle Eastern Studies*, Vol 34, No.1, pp 103–22, 106.

27. Kedourie, *In the Anglo-Arab Labyrinth*, pp 20–5.

28. For a more detailed discussion of British policy, see Jukka Nevakivi, *Britain, France, and the Middle East, 1914–1920* (Athlone Press, London: 1969) pp 13–45.

29. The paper 'British Desiderata in Turkey and Asia: Report, Proceedings and Appendices of a Committee Appointed by the Prime Minister, 1915', PRO CAB 27/1, pp 3–29 is substantively reproduced as Doc. 12 in J C Hurewitz, *The Middle East and North Africa in World Politics* (Yale University Press, New Haven: 1979), pp 26–45.

30. Dawn, *From Ottomanism to Arabism*, p 28.

31. George Antonius, *The Arab Awakening*, (Hamish Hamilton, London: 1938) p 79.

32. Dawn, 'The Amir of Mecca Al-Husayn Ibn-'Ali', p 24

33. Fromkin, *Peace to End all Peace*, pp 174–6.

34. Amir Abdullah to Ronald Storrs, 14 July 1915, in Great Britain, *Parliamentary Papers, 1939*, Misc. No 3, Cmd. 5957.

35. Ronald Storrs, *Orientations* (Nicholson & Watson, London: 1937), pp 160–1.

36. The correspondence can be found in Great Britain, *Parliamentary Papers, 1939*, Misc. No. 3, Cmd. 5957.

37. The following draws on Kedourie, *In the Anglo-Arab Labyrinth*, pp 65–137; Monroe, *Britain's moment in the Middle East* (Chatto and Windus, London: 1963)

Chapter 2, esp. pp 32–7; Isaiah Friedman, *The Question of Palestine 1914–1918: British-Jewish-Arab Relations* (Routledge & Kegan Paul, London: 1973) pp 65–96.

38. Kedourie, *In the Anglo-Arab Labyrinth*, p 4.

39. Ibid, p 120.

40. Fromkin, *Peace to End all Peace*, pp 176–80.

41. Friedman, *The Question of Palestine,* p 72.

42. Bruce Westrate, *The Arab Bureau: British Policy in the Middle East, 1916–1920* (Pennsylvania State University Press, University Park, PA: 1992) pp 26–9, 153; See Kedourie's views of Sykes in *England and the Middle East,* pp 67–87.

43. For Georges Picot's position as a strong backer of *la Syrie integrale* and his high standing among the imperial enthusiasts, Andrew and Kanya-Forstner, 'The French Colonial Party and French Colonial War Aims, 1914–1918', *Historical. Journal*, Vol 17 (1974) pp. 74–5.

44. For Grey's caution about interfering with France's aspirations see Kedourie, *In the Anglo-Arab Labyrinth*, p 55; Friedman, *The Question of Palestine,* pp 100–2.

45. For an outline of this thinking see Edward Peter Fitzgerald, 'France's Middle Eastern Ambitions, the Sykes-Picot Negotiations, and the Oil Fields of Mosul, 1915–1918', *Journal of Modern History*, Vol 66, No.4. (December 1994) pp 697–725.

46. Jan Karl Tanenbaum, 'France and the Arab Middle East, 1914–1920', *Transactions of the American Philosophical Society,* New Series, Vol 68, No.7 (1978) pp 1–50, 11.

47. Two useful assessments are in D K Fieldhouse, *Western Imperialism in the Middle East 1914–1958* (Oxford University Press: 2006) pp 52–8 and Yapp, *Making of the Modern Near East*, pp 281–6.

48. Dawn, 'The Amir of Mecca Al-Husayn Ibn-'Ali', pp 24–6.

16. Romania Enters the War

1. Keith Hitchins, *Ion I. C. Brătianu: Romania* (Haus Publishing, London: 2011) pp 18–64.
2. Gheorghe N Căzan and Şerban Rădulescu-Zoner, *Rumänien und der Dreibund 1878–1914* (Editura Academiei Republicii Socialiste România, Bucharest: 1983) pp 78–141, 206–49.
3. Anastasie Iordache, *Ion I. C. Brătianu* (Editura Albatros, Bucharest: 1994) pp 218–21.
4. Glenn E Torrey, *Romania and World War I* (The Center for Romanian Studies, Iaşi: 1998) pp 95–120.
5. Constantin Nuţu, *România în anii neutralităţii 1914–1916* (Editura Ştiinţifică, Bucharest: 1972) p 299.
6. V I Vinogradov, *Rumyniia v gody pervoi mirovoi voiny* (Izdatel'stvo Nauka, Moscow: 1969) pp 158–9.
7. I G Duca, *Amintiri politice*, Vol 1 (Jon Dumitru-Verlag, Munich: 1981) pp 276–7, 284.

17. America's Road to War

1. I am grateful to Grace Fraser and Professor Lester C Lamon for their helpful comments on the draft of this chapter.
2. John Palmer, *South Bend: Crossroads of Commerce* (Arcadia Publishing, Charleston, SC: 2003) pp 110–11.
3. Viscount Grey of Fallodon, *Twenty-five Years 1892–1916* (2 volumes, Hodder and Stoughton, London: 1925) Vol II, pp 83–4.
4. John Milton Cooper, Jr, *Woodrow Wilson: A Biography* (Vintage Books, New York: 2011) p 263.

5. A Scott Berg, *Wilson* (Simon & Schuster, London: 2013) Chapter 2; Cooper, *Woodrow Wilson*, Chapters 1–9, *passim*.

6. First Inaugural Address, Washington, D.C., 4 March 1913, quoted in James M McPherson (general ed), David Rubel (ed), *'To The Best of My Ability': The American Presidents* (Dorling Kindersley Publishing, New York: 2000) pp 401–2.

7. Paul Kennedy, *The Rise and Fall of the Great Powers: Economic and Military Conflict from 1500 to 2000* (Random House, New York: 1987), p 243, Table 21.

8. Kennedy, *The Rise and Fall of the Great Powers*, pp 242–9.

9. Burton J Hendrick, *The Life and Letters of Walter H. Page*, (William Heinemann, London: 1924) Part I, pp 366–7.

10. Grey, *Twenty-five Years*, Vol II, p 83.

11. Amanda Mackenzie Stuart, *Consuelo & Alva Vanderbilt: The Story of a Mother and a Daughter in the Gilded Age* (Harper Perennial, London: 2006).

12. Henry Cabot Lodge, *The Senate and the League of Nations* (Charles Scribner & Sons, New York: 1925) p 25.

13. Justus D Doenecke, *Nothing Less Than War: A New History of America's Entry into World War I* (The University Press of Kentucky, Lexington, KY: 2011) p 3.

14. Arthur Hertzberg, *The Jews in America, Four Centuries of an Uneasy Encounter: A History* (Simon and Schuster, New York: 1989) pp 225–6.

15. Dorothy Macardle, *The Irish Republic* (Victor Gollancz, London: 1937; 4th edition, Irish Press Ltd, Dublin: 1951) p 127.

16. Hildegard Biner Johnson, 'The Germans' in June
    Drenning Holmquist, (ed), *They Chose Minnesota:
    A Survey of The State's Ethnic Groups* (Minnesota
    Historical Society Press, St Paul, MN: 1981) pp 153–84.

17. William V Wallace, *Czechoslovakia* (Ernest Benn,
    London: 1976) pp 104–18.

18. 'Confidential to the President', 11 September 1914,
    quoted in Hendrick, *Life and Letters*, Part I, pp 325–6;
    Charles Seymour, *The Intimate Papers of Colonel House*
    (4 volumes, Houghton Mifflin Company, Boston and
    New York: 1925–8) Vol I, p 293.

19. Doenecke, *Nothing Less Than War*, pp 7–8.

20. Seymour, *Intimate Papers*, Vol I, pp 253–4; Godfrey
    Hodgson, *Woodrow Wilson's Right Hand: The Life of
    Colonel Edward M. House* (Yale University Press, New
    Haven and London: 2006).

21. Seymour, *Intimate Papers*, Vol I, pp 252–7.

22. Hodgson, *Wilson's Right Hand*, pp 100–1.

23. Hendrick, *Life and Letters*, Part II, pp 53–64; *The
    Times Documentary History of the War*, Vol III: Naval,
    Part I (The Times Publishing Company, London: 1917)
    Appendix.

24. Grey, *Twenty-five Years*, Vol II, pp 101–6.

25. Hendrick, *Life and Letters*, Part I, p 367 and Part II,
    pp 53–64; 'The Declaration of London', 25 February
    1909, *The Times Documentary History of the War* Vol
    III: Naval, Part 1, pp 429–84; Doenecke, *Nothing Less
    Than War* pp 42–3; Grey, *Twenty-five Years*, Vol II,
    pp 110–12.

26. Doenecke, *Nothing Less Than War*, pp 45–57.

27. Grey, *Twenty-five Years*, Vol II, pp 110–12.

28. Fritz Fischer, *Germany's Aims in the First World War* (Chatto & Windus, London: 1967) pp 282–3.

29. Doenecke, *Nothing Less Than War*, pp 58–63; Cooper, *Woodrow Wilson* pp 275–6; David Stevenson, *1914–1918 The History of the First World War* (Penguin Books, London: 2004) pp 255–6.

30. See Colin Simpson, *Lusitania* (Longman, London: 1972) *passim*; Doenecke, *Nothing Less Than War* pp 70–5; Berg, *Wilson* pp 362–9.

31. Cabot Lodge, *Senate and League* pp 32–3.

32. Franz von Papen, *Memoirs* Translated by Brian Connell (Andre Deutsch, London: 1952) pp 46–52; Barbara W Tuchman, *The Zimmermann Telegram* (Constable & Co Ltd, London: 1959), Chapter 5; Doenecke, *Nothing Less Than War* pp 130–1.

33. Macardle, *The Irish Republic* pp 191–2; Cooper, *Woodrow Wilson* pp 342–3.

34. Cooper, *Woodrow Wilson* pp 319–23.

35. Ibid, pp 334–6; Ross Gregory, *The Origins of American Intervention in the First World War* (W W Norton & Company, Inc., New York: 1971) pp 103–4.

36. Cooper, *Woodrow Wilson*, pp 362–9.

37. Fischer, *Germany's Aims*, pp 302–6; Gordon A Craig, *Germany 1866–1945* (Clarendon Press, Oxford: 1978) pp 379–81; Tuchman, *Zimmermann Telegram*, Chapter 9.

38. Cooper, *Woodrow Wilson*, pp 374–6.

39. Ian H Nish, *Alliance in Decline: A Study in Anglo-Japanese Relations 1908–23* (Athlone Press, London: 1972) pp 212–3.

40. Tuchman, *Zimmermann Telegram*, Chapter 9.

41. Keith Jeffery, *MI6: The History of the Secret Intelligence Service 1909–1949* (Bloomsbury, London: 2010) pp 114–15.
42. Tuchman, *Zimmermann Telegram*, Chapters 10 and 11; Doenecke, *Nothing Less Than War*, p 268.
43. Doenecke, *Nothing Less Than War*, pp 278–80; Cooper, *Woodrow Wilson*, pp 382–9; 'We Must Accept War', Message to Congress, 2 April 1917, quoted in Woodrow Wilson, *In Our First Year of War – Messages and Addresses to the Congress and the people – March 5, 1917 to January 8, 1918* (Harper & Brothers Publishers, New York and London: 1918; reprinted, Filiquarian Publishing, LLC/Qontro: nd) pp 11–19, printed in Great Britain by Amazon Ltd, Marston Gate.

War with Austria-Hungary did not come until December 1917 and the United States never declared war on the Ottoman Empire.

18. Central America, the Caribbean and the First World War

1. 'The Platt Amendment' in Charles I Bevans (ed), *Treaties and Other International Agreements of the United States of America, 1776–1949* (United States Government Printing Office, Washington: 1971) Vol 8, pp 1116–7.
2. Scott Nearing and Joseph Freeman, *Dollar Diplomacy: a Study in American Imperialism* (Heubsch, New York: 1925).
3. Regina Wagner, *Los Alemanes en Guatemala 1828–1944* (Editorial IDEA, Guatemala City: 2007) pp 250–3.
4. James N Cortada and James W Cortada, *US Foreign Policy in the Caribbean, Cuba and Central America* (Praeger, New York: 1986) pp 1–12.

5. Louis A Pérez, *Cuba and the United States: Ties of a Singular Intimacy* (University of Georgia Press, Athens, GA: 1990) p 124; Alan Dye, *Cuban Sugar in the Age of Mass Production: Technology and the Economics of Sugar Central, 1899–1929* (Stanford University Press, Redwood City, CA: 1998) p 9.

6. Hans Schmidt, *The United States Occupation of Haiti, 1915–1934* (Rutgers University Press, New Brunswick, NJ: 1971).

7. Hugh Thomas, *Cuba, or, in Pursuit of Freedom* (Da Capo Press, New York: 1998) p 546.

8. Cortada and Cortada, *US Foreign Policy in the Caribbean*, pp 1–12.

9. Michael Streeter, *Central America and the Treaty of Versailles* (Haus Publishing, London: 2010) *passim*.

19. In the Grasp of the United States

1. Loris Zanatta, *Storia dell'America Latina* (Editori Laterza, Roma-Bari: 2010) pp 9–21.

2. Michael Streeter, *South America and the Treaty of Versailles* (Haus, 2010) pp 28–9.

3. Ibid, p 57.

4. Ibid, p 54.

5. Ibid, pp 76–7.

6. Fredrick Braun Pike, *The Modern History of Peru* (Weidenfeld & Nicolson, 1967) p 254.

7. A Percy Martin, *Latin America and the War*, (The Johns Hopkins University Press, Baltimore, MA: 1925) pp 362–5.

8. Ibid, p 438.

9. Ibid, p 460.

10. Ibid, p 77; Martin, *Latin America and the War*, pp 479–80.

11. Ibid, pp 458–60.
12. Streeter, *South America*, p 10.
13. Martin, *Latin America and the War*, p 480.
14. Ibid, p 460.

20. Greece and the First World War

1. Michael Llewellyn Smith, *Ionian Vision: Greece in Asia Minor, 1919–1922* (Allen Lane, London: 1973) pp 12–18.
2. Reported by Venizelos; quoted in J Gennadius (ed), *The Vindication of Greek National Policy, 1912–1917* (Allen & Unwin, London: 1918) p 125; variant versions in E S Bagger, *Eminent Europeans* (Putnam, New York: 1922) p 103 and Prince Nicholas of Greece, *Political memoirs, 1914–1918* (Hutchinson, London: 1928) p 64.
3. Relevant documents cited in Geoffrey Miller, *Superior Force: the conspiracy behind the escape of Goeben and Breslau* (Geoffrey Miller, Flamborough, 1996), Chapters 11 and 12; www.manorhouse.clara.net/book1/contents. htm, accessed 13 March 2014.
4. Speech at Salonica, 25 November 1916; quoted in H A Gibbons, *Venizelos* (Fisher Unwin, London: 1921) p 202.
5. Hélène Venizelos, *A l'ombre de Veniselos* (Librairie de Médicis, Paris: 1955) pp 30–31.
6. Quoted by George B Leontaritis, *Greece and the First World War: from neutrality to intervention, 1917–1918* (East European Monographs, Boulder, CO: 1990) p 56. At the time when this remark is said to have been made, the former Nicholas II had been forced to abdicate and was under house arrest at Tsarskoe Selo.
7. Gennadius, *Vindication*, pp 148, 161.

21. Why on Earth was Siam a Participant in the First World War?

1. Andrew Dalby, *Prince Charoon and others: South East Asia* (Haus Publishing, London: 2010) *passim*.

22. Labourers in Place of Soldiers

1. Guoqi Xu, *Strangers on the Western Front: Chinese Workers in the Great War* (Harvard University Press, Cambridge, MA: 2011) p 13.

2. Russell Fifield, *Woodrow Wilson and the Far East: the Diplomacy of the Shantung Question* (Thomas Crowell Company, New York: 1952) p 25.

3. Stephen Craft, *V.K. Wellington Koo and the Emergence of Modern China* (University of Kentucky, Lexington, KY: 2004) p 38.

4. Ibid.

5. This also may have been Liang Shiyi's idea, since he proposed it in an article, 'China Must Be a Monarchy Again', in the *New York Times*, 4 June 1916. Although the paper billed him as 'the Brains of China', it seems not all his ideas were winners.

6. Xu, *Strangers*, p 29.

7. Fifield, *Woodrow Wilson*, pp 71–2.

8. 'China: The Early Republican Period', *Encyclopaedia Britannica DVD-ROM* (2001).

9. Quoted in John Fulton Lewis, *China's Great Convulsion 1894–1924* (Sun on Earth, Heathsville: 2005) p 81.

10. Michael Summerskill, *China on the Western Front* (Michael Summerskill, London: 1982) p 226.

11. Xu, *Strangers*, p 8.

12. Summerskill, *China*, pp 209–10.

23. The Wavering Road

1. Michael Streeter, *Epitácio Pessoa: Brazil*, (Haus Publishing, London: 2010) p 20; Joseph Smith, *A History of Brazil, 1500–2000: politics, economy, society, diplomacy* (Longman, London, 2002) p 87.

2. Steven Topik, *Trade and Gunboats: The United States and Brazil in the Age of Empire* (Stanford University Press, Palo Alto, CA: 1996) p 201.

3. Joseph Smith, *Unequal Giants: Diplomatic Relations between the United States and Brazil 1889–1930* (University of Pittsburgh Press: 1991) p 103.

4. S Emily Rosenberg, 'Anglo-American rivalry in Brazil', *Diplomatic History*, Vol 2, No. 2 (1978) pp 131– 52, 140.

5. Boris Fausto, *A Concise History of Brazil* (Cambridge University Press: 1999) p 187.

6. C Frederick Luebke, *Germans in Brazil* (Louisiana State University Press, Baton Rouge, LA: 1987) pp 68– 9.

7. Streeter, *Pessoa*, p 53.

8. Thomas Skidmore, *Brazil: Five Centuries of Change* (Oxford University Press: 1999) p 93.

9. Luebke, *Germans in Brazil*, p 85; Smith, *History of Brazil*, p 133.

10. Skidmore, *Brazil*, p 93.

11. Topik, *Trade and Gunboats*, pp 43– 5; Smith, *Unequal Giants*, p 104.

12. Smith, *Unequal Giants*, p 104; Smith, *A History of Brazil*, p 115.

13. Streeter, *Pessoa*, pp 56– 7.

14. Smith, *Unequal Giants*, p 107.

15. Ibid, pp 109–11.

16. Luebke, *Germans in Brazil*, p 149; Streeter, *Pessoa*, p 61.

17. Streeter, *Pessoa*, pp 62–3.

18. Luebke, *Germans in Brazil,* p 150.
19. Christopher,Clark, *The Sleepwalkers: How Europe went to War in 1914* (Penguin, London: 2013) p 180.
20. Streeter, *Pessoa,* pp 64– 5.
21. Ibid, p 53; Rosenberg, 'Anglo-American rivalry', pp 137– 9.
22. Luebke, *Germans in Brazil,* p 159.
23. P. Alvin Martin, *Latin America and the War,* (The John Hopkins University Press, Baltimore, MA: 1925) p 67; Luebke, *Germans in Brazil,* p 160.
24. Streeter, *Pessoa,* p 66.
25. Smith, *Unequal Giants,* p 117.
26. Martin, *Latin America and the War,* p 68.
27. Ibid, p 4.
28. Smith, *Unequal Giants,* p 117.
29. Smith, *A History of Brazil,* pp 93– 5.

24. Why Did Liberia Enter the First World War?

1. Charles M Wilson, *Liberia: Black Africa in Microcosm* (Harper and Row, New York: 1971) p 110.
2. Ibid, p 98.
3. George W Brown, *The Economic History of Liberia* (Associated Publishers, Washington: 1941) p 139.
4. Wilson, *Liberia,* p 105.
5. R Earle Anderson, *Liberia: America's African Friend* (University of North Carolina Press, Chapel Hill: 1952) p 88.
6. Wilson, *Liberia,* p xii.
7. Ibid, p 105.
8. Ibid, p 90.
9. Brown, *Economic History,* p 174.
10. Quoted in Wilson, *Liberia,* p 110.

11. Ibid, p 112.

25. From Fighting in Three Armies to the Proclamation of an Independent Poland

1. Janusz Pajewski, *Odbudowa państwa polskiego: 1914–1918* (Państwowe Wydawnictwo Naukowe, Warsaw: 1978) p 51.

2. Jerzy Holzer and Jan Molenda, *Polska w Pierwszej Wojnie Światowej* (Wiedza Powszechna, Warsaw: 1963) p 42.

3. Ibid, pp 42–3.

4. Jan Lewandowski, *Królewstwo Polskie pod okupacją austriacką 1914–1918* (Państwowe Wydawnictwo Naukowe, Warsaw: 1980) pp 25–7.

5. Holzer and Molenda, *Polska w Pierwszej*, p 45.

6. Lewandowski, *Królewstwo Polskie*, pp 25–9.

7. Wiktor Sukiennicki, *East Central Europe during World War I: From Foreign Domination to National Independence,* Vol I (East European Monographs, Boulder, CO: 1984) pp 119–20

8. Lewandowski, *Królewstwo Polskie*, pp 29–30.

9. Pajewski, *Odbudowa państwa polskiego*, pp 57–9.

10. Ibid, p 84.

11. Sukiennicki, *East Central Europe,* p 92.

12. Henryk Bagiński, *Wojsko Polskie na Wschodzie 1914–1920* (2nd edition, GRYF, Warsaw: 1990) pp 9–11.

13. Ibid, p 16

14. Holzer and Molenda, *Polska w Pierwszej*, p 52.

15. Sukiennicki, *East Central Europe,* pp 142–3.

16. Pajewski, *Odbudowa państwa polskiego*, pp 103–4.

17. Sukiennicki, *East Central Europe,* pp 268–9.

18. Anita J Prażmowska, *Ignacy Paderewski: Poland* (Haus Publishing, London: 2009) p 47.

19. Ibid, pp 53–4.

20. Sukiennicki, *East Central Europe,* pp 327–8.

21. The precise name was *Abteilung Polnische Wehrmach des General gouvernement Warschau.*

22. A Garlicki, *Józef Piłsudski, 1867–1935* (Scolar Press, Aldershot: 1995) pp 86–7.

23. Jan Zamoyski, *Powrót na mapę. Polski Komitet Narodow w Paryżu, 1914–1919* (Państwowe Wydawnictwo Naukowe, Warsaw: 1991) pp 52–3.

24. Sukiennicki, *East Central Europe*, pp 393–7

25. Garlicki, *Józef Piłsudski,* pp 88–9.

26. The End of the War and Peacemaking 1919

1. David Stevenson *With Our Backs to the Wall: Victory and Defeat in 1918* (Allen Lane, London: 2011) pp 30–169; Bullitt Lowry *Armistice 1918* (Kent State University Press, Kent, OH: 1996) *passim.*

2. Alan Sharp *The Versailles Settlement – Peacemaking after the First World War, 1919–1923* (2nd edition, Palgrave Macmillan, Basingstoke: 2008) pp 24–5.

3. Ibid, *passim*; Margaret MacMillan *Peacemakers: The Paris Conference of 1919 and Its Attempt to End War* (John Murray, London: 2001) *passim.* Manfred Boemeke, Gerald Feldman and Elisabeth Glaser (eds) *The Treaty of Versailles: A Reassessment after 75 Years* (Cambridge University Press: 1998) *passim.*

27. The Signature of the Treaty of Versailles

1. James Headlam-Morley, *A Memoir of the Paris Peace Conference 1919* (Methuen, London: 1972) p 178; Esme

Howard, *Diary 1919*, entry for 28 June, Howard papers in the Cumbria Archive Service, Carlisle.

2. Harry Harmer, *Friedrich Ebert: Germany* (Haus Publishing, London: 2008) p 112.

3. Sir William Orpen, *An Onlooker in France 1917–1919* (Williams and Norgate, London: 1924; reprinted Dodo Press, Gloucester: 2007) pp 125–6.

4. Headlam-Morley, pp 178–9; Harold Nicolson, *Peacemaking 1919* (Constable, London: 1933) pp 370–1; Howard, *Diary*; H W V Temperley (ed), *A History of the Peace Conference of Paris*, 6 volumes (H Frowde: London; Hodder and Stoughton: London; Oxford University Press: 1920–4) Vol II, p 19.

28. The Peace Settlement Reviewed

1. Robert Lansing's note, on behalf of the major allies, undertook 'to make peace with the Government of Germany on the terms of peace laid down in the President's address to Congress of January 8, 1918, and the principles of settlement enunciated in his subsequent Addresses': H W V Temperley (ed), *A History of the Peace Conference of Paris* (6 volumes; Oxford University Press, 1920–1969) Vol I, pp 379–80.

2. Percy to Temperley, 10 November 1920, in 'History of the Paris Peace Conference Correspondence 1919', File 16/2a, Archive of the Royal Institute of International Affairs, London.

3. George Egerton, *Great Britain and the Creation of the League of Nations: Strategy, Politics, and International Organization, 1914–1919* (Scolar Press, London: 1979) pp 63–109.

4. Ruth Henig, *The League of Nations* (Haus Publishing, London: 2010) pp 25–53; Alan Sharp, *The Versailles Settlement: Peacemaking after the First World War, 1918–1923* (2nd edition; Palgrave Macmillan, Basingstoke: 2008) pp 42–80.

5. MacMillan, *Peacemakers: The Paris Peace Conference of 1919 and its Attempt to End War* (John Murray, London: 2001) p 31.

6. Henig, Ruth, *The League of Nations*, (*passim.*

7. Quoted by Richard Debo, *Survival and Consolidation: The Foreign Policy of Soviet Russia 1918–1921* (McGill-Queen's University Press, Montreal: 1992) p 145.

8. Charlotte Alston *Piip, Meierovics, and Voldemaras: Estonia, Latvia and Lithuania* (Haus Publishing, London: 2010); Anita Prazmowska, *Ignacy Paderewski: Poland* (Haus Publishing, London: 2009); Peter Neville *Beneŝ, Masaryk: Czechoslovakia* (Haus Publishing, London: 2010).

9. Bryan Cartledge *Mihály Károlyi and István Bethlen: Hungary* (Haus Publishing, London: 2009) p 142. See also, Raymond Pearson, 'Hungary: A state truncated, a nation dismembered' in S Dunn and T G Fraser (eds) *Europe and Ethnicity: World War I and Contemporary Ethnic Conflict* (Routledge, New York: 1996) pp 88–109.

10. Jamie Bulloch, *Karl Renner: Austria* (Haus Publishing, London: 2010).

11. Harry Harmer, *Friedrich Ebert: Germany* (Haus Publishing, London: 2008).

12. See Stanislas Jeannesson, *Poincaré, La France et La Ruhr (1922–1924): Histoire d'une Occupation* (Presses Universitaires de Strasbourg, Strasbourg: 1998).

13. Antony Lentin, *Lloyd George and the Lost Peace: From Versailles to Hitler 1919–1940* (Palgrave Macmillan, Basingstoke: 2001) pp 67–88.

14. Comte de Saint-Aulaire, *Confession d'un Vieux Diplomate* (Flammarion, Paris: 1953) p 53.

15. Alan Sharp, *David Lloyd George: Great Britain* (Haus Publishing, London: 2008).

16. Sally Marks, *Paul Hymans: Belgium* (Haus Publishing, London: 2010).

17. Spencer Di Scala, *Vittorio Orlando: Italy* (Haus Publishing, London: 2010).

18. R J Crampton *Aleksaniŭr Stamboliĭski: Bulgaria* (Haus Publishing, London: 2009); Andrew Dalby, *Eleftherios Venizelos: Greece* (Haus Publishing, London: 2010); Dejan Djokic, *Pasic and Trumbic: The Kingdom of the Serbs, Croats and Slovenes* (Haus Publishing, London: 2010).

19. Andrew Mango, *From the Sultan to Ataturk: Turkey* (Haus Publishing, London: 2009).

20. Robert McNamara, *The Hashemites: The Dream of Arabia* (Haus Publishing, London: 2009).

21. D Lloyd George, *The Truth about the Peace Treaties* (2 volumes; Victor Gollancz, London: 1938) Vol II, p 1150.

22. T G Fraser, *Chaim Weizmann: The Zionist Dream* (Haus Publishing, London: 2009).

23. Anthony Clayton, '"Deceptive Might": Imperial Defence and Security, 1900–1968' in J Brown and W R Louis (eds), *Oxford History of the British Empire*, Vol IV: *The Twentieth Century* (Oxford University Press: 1999) pp 280–305.

24. Jonathan Clements, *Wellington Koo: China* (Haus Publishing, London: 2008).

25. Jonathan Clements, *Prince Saionji: Japan* (Haus Publishing, London: 2008).

26. Brian Morton, *Woodrow Wilson: United States* (Haus Publishing, London: 2008).

27. Alan Sharp, 'The Versailles Settlement: The Start of the Road to the Second World War?' in Frank McDonough (ed), *The Origins of the Second World War: An International Perspective* (Continuum, New York: 2011) pp 15–33.

28. Antony Lentin, *General Smuts: South Africa* (Haus Publishing, London: 2010) p x.

29. John Maynard Keynes, *The Economic Consequences of the Peace* (Macmillan, London: 1919).

30. For examples of recent more sympathetic treatments of the settlement, see Zara Steiner 'The Treaty of Versailles Revisited' in Michael Dockrill and John Fisher (eds), *The Paris Peace Conference 1919: Peace without Victory?* (Palgrave Macmillan, Basingstoke: 2001) pp 13–33; Mark Mazower, 'Two Cheers for Versailles', *History Today*, Vol 49 (1999) pp 8–14; MacMillan, *Peacemakers, passim*; Alan Sharp, *Consequences of Peace: The Versailles Settlement, Aftermath and Legacy, 1919–2010* (Haus Publishing, London: 2010) pp 1–40 and 211–19; Sally Marks, 'Mistakes and Myths: The Allies, Germany and the Versailles Treaty, 1918–1921', *Journal of Modern History*, Vol 85 (September 2013), pp 632–59. Others remain unconvinced, though the bibliographies in David Andelman, *A Shattered Peace: Versailles 1919 and the Price We Pay Today* (John Wiley & Sons, Hoboken: 2008) or Norman Graebner and Edward Bennett, *The Versailles Treaty and Its Legacy: The*

Failure of the Wilsonian Vision (Cambridge University Press: 2011) are both distinctly dated.

Chronology

YEAR	DATE	
1914	*28 June*	Archduke Franz Ferdinand assassinated in Sarajevo
	5 July	Kaiser Wilhelm II promises German support for Austria-Hungary against Serbia
	28 July	Austria-Hungary declares war on Serbia
	1 August	Germany declares war on Russia
	2 August	Italy formally declares neutrality
	3 August	Germany declares war on France and attacks Belgium
	4 August	Germany declares war on Belgium. The British Empire declares war on Germany
	5 August	Montenegro declares war on Austria-Hungary
	6 August	Austria-Hungary declares war on Russia and Serbia declares war on Germany
	8 August	Montenegro declares war on Germany
	12 August	Britain and France declare war on Austria-Hungary
	23 August	Germany invades France and Japan declares war on Germany

YEAR	DATE	
	25 August	Austria-Hungary declares war on Japan
	28 August	Austria-Hungary declares war on Belgium
	5 September	Treaty of London, Britain, Russia and France agree not to make peace separately.
	29 October	Turkey opens the war on Germany's side
	1 November	Russia declares war on Turkey
	5 November	Britain and France declare war on Turkey
	6 November	Serbia declares war on Turkey
1915	18 January	Japan issues 'Twenty One Demands' to China
	26 April	Treaty of London between Britain, France, Russia and Italy
	23 May	Italy declares war on Austria-Hungary
	3 June	San Marino declares war on Austria-Hungary
	14 October	Bulgaria declares war on Serbia
	15 October	Britain declares war on Bulgaria
	16 October	France declares war on Bulgaria
	19 October	Russia declares war on Bulgaria
	24 October	Britain promises Sherif Hussein an independent Arab state
1916	21 February	Battle of Verdun
	9 March	Germany declares war on Portugal
	15 March	Austria-Hungary declares war on Portugal
	16 May	Sykes-Picot Agreement
	31 May	Battle of Jutland
	5 June	Arab revolt against the Ottoman Empire begins

YEAR	DATE	
	1 July	Battle of the Somme
	28 August	Italy declares war on Germany
	30 August	Turkey declares war on Romania
	1 September	Bulgaria declares war on Romania
	7 December	Lloyd George becomes British Prime Minister
1917	1 February	Germany begins unrestricted U-boat warfare
	3 February	United States breaks off diplomatic relations with Germany
	15 March	Tsar Nicholas II abdicates
	6 April	United States Congress declares war on Germany
	7 April	Cuba and Panama declares war on Germany
	13 April	Bolivia officially breaks off relations with Germany
	27 June	Greece declares war on Austria-Hungary, Germany, Bulgaria and Turkey
	22 July	Siam declares war on Austria-Hungary and Germany
	14 August	China declares war on Austria-Hungary and Germany
	5 October	Peru breaks relations with Germany
	7 October	Uruguay breaks relations with Germany
	26 October	Brazil declares war on Germany
	2 November	Balfour Declaration
	7 November	Bolshevik revolution in Russia
	7 December	United States declares war on Austria-Hungary. Ecuador breaks relations with Germany
	10 December	Panama declares war on Austria-Hungary

YEAR	DATE	
	15 December	Armistice between Germany and Russia signed
1918	8 January	Wilson's Fourteen Points speech to Congress
	12 January	Liberia joins the war
	3 March	German-Soviet Russian Treaty of Brest-Litovsk
	23 April	Guatemala declares war on Germany
	7 May	Romanian-Central Powers Treaty of Bucharest
	8 May	Nicaragua declares war on Austria-Hungary and Germany
	23 May	Costa Rica declares war on Germany
	12 July	Haiti declares war on Germany
	18 July	Allied decisive counter-offensive opens in France
	19 July	Honduras declares war on Germany
	4 October	Germany requests armistice with Wilson
	30 October	Allies sign armistice with Turkey at Mudros
	3 November	Armistice signed between Allies and Austria-Hungary
	5 November	Lansing Note
	9 November	Abdication of Kaiser Wilhelm II, proclamation of German Republic
	11 November	Armistice signed between Allies and Germany
	12 November	Proclamation of Austrian Republic
	14 November	Proclamation of Czechoslovak Republic
	16 November	Proclamation of Hungarian Republic
	August to November	The Hundred Days Offensive achieves a decisive Allied Victory, leading to the fall of the German Empire

YEAR	DATE	
	1 December	Proclamation of the Kingdom of Serbs, Croats and Slovenes
1919	*8 January*	Wilson completes preliminary draft of the League Covenant then completed on the opening conference day
	18 January	Paris Peace Conference begins
	21 April	Italy walks out of Peace Conference
	28 April	Plenary session of Paris Peace Conference approves League Covenant. Eric Drummond appointed as first League Secretary-General
	6 May	Italy returns to the Conference
	7 May	Treaty text presented to Germany
	28 June	Treaty of Versailles signed in the Hall of Mirrors
	10 September	Treaty of St-Germain-en-Laye signed with Austria
	19 November	US Senate refuses to ratify the Treaty of Versailles and to join League

Bibliography

Primary sources
References to specific documents are given in the Notes.

Published documents

British and Foreign State Papers Vol.27 (HMSO, London: 1856).

Collected Diplomatic Documents Relating to the Outbreak of the European War (HMSO, London: 1915).

Papers Relating to the Foreign Relations of the United States: 1919: The Paris Peace Conference, 13 volumes (United States Government Printing Office, Washington, 1942–7).

Charles I Bevans (ed), *Treaties and Other International Agreements of the United States of America, 1776–1949* (United States Government Printing Office, Washington: 1971).

Vladimir Dedijer and Života Anić (eds), *Dokumenti o spoljnoj politici Kraljevine Srbije* (SANU, Belgrade: 1980).

Imanuel Geiss (ed), *July 1914, The Outbreak of the First World War: Selected Documents* (Batsford, London: 1967).

Frank Golder (ed), *Documents of Russian History 1914–1917* (The Century Company, New York: 1927).

G P Gooch and Harold Temperley (eds), *British Documents on the Origin of the War, 1898–1914*, 11 volumes (HMSO, London: 1926–38).

Istituto Giangiacomo Feltrinelli, *Dalle Carte di Giovanni Giolitti. Quarant'anni di politica italiana*, 3 volumes (Feltrinelli, Milan: 1962).

Paul Mantoux, *The Deliberations of the Council of Four (March 24 – June 28 1919: notes of the official interpreter, Paul Mantoux*, 2 volumes (Princeton University Press: 1992).

Portugal na Primeira Guerra Mundial (1914–1918), Vol I: *As Negociações Diplomáticas até à Declaração de Guerra* (Ministério dos Negócios Estrangeiros, Lisbon: 1997).

Alfred F Pribram, *The Secret Treaties of Austria-Hungary, 1879–1914* (Harvard University Press, Cambridge, Mass.: 1920).

Diaries, letters, memoirs, speeches

Albert de Bassompierre, *La Nuit du 2 au 3 août 1914 au Ministère des Affaires Étrangères de Belgique* (Librairie academique, Paris: 1916) in *Seeds of Conflict*, Series 5, *Germany and World Conflict*, Part I (Kraus Reprint, Nedeln: 1976).

Baron Eugène Beyens, *Deux Années à Berlin*, (2 volumes (Librairie Plon, Paris: 1931).

Ivanoe Bonomi, *Le vie nuove del socialismo* (Sestante, Rome: 1944).

Stephen Bonsal, *Suitors and Suppliants: The Little Nations at Versailles* (Prentice Hall, New York: 1946).

Michael and Eleanor Brock (eds), *H.H. Asquith Letters to Venetia Stanley* (Oxford University Press: 1982).

William C Bullitt, *The Bullitt Mission to Russia: Testimony before the Committee on Foreign Relations United States Senate* (B W Huebsch, New York: 1919).

Panta M Draškić, *Moji memoari* (SKZ, Belgrade: 1990).

Hugh S Gibson, *A Journal from Our Legation in Belgium* (Doubleday/Page, Garden City, New York: 1917).

Giovanni Giolitti, *Memorie della mia vita* (Garzanti, Milan: 1967).

Viscount Grey of Falloden, *Twenty-five Years*, 2 volumes (Hodder and Stoughton, London: 1925).

Vladimir Gurko, *Features and Figures of the Past: government and opinion in the reign of Nicholas II*, J E Wallace Sterling, Xenia Joukoff Eudin and H H Fisher (eds), trans Laura Matveev (Stanford University Press, Palo Alto, CA: 1939).

J W Headlam-Morley, *A Memoir of the Paris Peace Conference 1919* (Methuen, New York: 1972).

Burton J Hendrick, *The Life and Letters of Walter H. Page*, 3 volumes (William Heinemann, London,1922–5).

Herbert Hoover, *The Hoover Memoirs*, 3 volumes (Hollis and Carter, London: 1952).

Esme Howard, *Theatre of Life* (Hodder and Stoughton, London: 1936).

General Huguet, *Britain and the War: A French Indictment* (Cassell, London: 1928).

Guglielmo Imperiali, *Diario (1915–1919)* (Rubbettino, Catanzaro: 2006).

Count M Károlyi, *Faith Without Illusion* (Jonathan Cape, London,: 1956).

John Maynard Keynes, *The Economic Consequences of the Peace* (Macmillan, London: 1919).

Arturo Labriola, *Storia di dieci anni* (Il Viandante, Milan: 1910).

David Lloyd George, *War Memoirs*, 2 volumes (Odhams, London, 1938 edition).

——, *The Truth about the Peace Treaties*, 2 volumes (Victor Gollancz, London, 1938).

Frances Lloyd George, *The Years That Are Past* (Hutchinson, London: 1967).

Henry Cabot Lodge, *The Senate and the League of Nations* (Charles Scribner's Sons, New York and London: 1925).

Marvin Lyons (ed), *Vladimir Mikhailovich Bezobrazov: Diary of the Commander of the Russian Imperial Guard 1914–1917* (Dramco Publishers, Boynton Beach, Florida: 1994).

Olindo Malagodi, *Conversazioni della Guerra 1914–1919* (Ricciardi, Milan-Naples: 1960).

Kenneth Morgan (ed), *Lloyd George Family Letters, 1885–1936* (Oxford University Press: 1973).

Maurice Paléologue, *La Russe des Tsars pendant la Grande Guerre* (Librairie Plon, Paris: 1921).

Franz von Papen, *Memoirs*, trans Brian Connell (Andre Deutsch, London: 1952).

Raymond Poincaré, *Les Origines de la Guerre, Conférences prononcées en 1921* (Librairie Plon, Paris: 1921).

——, *Au Service de la France, Neuf Années de Souvenirs*, 11 volumes (Librairie Plon, Paris: 1926–74).

——, *Les Responsibilités de la Guerre, Quatorze Questions par René Gerin, Quatorze Réponses par Raymond Poincaré* (Payot, Paris: 1930).

Morgan Phillips Price, *My Three Revolutions* (Allen and Unwin, London: 1969).

Comte de Saint-Aulaire, *Confession d'un Vieux Diplomate* (Flammarion, Paris:1953).

Antonio Salandra, *La neutralita' italiana 1914–1915* (Mondadori, Milan: 1928).

Sergei Sazanov, *Fateful Years 1906–1916* (Jonathan Cape, London: 1928).

Hugh Seton-Watson, et al. (eds), *R.W. Seton-Watson and the Yugoslavs: Correspondence, 1906–1941*, 2 volumes (British Academy and University of Zagreb, Institute of Croatian History: 1976).

Charles Seymour, *The Intimate Papers of Colonel House*, 4 volumes (Houghton Mifflin Company, New York: 1926–8).

Sidney Sonnino, *Carteggio 1914–1916* (Laterza, Rome: 1974).

H W V Temperley (ed), *A History of the Peace Conference of Paris*, 6 volumes (H Frowde: London; Hodder and Stoughton: London; Oxford University Press: 1920–4).

René Viviani, *As We See It, France and the truth about the War* (Hodder and Stoughton, London: 1923).

Brand Whitlock, *Belgium, a Personal Narrative* (D Appleton, New York: 1919).

Woodrow Wilson, *In Our First Year of War: Messages and Addresses to the Congress and the people, March 5, 1917 to January 8, 1918* (Harper & Brothers, New York: 1918).

Secondary sources

The Makers of the Modern World (Haus Publishing, London)

Charlotte Alston, *Antonius Piip, Zigfrids Meierovics and Augustinas Voldermaras: The Baltic States* (2010).

Carl Bridge, *William Hughes: Australia* (2011).

Jamie Bulloch, *Karl Renner: Austria* (2010).

Bryan Cartledge, *Mihály Károlyi and István Bethlen: Hungary* (2009).

R J Crampton, *Aleksandŭr Stamboliĭski: Bulgaria* (2009).

Jonathan Clements, *Wellington Koo: China* (2008).

——, *Prince Saionji: Japan* (2008).

Andrew Dalby, *Eleftherios Venizelos: Greece* (2010).

——, *Prince Charoon and others: South East Asia* (2010).

Filipe Ribeiro de Meneses, *Afonso Costa: Portugal* (2010)

Spencer Di Scala, *Vittorio Orlando: Italy* (2010).

Dejan Djokic, *Nikola Pašić and Ante Trumbić: The Kingdom of the Serbs, Croats and Slovenes* (2010).

T G Fraser, *Chaim Weizmann: The Zionist Dream* (2009).

Harry Harmer, *Friedrich Ebert: Germany* (2008).

Ruth Henig, *The League of Nations* (2010).

Keith Hitchins, *Ion I. C. Brătianu. Romania* (2011).

Antony Lentin, *General Smuts: South Africa* (2010).

Andrew Mango, *From the Sultan to Atatürk: Turkey* (2009).

Sally Marks, *Paul Hymans: Belgium* (2010).

Robert McNamara, *The Hashemites: The Dream of Arabia* (2009).

Brian Morton, *Woodrow Wilson: United States* (2008).

Peter Neville, *Eduard Beneš and Tomáš Masaryk: Czechoslovakia* (2010).

Anita Prazmowska, *Ignacy Paderewski: Poland* (2009).

Hugh Purcell, *The Maharaja of Bikaner: India,* (2010).

Alan Sharp *David Lloyd George: Great Britain* (2008).

——, *Consequences of Peace: The Versailles Settlement, Aftermath and Legacy, 1919–2010* (2010).

Michael Streeter, *Central America and the Treaty of Versailles* (2010).

——, *Epitácio Pessoa: Brazil,* (2010).

——, *South America and the Treaty of Versailles,* (2010).

Martin Thornton, *Sir Robert Borden: Canada,* (2010).

David Watson, *Georges Clemenceau: France,* (2009)

James Watson, *W.F. Massey New Zealand* (2010).

Books

Luigi Albertini, *The Origins of the War of 1914*, 3 volumes, trans and ed Isabella M Massey (Oxford University Press: 1953 [Milan, 1942]).

René Albrecht-Carrié, *A Diplomatic History of Europe since the Congress of Vienna* (Harper's, New York: 1958).

David Andelman, *A Shattered Peace: Versailles 1919 and the Price We Pay Today* (John Wiley & Sons, Hoboken, NJ: 2008).

William C Askew, *Europe and Italy's Acquisition of Libya, 1911–1912* (Duke University Press, Durham, NC: 1942).

Zourab Avalishvili, *The Independence of Georgia in International Politics 1918–1921* (Headley Brothers, London: 1940).

Jànos M Bak, et al. (eds), *Uses and Abuses of the Middle Ages: Nineteenth to Twenty First Century* (Wilhelm Fink, Munich: 2009).

Sarah Badcock, *Politics and the People in Revolutionary Russia: a provincial history* (Cambridge University Press: 2007).

Henryk Bagiński, *Wojsko Polskie na Wschodzie 1914–1920* (2nd edition, GRYF, Warsaw: 1990).

Ivo Banac, *The National Question in Yugoslavia: Origins, History, Politics* (Cornell University Press, Ithaca, NY: 1984).

W G Beasley, *Japanese Imperialism* (Clarendon Press, Oxford: 1991).

Jean-Jacques Becker, *Le Carnet B, Les Pouvoirs Publics et l'antimilitarisme avant la Guerre de1914* (Editions Klincksieck, Paris: 1973).

——, *L'Armée 14* (Armand Colin, Paris: 2004).

Jean-Jacques Becker and Gerd Krumeich, *La Grande Guerre, Une Histoire Franco-Allemande* (Editions Tallardier, Paris: 2008).

P M H Bell, *France and Britain 1900–1940 Entente and Estrangement* (Longman, New York: 1996).

Max Beloff, *Britain's Liberal Empire: Imperial Sunset 1897–1921* (Methuen, London: 1969).

A Scott Berg, *Wilson* (Simon & Schuster, London: 2013).

Volker Berghahn, *Germany and the Approach of War in 1914* (Macmillan, London: 1973).

David Blackbourn and Geoff Eley, *The Peculiarities of German History: Bourgeois Society and Politics in Nineteenth-Century Germany* (Oxford University Press: 1984).

Manfred Boemeke, Gerald Feldman and Elisabeth Glaser (eds), *The Treaty of Versailles: A Reassessment after 75 Years* (Cambridge University Press: 1998).

Judith M Brown and R Louis (eds), *The Oxford History of the British Empire*, 5 volumes (Oxford University Press: 1998–9), Vol IV: *The Twentieth Century*.

H James Burgwyn, *The Legend of the Mutilated Victory: Italy, the Great War, and the Paris Peace Conference, 1915–1919* (Greenwood Press, Westport, CT: 1993).

Giorgio Candeloro, *Storia dell'Italia moderna* (Feltrinelli, Milan: 1989).

William Carr, *A History of Germany 1815–1985* (3rd edition, Edward Arnold, London: 1987).

Bryan Cartledge, *The Will to Survive: A History of Hungary* (3rd edition, C Hurst and Co., London: 2011).

Gheorghe N Căzan and Şerban Rădulescu-Zoner, *Rumänien und der Dreibund 1878–1914* (Editura Academiei Republicii Socialiste România, Bucharest: 1983).

Christopher Clark, *The Sleepwalkers: How Europe Went to War in 1914* (Penguin, London: 2013).

John Milton Cooper Jr, *Woodrow Wilson: A Biography* (Vintage Books, New York: 2011).

James N Cortada and James W Cortada, *US Foreign Policy in the Caribbean, Cuba and Central America* (Praeger, New York: 1986).

Stephen Craft, *V.K. Wellington Koo and the Emergence of Modern China* (University Press of Kentucky, Lexington, KY: 2004).

Gordon A Craig, *Germany 1866–1945* (Clarendon Press, Oxford: 1978).

Vasa Čubrilović (ed), *Velike sile i Srbija pred Prvi svetski rat* (SANU, Belgrade: 1976).

George Dangerfield, *The Damnable Question: A Study in Anglo-Irish Relations* (Quartet Books, London: 1979).

Richard Debo, *Survival and Consolidation: The Foreign Policy of Soviet Russia 1918–1921* (McGill-Queen's University Press, Montreal: 1992).

Vladimir Dedijer, *The Road to Sarajevo* (MacGibbon & Key, London: 1967).

——, *Sarajevo 1914*, 2 volumes (Prosveta, Belgrade: 1978).

Robert Devleeshouwer, *Les Belges et le danger de guerre, 1910–1914* (Éditions Nauwelaerts, Leuven: 1958).

Spencer Di Scala, *Dilemmas of Italian Socialism: The Politics of Filippo Turati* (University of Massachusetts Press, Amherst, MA: 1980).

Dimitrije Djordjević, *Carinski rat Austro-ugarske i Srbije, 1906–1911* (Istorijski institut, Belgrade: 1962).

Michael Dockrill and John Fisher (eds), *The Paris Peace Conference, 1919: Peace Without Victory?* (Palgrave, Basingstoke: 2001).

Justus D Doenecke, *Nothing Less Than War: A New History of America's Entry into World War I* (University Press of Kentucky, Lexington, KY: 2011).

Jacques Droz, *Les causes de la Première Guerre Mondiale: Essai d'Historiographie* (Editions du Seuil, Paris: 1973).

I G Duca, *Amintiri politice,* Vol 1 (Jon Dumitru-Verlag, Munich: 1981).

S Dunn and T G Fraser (eds), *Europe and Ethnicity: World War I and Contemporary Ethnic Conflict* (Routledge, London: 1996).

Gustave Dupin, *M Poincaré et la Guerre de 1914,* (Librairie du Travail, Paris: 1935).

Alan Dye, *Cuban Sugar in the Age of Mass Production: Technology and the Economics of Sugar Central, 1899–1929* (Stanford University Press, Palo Alto, CA: 1998).

Thomas A Emmert, *Serbian Golgotha: Kosovo, 1389* (East European Monographs, Boulder, NY: 1990).

Thomas A Emmert and Wayne S Vucinich (eds), *Kosovo: Legacy of a Medieval Battle* (University of Minnesota Press, Minneapolis, MN: 1991).

Richard Evans (ed), *Society and Politics in Wilhelmine Germany* (Croom Helm, London: 1978).

R J W Evans and H Pogge von Strandmann (eds), *The Coming of the First World War* (Oxford University Press: 1988).

Boris Fausto, *A Concise History of Brazil* (Cambridge University Press: 1999).

Sidney Fay, *The Origins of the First World War*, 2 volumes (Macmillan, New York: 1928).

Niall Ferguson, *The Pity of War* (Allen Lane, London: 1998).

Russell Fifield, *Woodrow Wilson and the Far East: the Diplomacy of the Shantung Question* (Thomas Crowell Company, New York: 1952).

Fritz Fischer, *Griff Nach der Weltmacht* (Droste Verlag, Düsseldorf, 1961), translated as *Germany's Aims in the First World War* (Chatto and Windus, London: 1967).

——, *Krieg der Illusionen* (Droste Verlag, Düsseldorf: 1969), translated as *War of Illusions* (Chatto and Windus, London: 1975).

Edith Rogovin Frankel, Jonathan Frankel and Baruch Knei-Paz (eds), *Revolution in Russia: Reassessments of 1917* (Cambridge University Press: 1991).

David Fromkin, *A Peace to End All Peace* (Holt, New York: 1989).

——, *Europe's Last Summer: Who Started the Great War in 1914?* (Vintage Books, New York: 2004).

Lieutenant General Emile Galet, *Albert, King of the Belgians in the Great War,* trans Major-General Sir Ernest Swinton (Houghton Mifflin, New York: 1931).

A Garlicki, *Józef Piłsudski, 1867–1935* (Scolar Press, Aldershot: 1995).

Peter Gatrell, *Government, Industry and Rearmament in Russia 1900–1914: the last argument of tsarism* (Cambridge University Press: 1994).

——, *Russia's First World War: A Social and Economic History* (Pearson Longman, Harlow: 2005).

——, *A Whole Empire Walking: Refugees in Russia during World War One* (Indiana University Press, Bloomington, IN: 2005).

Norman Graebner and Edward Bennett *The Versailles Treaty and Its Legacy: The Failure of the Wilsonian Vision* (Cambridge University Press: 2011).

Malbone W Graham, *Diplomatic Recognition of the Border States,* 3 volumes (California University Press, 1935–41).

Ross Gregory, *The Origins of American Intervention in the First World War* (W W Norton, New York: 1971).

John Grigg, *Lloyd George: From Peace to War 1912–1916* (Harper Collins, London: 1997).

J A S Grenville, *Lord Salisbury and Foreign Policy* (Athlone Press, London: 1970).

Henri Haag, *Le comte Charles de Broqueville*, Vol 1 (Collêge Érasme, Louvain-la-Neuve: 1990).

J W Hall, et al. (eds), *Cambridge History of Japan*, 6 volumes, Cambridge University Press: 1988–99).

Max Hastings, *Catastrophe: Europe Goes to War 1914* (William Collins, London: 2013).

M B Hayne, *The French Foreign Office and the Origins of the First World War 1898–1914* (Clarendon Press, Oxford: 1993).

Ruth Henig, *The Origins of the First World War* (Routledge, London: 1989).

David G Herrmann, *The Arming of Europe and the Making of the First World War* (Princeton University Press, 1996).

Arthur Hertzberg, *The Jews in America. Four Centuries of an Uneasy Encounter: A History* (Simon and Schuster, New York: 1989).

Gilles Heuré, *Gustave Hervé, Itinéraire d'un provocateur* (Edition La Découverte, Paris: 1997).

Michael C Hickey (ed), *Competing Voices from the Russian Revolution* (Greenwood, Oxford: 2007).

F H Hinsley (ed), *British Foreign Policy under Sir Edward Grey* (Cambridge University Press: 1977).

Godfrey Hodgson, *Woodrow Wilson's Right Hand: The Life of Colonel Edward M. House* (Yale University Press, New Haven, CT: 2006).

June Drenning Holmquist (ed), *They Chose Minnesota: A Survey of The State's Ethnic Groups* (Minnesota Historical Society Press, St Paul, MN: 1981).

Jerzy Holzer and Jan Molenda, *Polska w Pierwszej Wojnie Światowej* (Wiedza Powszechna, Warsaw: 1963).

Michael Howard, *The Continental Commitment: The Dilemma of British Defence Policy in the Era of Two World Wars* (Pelican, London: 1972).

Anastasie Iordache, *Ion I. C. Brătianu* (Editura Albatros, Bucharest: 1994).

Stanislas Jeannesson, *Poincaré, La France et La Ruhr (1922–1924): Histoire d'une Occupation* (Presses Universitaires de Strasbourg, Strasbourg: 1998).

Keith Jeffery, *MI6: The History of the Secret Intelligence Service 1909–1949* (Bloomsbury, London: 2010).

James Joll, *The Second International 1889–1914* (Weidenfeld and Nicolson, London: 1955).

Dragoljub Jovanović, *Političke uspomene*, 12 volumes (Kultura, Belgrade: 1997).

Jovan M Jovanović, *Borba za narodno ujedinjenje, 1914–1918* (Geca Kon, Belgrade: 1935).

Slobodan Jovanović, *Apis. Moji savremenici*, Vol 10 (Avala, Windsor, Canada: 1962).

John Keiger, *France and the Origins of the First World War* (Macmillan, Basingstoke: 1983).

——, *Raymond Poincaré* (Cambridge University Press: 1997).

Peter Kenez, *Civil War in South Russia* (University of California Press: 1971).

Paul Kennedy, *The Rise and Fall of the Great Powers: Economic and Military Conflict from 1500 to 2000* (Random House, New York: 1987).

Annie Kriegel and Jean-Jacques Becker, *1914 La Guerre et le Mouvement Ouvrier Français* (Librairie Armand Colin, Paris: 1964).

Gerd Krumeich, *Armaments and Politics in France on the eve of the First World, War: The Introduction of Three Year Conscription 1913–1914* (Berg, Leamington Spa: 1984).

Ivo J Lederer, *Yugoslavia at the Paris Peace Conference: A Study in Frontier making* (Yale University Press, New Haven, CT: 1963).

John Fulton Lewis, *China's Great Convulsion 1894–1924* (Sun on Earth, Heathsville: 2005). Antony Lentin, *Lloyd George and the Lost Peace* (Palgrave Macmillan, Basingstoke: 2001). Dominic Lieven, *Russia and the Origins of the First World War* (Macmillan, Basingstoke: 1983).

C Frederick Luebke, *Germans in Brazil* (Louisiana State University Press, Baton Rouge, LA: 1987).

Jan Lewandowski, *Królewstwo Polskie pod okupacją austriacką 1914–1918* (Państwowe Wydawnictwo Naukowe, Warsaw: 1980).

Dorothy Macardle, *The Irish Republic* (Victor Gollancz, London: 1937; 4th edition, Irish Press Ltd, Dublin: 1951).

David MacKenzie, *Apis: The Congenial Conspirator: The Life of Colonel Dragutin T. Dimitrijević* (East European Monographs, Boulder, NY: 1989).

——, *The 'Black Hand' on Trial, Salonika, 1917* (East European Monographs, Boulder, NY: 1995).

Margaret MacMillan *Peacemakers: The Paris Conference of 1919 and Its Attempt to End War* (John Murray, London: 2001).

——, *The War That Ended Peace: How Europe Abandoned Peace for the First World War* (Profile Books, London: 2013).

Frank McDonough (ed), *The Origins of the Second World War: An International Perspective* (Continuum, London: 2011).

Sean McMeekin, *The Russian Origins of the First World War* (Belknap of Harvard University Press, Cambridge, MA: 2011).

——, *July, 1914: Countdown to War* (Icon Books, London: 2013).

James M McPherson and David Rubel (eds), 'To The Best of My Ability': The American Presidents (Dorling Kindersley Publishing, Inc., New York: 2000).

Noel Malcolm, Bosnia: A Short History (Macmillan, London: 1996).

Andrew Mango, Atatürk (John Murray, London: 1999).

A H de Oliveira Marques (ed), O Segundo Governo de Afonso Costa, 1915–1916 (Publicações Europa-América, Lisbon: 1974).

A Percy Martin, Latin America and the War, (Johns Hopkins Press, Baltimore MA: 1925).

B F Martin, The Hypocrisy of Justice in the Belle Epoque, (Louisiana State University Press, Baton Rouge: 1984).

Veselin Masleša, Mlada Bosna (IP 'Veselin Masleša', Sarajevo: 1964).

Robert K Massie, Nicholas and Alexandra (Victor Gollancz, London: 1967).

Evan Mawdsley, The Russian Civil War (Unwin Hyman, Boston, MA: 1987).

Andrej Mitrović, Jugoslavija na Konferenciji mira, 1919–1920 (Zavod za izdavanje udžbenika, Belgrade: 1969).

——, Prodor na Balkan i Srbija, 1914–1918 (Zavod za udžbenike, Belgrade: 2011; first published 1981).

——, Srbija u Prvom svetskom ratu (2nd edition, Stubovi kulture, Belgrade: 2004)

——, Serbia's Great War, 1914–1918, (C Hurst & Co., London: 2007).

Annika Mombauer, The Origins of the First World War: Controversies and Consensus (Longman, London: 2002).

G W Monger, The End of Isolation: British Foreign Policy1900–1907 (Nelson, Edinburgh and London: 1963).

Kenneth Morgan, *Lloyd George* (Book Club Associates, London: 1974).

William Mulligan, *The Origins of the First World War* (Cambridge University Press: 2010).

Jean-Yves Le Naour, *L'Affaire Malvy* (Hachette, Paris: 2007).

Scott Nearing and Joseph Freeman, *Dollar Diplomacy: a Study in American Imperialism* (Heubsch, New York: 1925).

Keith Neilson, *Strategy and Supply: The Anglo-Russian Alliance 1914–1917* (Allen & Unwin, London: 1984).

Harold Nicolson, *Lord Carnock* (Constable, London: 1930).

Ian H Nish, *Alliance in Decline: A Study in Anglo-Japanese Relations 1908–23* (Athlone Press, London: 1972).

Constantin Nuțu, *România în anii neutralității 1914–1916* (Editura Științifică, Bucharest: 1972).

Robin Okey, *Taming Balkan Nationalism* (Oxford University Press: 2007).

Sir William Orpen, *An Onlooker in France 1917–1919* (Williams and Norgate, London: 1924; reprinted Dodo Press, Gloucester: 2007.)

M E Page (ed), *Africa and the First World War* (Macmillan, Basingstoke: 1987).

John Palmer, *South Bend. Crossroads of Commerce* (Arcadia Publishing, Charleston, SC: 2003).

Michael R Palmer, 'The British Nexus and the Russian Liberals 1905–1917', PhD thesis (University of Aberdeen, 2000).

Milada Paulová, *Jugoslovenski odbor: Povijest jugoslovenske emigracije za svjetskog rata od 1914–1918* (Prosvjetna nakladna zadruga, Zagreb: 1924).

Aleksandar-Aca Pavlović, *1914: Ljudi i događaji, ideje i ideali* (Jelena-Lela Pavlović, Belgrade: 2002).

Stevan K Pavlowitch, *Serbia: The History Behind the Name* (C Hurst & Co., London: 2002).

Louis A Pérez, *Cuba and the United States: Ties of a Singular Intimacy* (Georgia University Press, Athens, GA: 1990).

Bryan Perrett and Anthony Lord, *The Czar's British Squadron* (William Kimber and Co., London: 1981).

Michael Boro Petrovich, *A History of Modern Serbia*, 2 volumes (Harcourt Brace Jovanovich, New York: 1976).

Fredrick Braun Pike, *The Modern History of Peru* (Weidenfeld & Nicolson, London: 1967).

Janusz Pajewski, *Odbudowa państwa polskiego: 1914–1918* (Państwowe Wydawnictwo Naukowe, Warsaw: 1978).

Novica Rakočević, *Crna Gora u Prvom svjetskom ratu, 1914–1918* (ITP 'Unireks', Podgorica, Montenegro: 1997).

Matthew Rendle, *Defenders of the Motherland: The Tsarist Elite in Revolutionary Russia* (Oxford University Press: 2010).

Aaron Retish, *Russia's Peasants in Revolution and Civil War: citizenship, identity and the creation of the Soviet State 1914–1922* (Cambridge University Press: 2008).

Jean-Pierre Rioux, *Jean Jaurès* (Perrin, Paris: 2005).

Hans Rogger, *Russia in the Age of Modernisation and Revolution 1881–1917* (Longman, London: 1983).

A William Salomone, *Italy in the Giolittian Era: Italian Democracy in the Making 1900–1914* (University of Pennsylvania Press, Philadelphia, PA: 1945; 1960 edition).

Charles Sarolea, *Europe's Debt to Russia* (Heinemann, London: 1915).

Hans Schmidt, *The United States Occupation of Haiti, 1915–1934* (Rutgers University Press, New Brunswick, NJ: 1971).

Alfred Senn, *Emergence of Modern Lithuania* (Colombia University Press, New York: 1959).

R W Seton-Watson, *The Southern Slav Question and Habsburg Monarchy* (Constable, London: 1911).

——, *Sarajevo: A Study in the Origins of the War* (Hutchinson, nd [1926]).

Robert Service, *Lenin: A Biography* (Macmillan, Basingstoke: 2000).

Alan Sharp, *The Versailles Settlement: Peacemaking After the First World War, 1919–1923* (2nd edition, Palgrave Macmillan, Basingstoke: 2008).

Lewis Siegelbaum, *The Politics of Industrial Mobilization in Russia, 1915–1917: A Study of the War Industries Committees* (Palgrave Macmillan, Basingstoke: 1984).

Colin Simpson, *Lusitania* (Longman, London: 1972).

James Simpson, *The Self-Discovery of Russia* (Constable, London: 1916).

Vladislav Škarić, Osman Nuri Hadžić and Nikola Stojanović, *Bosna i Hercegovina pod austrougarskom upravom* (Geca Kon, Belgrade: 1938).

Thomas Skidmore, *Brazil: Five Centuries of Change*, (Oxford University Press: 1999).

Joseph Smith, *Unequal Giants: Diplomatic Relations between the United States and Brazil 1889–1930* (University of Pittsburgh Press: 1991).

——, *A History of Brazil, 1500–2000: Politics, Economy, Society, Diplomacy* (Longman, London and New York: 2002).

Jon Smele, *Civil War in Siberia: the Anti-Bolshevik Government of Admiral Kolchak 1918–1920* (Cambridge University Press: 1996).

Jonathan Steinberg, *Yesterday's Deterrent: Tirpitz and the Birth of the German Battle Fleet* (Macdonald, London: 1965).

Zara Steiner, *The Foreign Office and Foreign Policy 1898–1914* (Cambridge University Press: 1969).

———, *Britain and the Origins of the First World War* (Macmillan, London: 1977).

Norman Stone, *The Eastern Front 1914–1917* (Hodder and Stoughton, London: 1975).

Hew Strachan, *The First World War*, Vol I: *To Arms* (Oxford University Press: 2001).

Amanda Mackenzie Stuart, *Consuelo & Alva Vanderbilt: The Story of a Mother and a Daughter in the Gilded Age* (Harper Perennial, London: 2005).

Wiktor Sukiennicki, *East Central Europe during World War I: From Foreign Domination to National Independence,* 2 volumes (East European Monographs, Boulder, NY: 1984).

Michael Summerskill, *China on the Western Front* (Michael Summerskill, London: 1982).

Djordje Stanković, *Nikola Pašić i jugoslovensko pitanje* (2 volumes, BIGZ, Belgrade, 1985).

Geoff Swain, *The Origins of the Russian Civil War* (Longman, London: 1996).

Daniel H Thomas, *The Guarantee of Belgian Independence and Neutrality in European Diplomacy, 1830s–1930s* (D H Thomas Publishing Co, Kingston, Rhode Island: 1983).

Hugh Thomas, *Cuba, or, in Pursuit of Freedom* (Da Capo Press, New York: 1998).

John M Thompson, *Russia, Bolshevism and the Versailles Peace* (Princeton University Press: 1966).

Mark Thompson, *The White War: Life and Death on the Italian Front 1915–1918* (Basic Books, New York: 2008).

Steven Topik, *Trade and Gunboats: The United States and Brazil in the Age of Empire* (Stanford University Press, Stanford, CA: 1997)

Glenn E Torrey, *Romania and World War I* (The Center for Romanian Studies, Iaşi: 1998).

G M Trevelyan, *Grey of Falloden* (Longmans, London: 1937).

Barbara Tuchman, *The Zimmermann Telegram* (Constable, London: 1958).

Mitja Velikonja, *Religious Separation and Political Intolerance in Bosnia-Herzegovina* (Texas A & M University Press, College Station, TX: 2003).

G Vermes, *István Tisza* (Colombia University Press, New York: 1985).

Laurent Villatte *La République du Diplomates, Paul et Jules Cambon 1843–1935* (Science Infuse, Paris: 2002).

V I Vinogradov, *Rumyniia v gody pervoi mirovoi voiny* (Izdatel'stvo Nauka, Moscow: 1969).

Andrew B Wachtel, *Making a Nation, Breaking a Nation: Literature and Cultural Politics in Yugoslavia* (Stanford University Press, Palo Alto, CA: 1998).

Regina Wagner, *Los Alemanes en Guatemala 1828–1944* (Editorial IDEA, Guatemala City: 2007).

Neville Waites (ed), *Troubled Neighbours: France-British Relations in the Twentieth Century* (Weidenfeld and Nicolson, London: 1971).

Donald Mackenzie Wallace, *Our Russian Ally* (Macmillan, London: 1914).

William V Wallace, *Czechoslovakia* (Ernest Benn Limited, London: 1976).

David Robin Watson, *Georges Clemenceau: A Political Biography* (Eyre Methuen, London: 1974).

Samuel R Williamson, *The Politics of Grand Strategy: Britain and France Prepare for War, 1904–1914* (Ashfield, London: 1990).

Keith Wilson, *The Policy of the Entente: Essays on the Determinants of British Foreign Policy, 1904–1914* (Cambridge University Press: 1985).

—— (ed), *Decisions for War, 1914* (UCL Press, London: 1995).

—— (ed) *Forging the Collective Memory: Government and International Historians through Two World Wars* (Berghahn, Oxford: 1996).

Guoqi Xu, *Strangers on the Western Front: Chinese Workers in the Great War* (Harvard University Press, Cambridge, MA: 2011).

Jan Zamoyski, *Powrót na mapę. Polski Komitet Narodow w Paryżu, 1914–1919* (Państwowe Wydawnictwo Naukowe, Warsaw: 1991).

Loris Zanatta, *Storia dell'America Latina*, (Editori Laterza, Roma-Bari: 2010).

Z A B Zeman, *A Diplomatic History of the First World War* (Weidenfeld and Nicolson, London: 1971).

Milan Živanović, *Pukovnik Apis: Solunski proces 1917* (Self-published, Belgrade: 1955).

Book chapters

Christopher Andrew, 'The Entente Cordiale from its
    Origins to 1914' in Waites, *Troubled Neighbours*,
    pp 11–39.

Anthony Clayton, '"Deceptive Might": Imperial Defence
    and Security, 1900–1968' in Brown and Louis *Oxford
    History of the British Empire*, Vol IV, pp 280–305.

Mark Cornwall, 'Serbia' in Wilson *Decisions for War, 1914*,
    pp 55–96.

Dejan Djokić ,'Whose Myth? Which Nation? The Serbian
    Kosovo Myth Revisited' in Bak, *Uses and Abuses of
    the Middle Ages: Nineteenth to Twenty First Century*,
    pp 215–33.

Michael Ekstein and Zara Steiner, 'The Sarajevo Crisis' in
    Hinsley, *British Foreign Policy*, pp 397–410.

Fritz Fellner, 'Austria-Hungary' in Wilson, *Decisions for
    War*, pp 9–25.

——, 'Die "Mission Hoyos"' in Čubrilović, *Velike sile i
    Srbija pred Prvi svetski rat*, pp 387–410.

Ronald Hyam, 'The British Empire in the Edwardian
    Era' in Brown and Louis *Oxford History of the British
    Empire* Vol IV, pp 47–63.

Alexander Hoyos, 'Meine Mission Nach Berlin' in
    Čubrilović, *Velike sile i Srbija pred Prvi svetski rat*,
    pp 411–18.

Hata Ikuhiko, 'Continental Expansion 1905–1941' in Peter
    Duus (ed), *Cambridge History of Japan, Vol 6: The
    Twentieth Century* (Cambridge University Press: 1989),
    pp 271–314.

Hildegard Biner Johnson, 'The Germans' in Holmquist,
    They Chose Minnesota, pp 153–84.

W D McIntyre, 'Australia, New Zealand, and the Pacific Islands' in Brown and Louis, *Oxford History of the British Empire*, Vol IV, pp 667–92.

David Mandel, 'October in the Ivanovo-Kineshma industrial region' in Frankel, Frankel and Knei-Paz *Revolution in Russia*, pp 157–87.

J K Matthew, 'Reluctant Allies: Nigerian responses to military recruitment 1914–1918' in Page *Africa and the First World War*, pp 95–114

Keith Neilson, 'Russia' in Wilson, *Decisions for War*, pp 97–120.

——, 'That Elusive Entity British Policy in Russia: The Impact of Russia on British Policy at the Paris Peace Conference' in Dockrill and Fisher, *Paris Peace Conference*, pp 67–101.

Raymond Pearson, 'Hungary: A state truncated, a nation dismembered' in Dunn and Fraser *Europe and Ethnicity*, pp 88–109.

John Röhl, 'Germany' in Wilson, *Decisions for War*, pp 27–54.

Alan Sharp, 'The Versailles Settlement: The Start of the Road to the Second World War?' in McDonough *The Origins of the Second World War*, pp 15–33

D W Spring, 'Russia and the Coming of War' in Evans and von Strandmann, *The Coming of the First World War*, pp 57–86

Jean Stengers, 'Belgium' in Wilson, *Decisions for War*, pp 151–74.

D W Sweet and R T B Langhorne, 'Great Britain and Russia, 1907–1914' in Hinsley *British Foreign Policy*, pp 236–55.

Beryl Williams, 'Great Britain and Russia, 1905 to the 1907 Convention' in Hinsley *British Foreign* Policy, pp 133–47.

Keith Wilson, 'Britain' in Wilson, *Decisions for War*, pp 175–208.

Articles

René Albrecht-Carrié, 'The Present Significance of the Treaty of London of 1915',*The Political Science Quarterly*, Vol 54, No. 3 (September 1939), pp 364–90

——, 'Italian Colonial Problems in 1919', *Political Science Quarterly*, Vol 58, No. 4 (December, 1943) pp 562–80.

——, 'Italian Colonial Policy' *Journal of Modern History*, Vol 18, No. 2 (June 1946) pp 123–47.

Charlotte Alston, 'The Suggested Basis for a Russian Federal Republic: Britain, Anti-Bolshevik Russia and the Border States at the Paris Peace Conference, 1919', *History*, Vol. 91, No. 301 (January 2006) pp 24–44.

Ronald Bobroff, 'Behind the Balkan Wars: Russian Policy toward Bulgaria and the Turkish Straits, 1912–13', *Russian Review*, Vol 59, No. 1 (2000) pp 76–95.

John and Peter Coogan, 'The British Cabinet and the Anglo-French Staff Talks, 1905–1914: Who Knew What and When Did He Know It?', *Journal of British Studies*, Vol 24 (January 1985) pp 110–31.

Spencer Di Scala, 'Parliamentary Socialists, the Statuto, and the Giolittian System', *The Australian Journal of Politics and History*, Vol 25, No. 2 (August 1979) pp 155–68.

Edith M Durham, 'Fresh Light on the Sarajevo Crime', *Contemporary Review* (January 1925) pp 39–49.

Sidney Bradshaw Fay, 'The Black Hand Plot That Led to the World War', *Current History*, Vol 23, No. 2 (November 1925) pp 196–207.

W Harrison, 'Mackenzie Wallace's View of the Russian
  Revolution of 1905–1907', *Oxford Slavonic Papers,* New
  Series 4 (1971) pp 73–82.

Michael Hughes, 'Bernard Pares, Russian Studies and the
  Promotion of Anglo-Russian Friendship 1907–1914',
  Slavonic and East European Review, Vol 78, No. 3 (July
  2000) pp 510–35.

——, 'Searching for the Soul of Russia: British Perceptions
  of Russia during the First World War', *Twentieth
  Century British History*, Vol 20, No. 2 (2009)
  pp 198–226.

Ljuba [Ljubomir] Jovanović, 'Posle Vidova Dana 1914.
  godine' in Jovanović, *1914–1924. Krv slovenstva:
  Spomenica desetogodišnjice svetskog rata* (Štamparija
  Save Radenkovića i brata, Belgrade: 1924) pp 9–23;
  translated into English as 'The Murder of Sarajevo' in
  Journal of the British Institute of International Affairs,
  Vol 4, No. 2 (March 1925) pp 57–69.

Sally Marks, 'Mistakes and Myths: The Allies, Germany
  and the Versailles Treaty, 1918–1921', *Journal of Modern
  History,* Vol 85 (September 2013) pp 632–59.

Mark Mazower, 'Two Cheers for Versailles', *History
  Today*, Vol 49 (1999) pp 8–14.

Keith Neilson, '"Joy Rides"? British Intelligence and
  Propaganda in Russia, 1914–1917', *Historical Journal*,
  Vol 24 (1981) pp 885–906.

——, 'Watching the "steamroller": British observers and the
  Russian army before 1914', *Journal of Strategic Studies*,
  Vol 8, No. 2 (1985) pp 199–217.

S Emily Rosenberg, 'Anglo American rivalry in Brazil',
  Diplomatic History Vol 2, No. 2 (1978) pp 131–52.

Joshua Sanborn, 'The Mobilization of 1914 and the Question of the Russian Nation: A Reexamination', *Slavic Review*, Vol 59, No. 2 (2000) pp 267–89.

——, 'Russian Historiography on the Origins of the First World War since the Fischer Controversy', *Journal of Contemporary History*, Vol 48, No. 2 (2013) pp 350–62.

M L Sanders, 'British Film Propaganda during the First World War', *Historical Journal of Film, Radio and Television*, Vol 3 (1983) pp 117–29.

Jon Smele, 'Mania grandiosa' and 'The Turning Point in World History': Kerensky in London in 1918', *Revolutionary Russia*, Vol 20, No. 1 (June 2007) pp 1–34.

Russell E Snow, 'The Russian Revolution of 1917–18 in Transbaikalia', *Soviet Studies*, Vol 23 No. 2 (1971) pp 201–15.

Leo Valiani, 'Documenti francesi sull'Italia e il movimento Yugoslavo', *Rivista Storica Italiana*, Vol 80, No. 2 (1968) pp 351–64.

Newspapers and periodicals

Bulletin of the Russian Liberation Committee
Daily Mail
The New York Times
Nineteenth Century
The Russian Commonwealth
The Russian Outlook
The Times

Author Biographies

Charlotte Alston is Senior Lecturer in History at Northumbria University, Newcastle upon Tyne. She is the author of three books: *Russia's Greatest Enemy? Harold Williams and the Russian Revolutions* (I B Tauris, 2007); *Piip, Meierovics, Voldermaras: The Baltic States*, in the series Makers of the Modern World: The Peace Conferences and their Aftermath (Haus, 2010); and *Tolstoy and his Disciples: the history of a radical international movement* (I B Tauris, 2013). She has published journal articles and book chapters on Russia's relations (both cultural and diplomatic) with the West, the history of the Russian revolution and civil war, the post-First World War peace settlements, and the international influence of Tolstoy's thought.

Edoardo Braschi is a freelance author. He earned a Master's Degree in Contemporary History at the University of Florence with a thesis on the German occupation of Italy during World War Two. His main field of research lies in both local and national contemporary Italian history. His publications include *Lavoravo alla Todt. La costruzione della Linea Gotica in Mugello* (2010), *Dal Chianti alla Nazione. Patria,* *comunità e peasaggio nel Risorgimento italiano* (2011), *Patria, Libertà, Progresso. Storia e simboli di Mutuo Soccorso dall'archivio della Fratellanza artigiana di Greve in Chianti 1882–1956* (2013).

Bryan Cartledge is a retired diplomat, who served in Sweden, the Soviet Union and Iran before being appointed, in 1977, to be Private Secretary (Overseas Affairs) to the British Prime Minister; he served both James Callaghan and Margaret Thatcher in that capacity before taking up his first ambassadorial appointment as British Ambassador to Hungary, in 1980. After serving for three years as British Ambassador to the USSR, Cartledge left the Diplomatic Service in 1988 on his election to be Principal of Linacre College, Oxford. Earlier in his career, he was enlisted to assist Sir Anthony Eden (later the Earl of Avon) with the first volume of his memoirs. At Oxford, he edited six books on environmental issues. He holds diplomas in the Hungarian language from the Universities of Westminster and Debrecen (Hungary). His well-received history of Hungary, *The Will to Survive*, fulfils an aspiration which grew out of his deep interest in that country, where he lived for three years.

Jonathan Clements is a Visiting Professor at the Shaanxi Key Laboratory of E-Commerce and E-Government, Xi'an Jiaotong University, China. He is the author of the volumes in the Makers of the Modern World series on both Wellington Koo (China) and Prince Saionji (Japan). His other books include a new translation of Sun Tzu's *Art of War* and volumes on modern China and Japan in Hodder's *All That Matters* series.

Andrew Dalby is a historian, linguist and translator, who has worked on early and medieval Greece (notably *Rediscovering Homer*, 2006) and on South East Asia. He has also written on the social history of languages (*Language in Danger*, 2002) and on food history, including *The Breakfast Book* (2013) and the acclaimed *Siren Feasts: a history of food and gastronomy in Greece* (1996), which won a Runciman Award.

Dejan Djokić is Reader in History and Director of the Centre for the Study of the Balkans, Goldsmiths, University of London. He is the author of, among other works, *Elusive Compromise: A History of Interwar Yugoslavia* (2007) and *Pašić & Trumbić: The Kingdom of Serbs, Croats and Slovenes* (2010), and is currently working on *A Concise History of Serbia* for Cambridge University Press.

Irene Fattacciu is a research fellow at the University of Turin. She earned her PhD at the European University Institute (Florence, Italy) with a thesis investigating the mechanisms and implications of appropriation and diffusion of chocolate through Atlantic and Spanish networks during the 18th century. She has published several articles and essays in international publications, such as 'The Resilience and Boomerang Effect of Chocolate: A Product's Globalization and Commodification' in B. Yun Casalilla, B. Aram Worzella ed., *American Products in the Spanish Empire. Globalization, Resistance and Diversity, 1492–1824.* (London: Palgrave Macmillan, forthcoming 2014) and 'Alexis E. Frye y la experiencia de los maestros Cubanos en Harvard en el 1900' in A. Lorini ed., *An intimate and contested relation: the United States and Cuba in the late 19th and early 20th centuries,* (Florence: Firenze University Press, 2007). Her present research focuses on visual culture and racial categorization in the Caribbean area during the 19th century, exploring strategies of self-representation and resistance to racial stereotypes by free people of colour in New Orleans and Havana through photographic portraiture.

T G Fraser, MBE, is Emeritus Professor of History and Honorary Professor of Conflict Research at the University of Ulster, previously Provost of its Magee campus. In 1983–4 he was Fulbright Scholar-in-Residence at Indiana University at South Bend. With Haus Publishing he has published: *Chaim Weizmann. The Zionist Dream* (2009), with Andrew Mango and Robert McNamara, *The Makers of the Modern Middle East* (2011); and contributed to *East-West Divan. In Memory of Werner Mark Linz* (The Gingko Library, 2014). He is a Fellow of the Royal Asiatic Society, the Royal Historical Society and the Royal Society of Arts.

Keith Hitchins is Professor of History at the University of Illinois and specialises in Southeastern Europe, Romania, Transylvania, the Kurds, Central Asia, and nationalism. Among his more recent books are *Rumania, 1866– 1947*, in the Oxford History of Modern Europe series (Oxford: Clarendon Press, 1994), *The Romanians, 1774–1866* (Oxford: Clarendon Press, 1996), *A Nation Discovered: Romanian Intellectuals in Transylvania and the Idea of Nation, 1700–1848* (Bucharest: Encyclopaedic Publishing House, 1999), *A Nation Affirmed: The Romanian National Movement in Transylvania, 1860–1914* (Bucharest: Encyclopaedic Publishing House, 1999), *Ion I. C. Brătianu: Romania* (Haus Publishing, London: 2011) and *A Concise History of Romania* (Cambridge University Press, Cambridge: 2014). He has a

Ph.D from Harvard University and holds honorary degrees from the universities of Cluj, Sibiu, Alba Iulia, Târgu Mureş, and Timişoara in Romania. He is an honorary member of the Romanian Academy.

Mariella Hudson is an undergraduate English and History student at the pioneering New College of the Humanities in Bloomsbury, where she is part of the editorial team and a regular contributor to *Anchor* newspaper and *The Parturient*, a creative arts journal. She is a playwright as well as a non-fiction writer, and her first play, *Things Made to Last*, won the Arthur Cotterell Theatre One-Act Playwriting Competition for the south-east of England.

Antony Lentin is a Senior Member of Wolfson College, Cambridge, a Fellow of the Royal Historical Society and a Barrister. Formerly a Professor of History and Law Tutor at the Open University, he is the author of *Guilt at Versailles: Lloyd George and the Pre-History of Appeasement* (1985), *Lloyd George and the Lost Peace* (2001), and *General Smuts* in the series 'Makers of the Modern World: the peace conferences of 1919–1923 and their aftermath' published by Haus. He has published *The Last Political Law Lord: Lord Sumner (1859–1934)* (2008) and is currently writing a biography of another controversial judge, Sir Henry McCardie (1869–1933). His most recent book, *Banker, Traitor, Scapegoat, Spy: The Troublesome Case of Sir Edgar Speyer*, was published by Haus in 2013.

Andrew Mango is the author of the definitive biography of *Atatürk* (2002), as well as an account of modern Turkey, *The Turks Today* (2004). He was for 14 years in charge of broadcasting in Turkish for the BBC and later headed the BBC's South European Service and its French Language Service.

Sally Marks is an American independent historian specializing in interwar European (and some American) international politics, particularly in the pre-Hitlerian era from 1918 to 1933. Her dissertation at the University of London dealt with the Paris peace settlement, as have her works since. A recipient of awards from the American Council of Learned Societies and the AHA, she has published numerous articles and chapters, especially about the controversial question of German reparations payments. Her books include: *The Illusion of Peace: International Relations in Europe, 1918–1933* (Macmillan-St. Martin's-Palgrave, 1976, 2nd ed. 2003); *Innocent Abroad: Belgium at the Paris Peace Conference of 1919* (University of North Carolina Press, 1981), which won the George Louis Beer prize of the AHA and Phi Alpha Theta's senior scholar award; *The Ebbing of European Ascendancy: An International History of the World, 1914–1945* (Edward Arnold, 2002) and *Paul Hymans: Belgium* (Haus Publishing, London: 2010). She has served on the AHA's program committee and Beer prize committee, which she chaired, and is a member of the editorial board of H-Diplo. She recently published an article reassessing the Versailles Treaty.

Robert McNamara, a graduate of University College Cork, is currently a Senior Lecturer in International History at the University of Ulster. His publications include: with Tom Fraser and Andrew Mango, *The Makers of the Modern Middle East* (2011); *The Hashemites: The Dream of Arabia* (2010); *Britain, Nasser and the Balance of Power in the*

Middle East from Egyptian Revolution to the Six Day War (2003) and the edited collection *The Churchills in Ireland* (2012)

Filipe Ribeiro de Meneses is Professor of History at the National University of Ireland Maynooth. In 2005–6 and again 2011–12 he was an Irish Research Council Research Fellow, and in 2012–13 he was a Visiting Professor at Brown University. A specialist in contemporary Portuguese and Spanish history, his publications include *Franco and the Spanish Civil War* (2001), *Portugal 1914–1926: From the First World War to Military Dictatorship* (2004), and *Salazar: A Political Biography* (2009), which was also published in Portugal and Brazil. He is currently writing on the subject of Portuguese decolonization.

Anita Prazmowska teaches courses at the Department of International History at the London School of Economics and Political Science. In her research, Professor Prazmowska focuses mainly on areas related to Modern Polish and East European History. Her publications principally analyse Polish foreign policy before and during the Second World War. Additionally, she has written more general commentaries on Poland's place in Europe. Publications include *Britain, Poland and the Eastern Front, 1939* (Cambridge University Press, Cambridge: 1987), *Britain and Poland 1939–1943. The Betrayed Ally* (Cambridge University Press, Cambridge: 1995) and *Civil War in Poland, 1941–1948* (Palgrave Macmillan, Basingstoke: 2004). Her *Eastern Europe and the Origins of the Second World War* (Macmillan, Basingstoke: 2000) is an aid to teaching. Her general commentaries include *A History of Poland,* (Palgrave Macmillan, Basingstoke: 2004) and *Poland. A Modern History*, (I B Tauris, London: 2010). Her most recent work is *Władysław Gomułka. A Political Biography*, soon to be published by I B Tauris in their series of Communist Lives. Professor Prażmowska also commentates for TV and radio on contemporary Polish history and politics.

Spencer Di Scala is Professor of History and past History Graduate Program Director at the University of Massachusetts, Boston. He is the author of numerous scholarly books and articles on Italian and European politics and culture, serves on the editorial boards of scholarly journals, and has edited a book series on Italian and Italian American Studies. He taught at the University of Kentucky and in 1970 began teaching at the University of Massachusetts, Boston. Among other books, he has published *Dilemmas of Italian Socialism: The Politics of Filippo Turati, Renewing Italian Socialism: Nenni to Craxi, Italy: From Revolution to Republic: 1700 to the Present*, chosen as an alternate of the History Book Club and which has gone into several editions, *European Political Thought, 1815–1989* (co-author) and *Europe's Long Century: Society, Politics and Culture 1900–Present*. In 1983 he was named a Senior Fulbright Research Fellow in Rome and in 1997 Research Professor by the University of Massachusetts. In 1995 he was named a Commendatore (Commander) in the Order of Merit of the Italian Republic.

Alan Sharp is Emeritus Professor of International History at the University of Ulster from which he retired as Provost of the Coleraine campus in 2009. His books include *The Versailles Settlement: Peacemaking after the First World War, 1919–1923* (Macmillan 1991, second ed. 2008) and *David*

Lloyd George: Great Britain (Haus 2008); and *Consequences of Peace, The Versailles Settlement: Aftermath and Legacy 1919–2010* (Haus, 2010) in the *Makers of the Modern World* series, of which he was the general editor.

David Robin Watson was senior lecturer in History at the University of Dundee for many years until his retirement. His field is European history, especially French; after writing a major biography of Clemenceau more than 30 years ago, he continued to research and write upon his life and on related topics in French and European history. His principal publications are *The Nationalist Movement in Paris 1900–1906* (1962), 'Marcel Proust and Joseph Reinach', *Modern Languages Review* (1966), 'The Treaty of Versailles' in N Waites (ed.), *Troubled Neighbours* (1971), *Life of Charles I* (1972), *Clemenceau, A Political Biography* (1974), 'France, Europe and the World since 1880' in J McMillan (ed.), *The Oxford History of Modern France* (2003). He has also published a large number of articles in academic periodicals and in collective works including 'The Franco-Soviet negotiations of 1924–7' in G Johnson (ed.), *Locarno Revisited, European Diplomacy 1920–29* (2004), 'Les contacts de Clemenceau avec Angleterre' in S Brodziak (ed.), *Clemenceau et le Monde Anglo-Saxon* (2005) and 'Clemenceau's contacts with England' in *Diplomacy and Statecraft* (17 December 2006).

Index